Palgrave Studies in Religion, Politics, and Policy

Series Editor
Mark J. Rozell
Schar School of Policy and Government
George Mason University
Arlington, VA, USA

This series originated under the co-editorship of the late Ted Jelen and Mark J. Rozell. A generation ago, many social scientists regarded religion as an anachronism, whose social, economic, and political importance would inevitably wane and disappear in the face of the inexorable forces of modernity. Of course, nothing of the sort has occurred; indeed, the public role of religion is resurgent in US domestic politics, in other nations, and in the international arena. Today, religion is widely acknowledged to be a key variable in candidate nominations, platforms, and elections; it is recognized as a major influence on domestic and foreign policies. National religious movements as diverse as the Christian Right in the United States and the Taliban in Afghanistan are important factors in the internal politics of particular nations. Moreover, such transnational religious actors as Al-Qaida, Falun Gong, and the Vatican have had important effects on the politics and policies of nations around the world. Palgrave Studies in Religion, Politics, and Policy serves a growing niche in the discipline of political science. This subfield has proliferated rapidly during the past two decades, and has generated an enormous amount of scholarly studies and journalistic coverage. Five years ago, the journal Politics and Religion was created; in addition, works relating to religion and politics have been the subject of many articles in more general academic journals. The number of books and monographs on religion and politics has increased tremendously. In the past, many social scientists dismissed religion as a key variable in politics and government. This series casts a broad net over the subfield, providing opportunities for scholars at all levels to publish their works with Palgrave. The series publishes monographs in all subfields of political science, including American Politics, Public Policy, Public Law, Comparative Politics, International Relations, and Political Theory. The principal focus of the series is the public role of religion. "Religion" is construed broadly to include public opinion, religious institutions, and the legal frameworks under which religious politics are practiced. The "dependent variable" in which we are interested is politics, defined broadly to include analyses of the public sources and consequences of religious belief and behavior. These would include matters of public policy, as well as variations in the practice of political life. We welcome a diverse range of methodological perspectives, provided that the approaches taken are intellectually rigorous. The series does not deal with works of theology, in that arguments about the validity or utility of religious beliefs are not a part of the series focus. Similarly, the authors of works about the private or personal consequences of religious belief and behavior, such as personal happiness, mental health, or family dysfunction, should seek other outlets for their writings. Although historical perspectives can often illuminate our understanding of modern political phenomena, our focus in the Religion, Politics, and Policy series is on the relationship between the sacred and the political in contemporary societies.

More information about this series at
http://www.palgrave.com/gp/series/14594

Paul Christopher Manuel • Miguel Glatzer
Editors

Faith-Based Organizations and Social Welfare

Associational Life and Religion in Contemporary Western Europe

palgrave
macmillan

Editors
Paul Christopher Manuel
Government
American University
Washington, DC, USA

Miguel Glatzer
Political Science
La Salle University
Philadelphia, DC, USA

Palgrave Studies in Religion, Politics, and Policy
ISBN 978-3-319-77296-7   ISBN 978-3-319-77297-4 (eBook)
https://doi.org/10.1007/978-3-319-77297-4

Library of Congress Control Number: 2018935698

© The Editor(s) (if applicable) and The Author(s) 2019
This work is subject to copyright. All rights are solely and exclusively licensed by the Publisher, whether the whole or part of the material is concerned, specifically the rights of translation, reprinting, reuse of illustrations, recitation, broadcasting, reproduction on microfilms or in any other physical way, and transmission or information storage and retrieval, electronic adaptation, computer software, or by similar or dissimilar methodology now known or hereafter developed.
The use of general descriptive names, registered names, trademarks, service marks, etc. in this publication does not imply, even in the absence of a specific statement, that such names are exempt from the relevant protective laws and regulations and therefore free for general use.
The publisher, the authors and the editors are safe to assume that the advice and information in this book are believed to be true and accurate at the date of publication. Neither the publisher nor the authors or the editors give a warranty, express or implied, with respect to the material contained herein or for any errors or omissions that may have been made. The publisher remains neutral with regard to jurisdictional claims in published maps and institutional affiliations.

Cover credit: iStock / Getty Images

Printed on acid-free paper

This Palgrave Macmillan imprint is published by the registered company Springer International Publishing AG part of Springer Nature.
The registered company address is: Gewerbestrasse 11, 6330 Cham, Switzerland

PRAISE PAGE

"This timely book makes a distinctive contribution to the growing literature on welfare and religion in Europe. Drawing from political science perspectives, it is theoretically innovative and empirically rich. In-depth case studies bring to life the following paradox: the growing presence of the churches in the delivery of welfare in an increasingly secular Europe. I recommend it warmly."
—Grace Davie, *Professor of Sociology, University of Exeter, UK*

"This is a wonderfully illuminating book presenting a novel incisive assessment of the role played by religious-based organizations in deeply secularized Western Europe. By covering a representative selection of country cases, the volume addresses salient issues, such as their contribution to associational life, to the enrichment of the public debate and, therefore, to the advancement of democracy. Further, the analysis focuses on the activities deployed on behalf of the poor and the socially excluded, alleviating the long-lasting burden on welfare states generated by the crisis, intense immigration flows and deepening of inequalities. A must-read for both comparative welfare scholars and students and policy-makers."
—Ana M. Guillén, *Professor of Sociology, University of Oviedo, Spain*

"Raising the core question, 'what would happen to welfare services in Europe if faith-based organizations ceased to exist,' this book provides insight on a new approach to theoretical understanding of faith-based organizations in contemporary European society, grounded on empirical

solid information. Given the long-term tension between religious and secular, the historical churches—both Catholic and Protestant—have sought to compensate for their weakening in church membership and attendance and their normative influence on ethical life issues, by developing new forms of societal engagement in line with the principles of the social doctrine of the churches and, to that extent, introducing new types of solidarity. Faith-based organizations related to those churches have shown the ability to (re)create various kinds of mechanisms to promote to social capital and integration of individuals (immigrants, refugees, homeless people, marginalized) at various levels. In this regard, the book shows, in a comparative perspective, and in a valid way, that the religious institutions in Western Europe continue to play a key role in the social integration. As the editors emphasize, the faith-based organizations, following a strategic silence and a muted vibrancy, meet the failures of the welfare state and provide an indispensable service to democracy."
—Helena Vilaça, *Professor of Sociology, University of Porto, Portugal*

"The book is a fundamental contribution to social capital and social policy literature as it sheds new light on the influence of faith organizations, critically discussing the idea that secularization and losing importance of religion are the only phenomena at play. By analysing theoretical issues in eight different case studies, the book is a must-read for all scholars interested in better understanding the relation between religion, politics and society in twenty-first-century Western Europe."
—Emanuele Ferragina, *Assistant Professor of Sociology, Sciences Po-Paris, France*

"Understudied for too long, the relationship between religion and social policy is a key issue this volume tackles by providing detailed analysis of the social welfare involvement of faith-based organizations in eight Western European countries. This excellent volume suggests that, despite secularization, these organizations remain deeply involved in social provision, an area in which they exhibit 'muted vibrancy.' The volume is a must-read for scholars interested in the role of faith-based organizations in social policy."
—Daniel Béland, *Canada Research Chair and Professor in Public Policy, Johnson Shoyama Graduate School of Public Policy, Canada*

But if I am doing them, then have belief in the works even if you have no belief in me...
John 10:38

"To the rebirth of a Europe weary, yet still rich in energies and possibilities, the Church can and must play her part."
Pope Francis, at the reception of Charlemagne Prize, May 6, 2016

To Professor Ted Jelen (1952–2017)
With our gratitude to a giant in the scholarly field of religion and politics

Foreword

The issue of societies' secularization and associated political implications has long been an important focal point of political science and political sociology. Western European countries are collectively notable in having high degrees of secularization, often with attendant ramifications for political competition and outcomes. However, in recent years, "even" the most secular of Western European countries, such as France and the United Kingdom, have experienced increasing involvement of various types of religious or cultural actors, including explicitly political statements from churches and expressions of desire for equality from Muslims and other immigrant groups. Partly as a result, it is now widely agreed that secularization theory is significantly flawed because it predicted the demise of religion, when according to many scholars, the opposite is happening. Secularization theory anticipated that as countries developed economically and more generally became "modernized," they would as a result necessarily and irrevocably become more and more secular, leading eventually to the public "demise" of religion.[1] What happened, however, was different, defying secularization theory's prediction of the death of religion. "Even" in Western Europe, where regional countries without exception continue to exhibit clear signs of secularization, the issue is by no means as clear cut as once believed by many scholars.[2]

At the same time, it would be wrong to assume that religion continues simply to "return from the dead" in Western Europe, that is, demonstrating clear ability to apply more and more influence on political outcomes in regional countries, leading to a position where religion will again resume a position of authority in relation to secular political power. But what we are seeing in this regard is not simply the decline of secularization theory as a powerful explanatory tool for the relationship between religion and politics in Western Europe. Instead, we are witnessing novel forms of interaction, including in relation to social welfare delivery by faith-based organizations. Instead, there is what appears to be a "middle way" between, on the one hand, what secularization theory predicts (i.e., the claim that religion will eventually diminish substantially—or even disappear—as a public force) and the "return of religion" approach (i.e., the claim that religion is inexorably "returning" as a powerful and persuasive political actor, as a consequence of post-secularization and, as a result, reassuming a significant role in political discourse and competition in regional countries in Western Europe). In short, the premises of secularization theory remain a useful starting point to understand religion's current social and political roles in the countries of Western Europe. It is, however, very difficult to accept empirically all aspects of the theory, especially a core prediction: religion's universal public decline to irrelevance.

An area where faith-based organizations have been increasingly significant is in relation to social welfare and the delivery of associated benefits to those who need them. This is not to suggest that faith-based organizations use their capacity in relation to social welfare delivery to "entrap" the unwary and convert them to the faith-based organizations' faith tradition. Instead, more generally and, from a political science and political sociology point of view, more interesting, it may be that this is indicative of a growing socio-political involvement of "religion" in the countries of Western Europe in response to two developments. The first is partial withdrawal of the state from social welfare delivery because of the allegedly "unsupportable" costs of continuing to provide European-style "welfare states" and the associated unwillingness of (some or many) tax payers to support such governments and their "waste" of their pounds and Euros. The second issue is the symbiotic growth of civil society organizations, including faith-based organizations, which in many regional countries have sought to step into the breach in the absence of the state's inability or unwillingness any longer to meet its historic social welfare obligations and goals.

The case-studies of the current book are fascinating. It is great to have such well-written and comprehensive case-studies covering various countries in Western Europe, while the theoretical implications are covered impressively by the editors in the volume's thoughtful introductory chapter. Overall, the book is a delight to read, and while this is not of course the only purpose of a social scientific volume, it is a great boon in an era when good writing is at a premium.

London Metropolitan University   Jeffrey Haynes
London, UK

NOTES

1. Steve Bruce, *God is Dead: Secularization in the West* (London: Wiley/Blackwell, 2002).
2. Petr Kratochwil and Tomáš Doležal, *The European Union and the Catholic Church* (New York: Palgrave Macmillan, 2015); Lucien Leustean, *Representing Religion in the European Union* (London: Routledge, 2013).

ACKNOWLEDGMENTS

Miguel Glatzer and Paul Manuel first developed the idea for this volume at the July 2015 Annual Meeting of the Council for European Studies at the Institut d'Etudes Politiques de Paris (Sciences Po) in Paris, France. They were each presenting conference papers on different aspects of social welfare programs and religion in Europe, and thought that a volume such as this could make an original theoretical contribution.

There are many people who made this volume possible. We are especially thankful to Ted Jelen and Mark Rozell, the series editors at Palgrave Studies in Religion, Politics, and Policy, who believed in this project. Thanks also to Chris Robinson and Michelle Chen, our editors at Palgrave Macmillan, as well as to John Stegner, our wonderful editorial assistant at Palgrave Macmillan. We are most grateful to Heather Dubnick for her masterful copyediting job. We are indebted to the anonymous reviewers of the original proposal for the book for their very useful comments. Our project enjoyed the generous support from the provost's office at LaSalle University. We would like to thank our families for their patience, encouragement, and support of our work.

Paul Manuel presented an earlier version of the introduction and the chapter on Portugal at the Annual Meeting of the Council of European Studies at the Institut d'Etudes Politiques in Paris on July 8, 2015. He is grateful to the panel chair, Simon Griffiths (Goldsmiths, University of London), and the panel discussant, Priska Daphi (Goethe University Frankfurt/Main), for their helpful and insightful comments. Paul Manuel is also grateful to another set of people who provided insights and edits: Madalena Eça de Abreu; Rui Branco; Ana Carvalho; Maria Cláudia

Mendes Dimitre; Tiago Fernandes; Silvia Ferreira; Robert Fishman; Miguel Glatzer; Rev. Lino Maia; Rev. Tom Massaro, S.J.; Rev. Pedro McDade, S.J.; Rev. Manuel Morujão, S.J.; Madalena Resende; Rev. Hermínio Rico, S.J.; José Damião Rodrigues; Sonia Sousa; and Helena Vilaça.

Miguel Glatzer presented papers on civil society, the welfare state, and non-profit contracting at meetings of the Council for European Studies and the Society of the Advancement of Socio-Economics as well as at a conference at the University of Lisbon. He warmly thanks Ugo Ascoli, Rui Branco, Ana Guillen, Tiago Fernandes, Robert Fishman, Amilcar Moreira, Emmanuele Pavolini, Maria Petmesidou, and Dimitri Sotiropoulos for rich discussions and insightful comments.

A number of the contributors to this volume participated in the September 2017 European Consortium for Political Research (ECPR) in Oslo, at the "Religious Organizations in European Welfare States in the Twenty-First Century" panel, co-chaired by Matthias Kortmann of the Ludwig-Maximilians-Universität München and Josef Hien of the Università degli Studi di Milano. Annette Leis-Peters presented on the interaction of religious organizations as welfare providers and the public in Norway and Sweden; Xabier Itçaina presented on the relationship between moralizing capitalism and solidarity alternatives. This Oslo meeting also provided these volume contributors a wonderful opportunity to discuss the key themes of this present volume.

Sadly, Professor Ted Jelen, a giant in the field of religion and politics, and one of the editors of the Palgrave Studies on Politics, Religion, and Policy—of which this volume is a part—died during the final stages of this project. Ted's scholarly work, including the 16 books he authored, co-authored, or edited, as well as some 150 journal articles and book chapters, helped the academy rediscover the vital variable of religion in the larger processes of political, social, and cultural change. He was a big supporter of this volume. *It is our honor to dedicate this work to him.*

Washington, DC	Paul Christopher Manuel
Philadelphia, Fall 2017	Miguel Glatzer

Contents

1 "Use Words Only If Necessary": The Strategic Silence of Organized Religion in Contemporary Europe 1
Paul Christopher Manuel and Miguel Glatzer

Part I Countries with a Dominant Religious Society 19

2 The Entanglement and Disentanglement of Church and State in Irish Social Policy 21
Michele Dillon

3 Religiously Oriented Welfare Organizations in Italy Before and After the Great Recession: Toward a More Relevant Role in the Provision of Social Services? 47
Ugo Ascoli and Marco Arlotti

4 Muted Vibrancy and the Invisible Politics of Religion: Catholic Third Sector, Economic Crisis, and Territorial Welfare in Spain 75
Xabier Itçaina

5 The State, Religious Institutions, and Welfare Delivery: The Case of Portugal 103
Paul Christopher Manuel and Miguel Glatzer

6 Church–State Relations in Today's Crisis-Beset Greece:
  A Delicate Balance Within a Frantic Society 135
  Periklis Polyzoidis

Part II Countries with Competing Religious Societies and
        with a Formerly Dominant Church 159

7 Combining Secular Public Space and Growing Diversity?
  Interactions Between Religious Organizations as Welfare
  Providers and the Public in Sweden 161
  Annette Leis-Peters

8 Social Capital and Religion in the United Kingdom 185
  Steven Kettell

9 Faith-Based Organizations Under Double-Pressure:
  The Impact of Market Liberalization and Secularization
  on Caritas and Diakonie in Germany 205
  Josef Hien

Index 229

About the Editors

Miguel Glatzer is associate professor of Political Science and director of the Leadership and Global Understanding Program at La Salle University. In addition to journal articles and book chapters, his publications include *Globalization and the Future of the Welfare State* (2005, edited with Dietrich Rueschemeyer) and *Portugal: Strategic Options in a European Context* (2003, edited with Fátima Monteiro, José Tavares, and Angelo Cardoso). His current research focuses on social policy, labor market policy, the European sovereign debt crisis, financial literacy, and immigration. He holds a PhD in government from Harvard University.

Paul Christopher Manuel is distinguished scholar in residence in the department of government in the School of Public Affairs at American University. He is also a research fellow at the Berkley Center for Religion, Peace, and World Affairs at Georgetown University and a local affiliate at the Minda de Gunzburg Center for European Studies at Harvard University, where he co-chaired the Iberian Studies Group. His research interests address comparative democratization, comparative public policy, and the relationship between religion and politics. Manuel has authored or co-authored nine books and numerous articles. He holds an MTS from Boston College (Weston Jesuit School of Theology) and a PhD in government from Georgetown University.

Contributors

Marco Arlotti is researcher of Economic Sociology at the Politecnico di Milano (Italy).

Ugo Ascoli is professor of Economic Sociology and Social Policy at the Università Politecnica delle Marche, Ancona (Italy).

Michele Dillon is Class of 1944 professor of Sociology at the University of New Hampshire (USA).

Josef Hien is post-doctoral fellow at the University of Milan (Italy) and at the Berlin Social Science Center (WZB, Germany).

Xabier Itçaina is CNRS research director and director of the Centre Emile Durkheim at Sciences Po Bordeaux (France).

Steven Kettell is associate professor in the Department of Politics and International Studies at the University of Warwick (UK).

Annette Leis-Peters is associate professor of Theology, Diaconia and Leadership Studies, and Vice-Dean at VID Specialized University in Oslo (Norway).

Periklis Polyzoidis is associate professor in the Department of Social Administration and Political Science at Democritus University of Thrace, Komotiní (Greece).

LIST OF FIGURES

Fig. 1.1	Four dimensions of comparative inquiry	8
Fig. 2.1	Religious affiliation in the Republic of Ireland, 2016	22
Fig. 2.2	Change in religious affiliation in the Republic of Ireland, 1991–2016	23
Fig. 3.1	Change in religious affiliation in Italy, 1990–2012	51
Fig. 3.2	Religious affiliation in Italy, 2012	51
Fig. 3.3	Changes in the number of regular churchgoers (only Catholics) in Italy, 1990–2010	52
Fig. 4.1	Religious self-definition in Spain	78
Fig. 4.2	Believers in religions other than Catholicism in Spain	79
Fig. 5.1	Religious affiliation in Portugal, 2011	107
Fig. 5.2	Change in religious affiliation in Portugal, 1999–2011	108
Fig. 6.1	Change in religious affiliation in Greece, 1991–2016	140
Fig. 6.2	Religious affiliation in Greece, 2016	141
Fig. 7.1	Membership, Church of Sweden, 1991–2016	163
Fig. 7.2	Membership, Church of Sweden, 2016	164
Fig. 8.1	Change in religious affiliation in Britain, 1992–2016	196
Fig. 8.2	Religious affiliation in Britain, 2016	197
Fig. 9.1	Change in religious affiliation in Germany, 1990–2015	208
Fig. 9.2	Religious affiliation in Germany, 2011	209
Fig. 9.3	Frequent church attendance, Protestant Church and Catholic Church	214

LIST OF TABLES

Table 1.1	Size and projected growth of major religious groups in Europe	9
Table 1.2	Percentage of population identifying as Christian, by country	10
Table 3.1	"Otto per mille" projects, 2009; 2012; 2015	67
Table 3.2	A comparison between the territorial allocation of the "Otto per mille" resources and the territorial distribution of poor people, 2015	67
Table 4.1	Public perceptions of the Catholic Church in Spain	91
Table 4.2	Public perceptions of the institutions	92
Table 5.1	Religious affiliation in Portugal, 2011	106
Table 5.2	Categories of religious positions among believers (in percentages)	108
Table 5.3	Religious practices of Roman Catholics in Portugal, 2011 (in percentages)	109
Table 5.4	Would there be more poverty if there were no Roman Catholic Church in Portugal?	121
Table 5.5	Would many lack a purpose in life if there were no Roman Catholic Church in Portugal?	122
Table 5.6	Would many die without hope if there were no Roman Catholic Church in Portugal?	122
Table 5.7	Would there be more progress if there were no Roman Catholic Church in Portugal?	123
Table 5.8	Would there be more individual freedom if there were no Roman Catholic Church in Portugal?	123
Table 5.9	Would there be more religious freedom if there were no Roman Catholic Church in Portugal?	124

Table 9.1	Employees of faith-based welfare organizations in Germany, 1990–2012	206
Table 9.2	Employees of faith-based welfare organizations in Germany, 2012–2015	207

CHAPTER 1

"Use Words Only If Necessary": The Strategic Silence of Organized Religion in Contemporary Europe

Paul Christopher Manuel and Miguel Glatzer

The consideration of religious variables in comparative politics entered the scholarly discussion relatively late, but a number of important works over the past few years have considered the possibilities and obstacles religion presents to a democratic society.[1] Among other concerns, this literature examines how the work of religious interest associations might promote greater social capital, civic engagement, empowerment, and participation among the poor and other socially marginalized groups. This literature is consistent with the concept of muted vibrancy and builds on both the social capital and democratic deepening approaches.

The concept of muted vibrancy carves out a promising research area for how religion and politics, or even faith and culture, may interact in a society historically dominated by one religion. Derived from the work

P. C. Manuel (✉)
American University, Washington, DC, USA

M. Glatzer
La Salle University, Philadelphia, PA, USA

© The Author(s) 2019
P. C. Manuel, M. Glatzer (eds.), *Faith-Based Organizations and Social Welfare*, Palgrave Studies in Religion, Politics, and Policy, https://doi.org/10.1007/978-3-319-77297-4_1

on Roman Catholicism in France (traditionally referred to as the eldest daughter of the church) by a number of scholars, including historian René Rémond, Jesuit philosopher Paul Valadier, and historian Steven Englund in a notable 2001 review article in *Commonweal*, this concept suggests that social scientists need to move beyond the lens normally applied to the question of Catholicism in contemporary Europe (i.e., it is a dying, anti-modern, anti-rational, and conservative institution) and instead examine its ongoing societal functions.[2] Valadier, for instance, examines the continued relevance of Catholicism in French society in his 1999 book *L'Eglise en Procès: Catholicisme et Société Moderne*.[3] The Spanish Jesuit Gonzalo Villagrán has asked similar questions about the church in Spanish society.[4] For his part, Steven Englund, in "L'Eglise de France, The Church in a post-religious age," following Rémond, laments the ongoing anti-clericalism of the French intelligentsia, and asks "why is [French Catholicism] ... judged on its past and not its present."[5] The muted-vibrancy approach seeks to provide a nuanced understanding of the contemporary role of lived religion in a given society and therefore avoid the pitfalls of a facile reading of the role of religion in the public square.

We use the term *muted vibrancy* to denote two elements that are key to our understanding of the work of faith-based organizations in contemporary Western Europe. First, while acknowledging that reduced religious attendance, secularization, and increased religious pluralism constitute important trends, it is important not to overstate the case. As the chapters in this volume illustrate, identification with the dominant traditional religions (Roman Catholicism, Anglican, Lutheran, and Greek Orthodox Christianity) still plays a vital role in the lives of large percentages of the population. Traditional religious observance and identity is diminished, but is certainly not dead.

Second, we recognize that churches have lost most of the high-profile battles on moral issues that dominate much of the press coverage and discussion. Whereas many states once took their cues explicitly or implicitly from religious traditions on matters of divorce, abortion, and homosexuality, particularly in countries where Catholicism or Greek Orthodoxy was dominant, the battles to preserve such traditions have been decisively lost. Legalization, or in some cases, decriminalization, of abortion, divorce, and gay marriage now constitutes an important part of law across Western Europe; further, these previously controversial positions now enjoy majority support in virtually every Western European country.

Having lost these battles, churches essentially face three choices: they could perhaps continue to loudly proclaim their opposition; second, they could engage in doctrinal or structural reform to reflect contemporary social views (expanded roles for women, or the ability of the divorced to receive communion); or, third, they could possibly focus on other relatively non-controversial issues (compassion, good works), or where public opinion is still in flux (policy on migration and refugees). Building on that third option, this volume argues that while churches may have lost power and prestige relative to the past, they remain powerful, if often unheralded, vital actors in social services and welfare provision; we use the concept of muted vibrancy as a lens through which to understand their contribution to West European civil society.

This theoretical approach also helps us overcome—as several of the authors in this volume note—a seeming paradox. That is, even as formal religious adherence declines and as the prestige of the church, rocked in some cases by scandals, diminishes, its role in the provision of services continues to grow. While the church may be muted in some respects (experiencing declines in attendance, rising secularism, losing battles on moral issues, and, in some cases, choosing to downplay its continued opposition to society's new positions), it is vibrant in others, namely in its commitment to serving the poor and vulnerable.

Muted vibrancy is also in harmony with the notion of *strategic silence*. The "strategic actor" model, most notably developed by Carolyn Warner in *Confessions of an Interest Group*, contends that the post–Vatican II institutional Catholic Church has comported itself not unlike an interest group in the European public square—and this insight can be certainly be applied to other religious groupings in Europe.[6] There have been multiple efforts to influence public policies to ensure that health and welfare benefits are available to those in need, for example. At the same time, in some of our cases, the Catholic Church has been remarkably muted on national debates over abortion and same-sex marriage. We wonder if this represents a sort of "strategic silence" on behalf of the religious groupings to de-emphasize politically divisive social issues where the battle has been lost in favor of the important work of meeting basic human needs and of advocacy on issues not yet settled in the public arena.

We argue that the literature on social capital and civic engagement is consistent with the emphasis on social services, attention to socioeconomic needs, and response to new social risks that the concept of muted vibrancy tries to highlight. Putnam has argued that social capital, meaning "features of social life—networks, norms, and trust—that enable participants to act together more effectively to pursue shared objectives," is necessary to the promotion of a robust associational life in a democracy.[7] Likewise, Schmitter suggests that "interest associations may be important (if subsidiary) sites at which the legitimacy of democracy is accorded ... therefore the long-term viability of a given democratic regime may come to depend on the configuration and behavior of such."[8] Stepan has noted as well that "democracy should not be considered consolidated in a country unless, among other things, there is an opportunity for the development of a robust and critical civil society."[9] Combined, there is a shared concern that social scientists examine "bottom-up" civic associations—religious or secular—in order to effectively assess how well such social groupings add to democratic processes, legitimacy, and stability.

For its part, the deepening democracy scholarship is particularly concerned with how social divisions may prove to be an obstacle for democratic consolidation. Fishman argues that "the literature on the deepening of democracy emphasizes institutional factors in the opening—or closing—of spaces for effective participation by the poor and other socially subordinate sectors, but also examines social movements and social pressure from below."[10] If interest associations are to have a crucial legitimizing function in consolidating new democratic regimes, one of the critical questions involves how, exactly, they may accomplish that task. Archon Fung points to six contributions that civic associations make in the process of deepening democracy, including the intrinsic good of association and freedom to associate; civic socialization and political education; popular resistance and the checking of power; interest representation; public deliberation and the public sphere; and direct governance.[11] With these, Fung builds on Paul Hirst's argument in *Associative Democracy* that "the state should cede functions to such associations, and create the mechanisms of public finance whereby they can undertake them."[12] To the degree that religious organizations might perform these functions, they may indeed be promoting democratic deepening.

The scholarship on faith-based interest associations specifically asks how these groups might deepen associational life in a newly consolidated democratic regime and thereby facilitate and stabilize democratic regimes. For instance, Pazit Ben-Nun Bloom and Gizem Arikan have recently found "that communal aspect of religious social behavior increases political interest and trust in institutions, which in turn typically lead to more support for democracy."[13] Other research also supports these findings.

A related concern of this scholarship is how the charitable works of religious interest associations can serve as an important counter-weight to the dangers that unbridled free-market capitalism can pose to democratic equality. Casanova argues that "religion may remind individuals and societies of the need to check and regulate those impersonal market mechanisms to ensure that they ... may become more responsible to human needs."[14] Certainly, during times of economic upheavals, a political regime may need to rely on religious associations more fully than during normal periods to maintain social peace and bolster its governing coalition.

Although academic scholarship on the role of faith-based organizations in contemporary welfare states is a field with a high potential for growth, the role of churches in this area has not gone unnoticed by the general public. In many countries the most admired role of the church in contemporary society is precisely its work to meet the needs of the most vulnerable. While mass publics often exhibit distrust of the religious hierarchy or of the church's position on traditional high-profile moral issues, they admire the good that churches do on the ground. This volume examines these good works, the ways these are perceived, the intricate church–state relationships that have arisen to structure them, and some of the challenges they face.

Given its long history of *laïcité*, or a policy of strict separation between church and state based on the revolutionary principles of *liberté*, *égalité*, and *fraternité*, and the corollary notion that the secular state should exercise control over the society, *or étatisme*, France well encapsulates both the challenges and advantages of the secular state working with faith-based organizations to provide welfare services. As with most things in France, the issue of faith-based organizations and the secular welfare system has a long history; it derives from a centuries-long struggle between those favoring religious, traditional understandings of providing corporal works of mercy to those in need and those espousing anti-religious, enlightenment views of the fundamental need of the secular state to provide basic services to citizens. This religious–secular tension has given rise to many inconsistencies between stated objectives and actual policies, as political power has shifted between the two sides at different periods of history. Arguably, since the 1789 revolution, and certainly in the aftermath of the 1905 law of separation between the church and the state, the secular state has sought to restrict the practice of religion in the public square; ironically, this changed during the socialist administration of President Francois Mitterrand (1981–1995), when legislation was passed creating space for both local agencies and voluntary organizations to implement state policies, resulting in more cooperation and less hostility between church and state authorities in the delivery of welfare services.[15] We can note that history rarely follows a linear path, and faith-based organizations in France serve as a case in point: they provided social services before the revolution, were then significantly limited from doing so, and are again presently engaged in this work.[16] As Louella Moore has insightfully observed, "France has come full circle from banning nonprofit entities in 1791 to currently recognizing and working with social economy organizations to help deliver social welfare services."[17] To this point, İpek Göçmen also notes that "currently, secular voluntary associations such as *Secours Populaire* and *Restaux du Coeur* (est. 1983) fill an important gap in social welfare, especially in alleviating poverty and helping people in urgent situations. The most important faith-based social welfare provider is *Secours Catholique*, a Catholic charity organization established in 1946."[18]

This opening to faith-based providers in France appears to have taken place at a most opportune time. According to a 2011 OECD Social Expenditure Report, France spends a great deal on its welfare system: as a percent of GDP at factor cost, its net total social expenditure in 2007 was 30 percent.[19] Similarly, the 2010 Welfare and Religion in European Perspective (WREP) project found that as costs and need increase, the secular welfare state will need to rely on faith-based organizations to deliver welfare to the needy.[20] Likewise, Anders Bäckström and Grace Davie note the "increasing ... role of the majority churches in the voluntary sector, both as providers of welfare and as a 'critical voice' able to point out the less as well as more obvious deficiencies of the system. This is a situation where local knowledge counts for a great deal. Particularly important, for example, is the work of the churches amongst groups of individuals—particularly homeless people or asylum-seekers—who do not fit easily into the system.[21]"

Bäckström and Davie further observe that the ability of faith-based organizations to quickly cut through red tape, and to rapidly respond to crisis situations, is a strength. Relatedly, Ingo Bode notes that many faith-based organizations in France do not have many paid staffers but instead provide services through volunteer networks—arguably providing these organizations with a sort of barrier from sometimes burdensome state employment regulations on smaller enterprises. These observations bring us back to the concepts of both muted vibrancy and strategic silence; that is, France offers an interesting example of how faith-based organizations appear to be quietly involved in an array of welfare-delivery services. Other countries are facing similar challenges, as we shall see in the chapters in this volume.[22]

STRUCTURE OF THE VOLUME

This volume concerns the role and function of religious-based organizations in strengthening associational life in Europe. The essays in this volume search for larger political, sociological, cultural, and religious patterns that bind the European nations together. To that end, and as appropriate to the case-study, each chapter considers five key questions, three of which were developed by Jeffrey Haynes and Anja Henning.[23] *Grosso modo*, these five questions seek to identify the historical path, objectives, means, strategies, effects, and public perception of faith-based civic organizations in European society: (1) *path development*: each chapter establishes the current religious composition of the society and examines how the church–state relationship evolved in each country; (2) *objectives*: we wonder what religious actors intend to achieve in their public actions; (3) m*eans and strategies*: we examine how religious actors operate in the public square; (4) *effects*: the intended or unintended consequences of religious actors' political/public involvement are also considered, around the larger question of which pressures would be brought on the welfare state if these services were stopped; and (5) *public perception*: how the national population views the activities of faith-based activities.

Comparative Perspectives

We assembled a group of scholars who are specialists on different European countries. Each author offered a detailed examination of faith–culture relations in one of the eight European countries under examination, namely Germany, the United Kingdom, Ireland, Greece, Italy, Portugal, Spain, and Sweden. We asked the authors to examine questions related to how faith, culture, and politics interrelate in their case-study, and how the various national experiences resonated with other countries. The volume examines eight cases, selected to maximize variation along four comparative dimensions: type of religious marketplace, level of democratization, welfare state type, and vulnerability to the 2008 economic crisis (see Fig. 1.1).

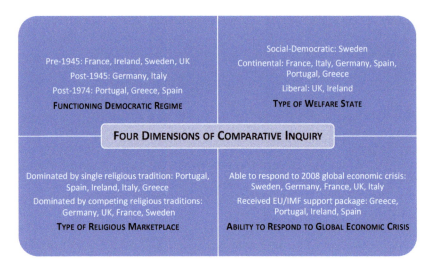

Fig. 1.1 Four dimensions of comparative inquiry

First Comparative Dimension: The Contemporary West European Religious Marketplace

As we gaze upon contemporary Western Europe in 2018, we find a complex range of cultural, political, and religious activities at the grassroots level of civil society. This activity calls out for serious scholarly attention. This volume takes up that call as it seeks to capture the rich, lived reality of religion and politics, as well as faith and culture, across eight European nations.

According to a recent Pew Research Center poll, as demonstrated in Table 1.1, Christianity is expected to remain the dominant religion in Europe in the near future, even if a gradual shift toward people unaffiliated with a specific religious denomination, or toward Islam, is also likely to occur.[24] Despite 100 million fewer Christians in Europe between 2010 and 2050, Pew predicts Christians in mid-century will nonetheless outnumber the unaffiliated by close to three to one. While variation by country is important, the notion of a broadly secular Europe is perhaps exaggerated.

The religious dynamic is an important, and yet understudied, element of contemporary European society. Europe retains a Christian cultural identity, as Table 1.2 indicates.[25] However, the exact nature of the practice of Christianity experiences wide variation among European countries.

Table 1.1 Size and projected growth of major religious groups in Europe

	2010 est. pop.	% in 2010	2050 projected pop.	% in 2050	Pop. growth 2010–2050	% increase 210–2050	Compound actual growth rate (%)
Christians	553,280,000	74.5	454,090,000	65.2	−99,190,000	−17.9	−0.5
Unaffiliated	139,890,000	18.8	162,320,000	23.3	22,420,000	16.0	0.4
Muslims	43,470,000	5.9	70,870,000	10.2	27,400,000	63.0	1.2
Jews	1,420,000	0.2	1,200,000	0.2	−220,000	−15.2	−0.4
Hindus	1,380,000	0.2	2,660,000	0.4	1,280,000	92.9	1.7
Buddhists	1,350,000	0.2	2,490,000	0.4	1,140,000	85.0	1.5
Other religions	890,000	0.1	1,100,000	0.2	210,000	23.3	0.5
Folk religions	870,000	0.1	1,590,000	0.2	720,000	83.1	1.5
Regional total	742,550,000	100.0	696,330,000	100.0	−46,220,000	−6.2	−0.2

Source: Pew Research Center, "Size, Projected Growth of Major Religious Groups in Europe, 2010–2050," March 27, 2015, http://www.pewforum.org/2015/04/02/europe/attachment/147/
Population estimates are rounded to the nearest 10,000. Percentages are calculated from unrounded numbers. Figures may not add to 100% because of rounding

Table 1.2 Percentage of population identifying as Christian, by country

Germany	<90%
Greece	<90%
France	<90%
Ireland	≥90%
Italy	<90%
Portugal	≥90%
Spain	<90%
Sweden	<90%
UK	<90%

Source: Pew Research Center, "Largest Religious Group, by Country," June 19, 2015, http://www.pewresearch.org/fact-tank/2015/06/22/what-is-each-countrys-second-largest-religious-group/ft_15-06-12religiousgroups_alargest640px-2/. Estimates for the year 2010. Followers of other religions do not make up the largest religion in any country

This volume goes beyond the macro-level that these numbers suggest and examines the lived reality of those faith-based organizations in eight representative European countries. Each chapter describes what they do and the services they provide and then measures their impact against the services provided by the secular state. Each chapter also includes a "what-if" exercise, asking what new pressures would be placed on the state if the faith-based organizations ceased to function. We do this to weigh the ongoing salience of faith-based organizations to the promotion of a healthy associational life in democratic Europe.

Adapting the theoretical model developed by Jelen and Wilcox, we can meaningfully classify our various case-studies in terms of *distinct forms of religious marketplaces, or societies*.[26] Several of the cases can be classified as *societies dominated by a single religious tradition*: Portugal, Spain, Ireland, Italy, and Greece. Roman Catholicism and Greek Orthodox remain the dominant religious organizations in these societies. The remaining four case-studies constitute cases of *competing religious societies, with a formerly dominant church*: Germany, Sweden, and the United Kingdom. Roman Catholicism still accounts for the largest confession in Germany, as does the Church of England in the United Kingdom and the Lutheran Church in Sweden, but there has been increased religious competition.

Second Comparative Dimension: Level of Democratization Across Western Europe

Our case-studies include countries whose history of democracy is long (pre-1945 in the United Kingdom, Sweden, Ireland, and France, which we include in this category as France's loss of democracy during World War II was due to military defeat rather than to internal factors), intermediate (post-1945 in Germany and Italy), and more recent (mid-1970s in Portugal, Spain, and Greece). Church–state relations were often altered as a result of the transition to democracy. In some cases, formal agreements with the Vatican, such as the Concordat, were changed, and privileges once enjoyed by the church in alliance with conservative dictatorships were reduced, while in others the opening of civil society extended to the church as well, increasing its ability to engage in public critique. Even in long democracies, however, church–state relations continued to evolve, as church involvement in education and health care in Ireland or the special labor provisions for church organizations in Germany indicate.

Third Comparative Dimension: Welfare State Type Across Western Europe

Adapting Esping-Andersen's *Three Worlds of Welfare Capitalism*, we classify these countries' welfare states as social democratic (Sweden), liberal (the UK and Ireland), and continental (the remaining countries).[27] While we are more interested in social services than in transfers, the *Three Worlds* scheme predicts high state involvement in direct state provision of services in social democracies, state funding of services delivered by civil society organizations in the continental model, and a heavy reliance on market mechanisms in the liberal model. Our study will allow us to assess the degree of fit of our cases with the ideal types that constitute this conceptualization of the worlds of welfare.

Fourth Comparative Dimension: Vulnerability to the 2008 Global Economic Crisis

Our cases exhibit variation in the degree to which they were affected by the 2008 economic crisis. Some experienced deep and long-lasting recessions (Portugal, Spain, and Ireland, with Greece's experience in several respects exceeding the Great Depression), while others suffered much less.

We make a distinction between countries that were subject to some form of external supervision and conditionality and those that were not. We include among countries that required foreign assistance those that received explicit bailouts (Greece, Portugal, and Ireland) or a bank bailout (Spain). While these countries were thus subject to externally imposed austerity measures, the depth of these measures and their compliance with them varied. We also note that some countries not subject to foreign conditionality embraced relatively deep austerity measures for domestic political reasons, most notably Britain. The recessions increased social need, and austerity reduced the ability of the government to cushion these needs. They thus serve as a sort of stress test for the capacity of religiously oriented welfare organizations to cope with increases in social suffering.

Our Comparative Dimensions: Summary

As discussed above, and illustrated in Table 1.2, this volume examines eight cases, selected to maximize variation along four comparative dimensions: type of religious marketplace, level of democratization, welfare state type, and vulnerability to the 2008 economic crisis. The cases are organized by type of religious marketplace: the first part of the volume groups those countries with a dominant religious society (Ireland, Italy, Spain, Portugal, and Greece), whereas the second part encompasses those countries with competing religious societies and with a formerly dominant church (Sweden, the United Kingdom, and Germany). In each of the case-studies, a central task is to shed light on the question of how much and in what ways faith-based organizations support the poor and marginalized and which new pressures would be brought to the secular welfare state if such activities were to cease. Will faith-based organizations remain vital actors in social services and welfare provision?

A Preliminary Assessment: Key Themes from the Case-Studies

At least six important themes emerge from the case-studies. First, the size of faith-based organizations involved in social service delivery is impressive. Xabier Itçaina points out that in Spain, *Cáritas* provided assistance in its reception centers to one million people in the depths of the recession in 2012. In 2015, Periklis Polyzoidis notes that the Greek Orthodox

Church served about 1.2 million people, close to 10 percent of the population. Ugo Ascoli and Marco Arlotti observe that affiliated Catholic organizations in Italy operate over 14,000 health and social service programs run by 420,000 workers, many of them volunteers. Germany's main Catholic and Protestant welfare organizations constitute the second largest employer in the country, surpassed only by the state itself. Ireland's largest charitable voluntary organization is the Saint Vincent de Paul Society.

Second, while crucial, the role of state funding varies across cases and is not always dominant. While two-thirds of the budget of *Cáritas* in Germany comes from the state, the public sector contributes just over one-quarter of the budget of *Cáritas* in Spain. Trends in state funding vary as well. In some countries, welfare states remain transfer-heavy (emphasizing programs such as pensions or unemployment insurance), while in others social and personal services have a longer history. Austerity, whether externally imposed or internally driven, meant substantial cuts in social service budgets or meager increases but in no case matched the increased need. Finally, in some countries new programs or the expansion of existing programs resulted in new streams of public money (as in the German case of increased federal subsidies for child care and elder care). The sources of state funding also vary. In some cases (e.g., Greece), clergy are civil servants, paid by the state. Some states allow individuals to allocate a part of their income taxes to their church. In others, the dominant form of state funding occurs through the allocation of contracts for welfare services.

Third, countries vary in the extent of internal regional variation in the capacity of faith-based organizations to provide social services. While the Greek Orthodox Church provides services even in isolated villages and islands—as is also the case of the Roman Catholic Church in Portugal—Spain and Italy are marked by substantial levels of internal variation. Interestingly, the variation is poorly correlated with regional differences in religiosity. Instead, the differences in capacities to respond to local need stem both from differences in funding streams (poorer regions have higher need but lower capacity to contribute) as well as the institutional capacity of regional governments and their willingness to partner effectively with third sector organizations in the delivery of social services. Northern and Central Italy perform better on these dimensions than Southern Italy. In Spain, the Basque region and Barcelona exhibit both the resources and capacity to partner with faith-based organizations, while Madrid, by contrast, although also wealthy, does less. Federalism and devolution of power to regions and local governments can have many positive effects, but one risk is geographical variation in the capacity and willingness to meet social needs. Although churches are complex national (indeed, often international) institutions, the important local dimensions of the parish and diocese in the response to social needs, as well as their dependence on local government, limits their capacity to redistribute resources geographically, unless the federal level of government plays a primary role in the distribution of funds according to need.

Fourth, church attention to the poor and the most vulnerable garners positive responses from public opinion, in some cases far exceeding approval rates for the church hierarchy. As Michelle Dillon argues, in an era marked by scandal and a sense that the church is often out of touch in Ireland, and indeed throughout Western Europe, this reservoir of positive feelings is an important resource for the church as a social institution. Nonetheless, the church faces pushback in some quarters from the ways it operationalizes its social service functions. In Germany, for example, and as noted by Josef Hien, exemptions from ordinary labor law, enacted in the 1950s, have led to contestation over the dismissal of employees who divorce or are gay. In addition, minority religions have contested the privileged status and access to funding of the dominant Catholic and Protestant service organizations. Germany has a much longer history of immigration than do Portugal, Spain, Greece, or Ireland, which don't yet face the issue of how to care for Muslim *gastarbeiter* (guest worker) entering frail old age. Nonetheless, as societies become more multicultural and religiously diverse, navigating the secular functions of faith-based organizations may at times become fraught.

Fifth, with respect to one of the animating questions of this volume—*what would happen to welfare services in Europe if faith-based organizations ceased to exist?*—there is no one answer. Where state funding is the dominant source, as in Germany, the state could arguably contract with secular third sector organizations to provide the services. In other cases, where civil society or the third sector remains relatively weak and where the state plays a relatively modest role, the disappearance of faith-based organizations would be likely to have a very substantial effect.

Finally, the chapters in this volume, and especially the contributions by Steven Kettell (UK) and Annette Leis-Peters (Sweden), raise the question of the implications a more secular society poses for the work performed by these faith-based organizations. Will they be able to recruit workers and volunteers as readily, for example? Will donations fall as the numbers of people disengaged from formal religion increase? The chapter on the United Kingdom in this volume offers a hopeful analysis, perhaps. Steven Kettell argues that the assumption that the religiously motivated donate or volunteer at higher rates than those without religious connections may be faulty. If so, support for charitable organizations is not doomed to fail. Indeed, if faith-based organizations are able both to reach out to and to recruit diverse populations, their work may be more sustainable, because the risk that they reinforce *bonding social capital* (develop an exclusionary sub-culture) over *bridging social capital* (bringing diverse populations together) would be mitigated.

In conclusion, while robust at present in all our case-studies, faith-based organizations face a number of challenges on the horizon. We wonder whether they will be able to maintain and expand the delivery of social services at a time of secular welfare state retrenchment and cutbacks. Also, as the number of secular non-profits expands, will they survive a more competitive third-sector environment? While religion continues to play a vital role in many Europeans' lives, will faith-based organizations be able to incorporate the growing share of the population that is secular or affiliated with minority religions? Will faith-based organizations remain a significant feature of European civil society in the future? For answers to these important questions, we await future research.

NOTES

1. These works include Scott R. Appleby *The Ambivalence of the Sacred: Religion, Violence and Reconciliation* (New York: Rowman & Littlefield, 2000); Anders Backstrom and Grace Davie with Ninna Edgardh and Per Petterson, eds., *Welfare and Religion in 21st Century Europe*, vol. 1 (Farnham, UK: Ashgate, 2010); Anders Backstrom, Grace Davie, Ninna Edgardh, and Per Petterson, eds., *Welfare and Religion in 21st Century Europe*, vol. 2 (Farnham, UK: Ashgate, 2011); Peter Berger, *The Sacred Canopy: Elements of a Sociological Theory of Religion* (Boston: Anchor, 1990); Ingo Bode, "A New Agenda for European Charity: Catholic Welfare and Organizational Change in France and Germany," *International*

Journal of Voluntary and Nonprofit Organizations 14, no. 2 (2003): 205–225; Jose Casanova, "Civil Society and Religion: Retrospective Reflections on Catholicism and Prospective Reflections on Islam Social Research," *Civil Society Revisited* 68, no. 4 (2001): 1041–1080; Ipek Gocmen, "The Role of Faith-Based Organizations in Social Welfare Systems: A Comparison of France, Germany, Sweden, and the UK," *Nonprofit and Voluntary Sector Quarterly* 42, no. 3 (2013): 495–516; Jeffrey Haynes and Anja Henning, *Religious Actors in the Public Square: Means, Objectives and Effects* (New York: Routledge, 2011); Ronald Inglehart and Christian Welzel, *Modernization, Cultural Change and Democracy: The Human Development Sequence* (Cambridge: Cambridge University Press, 2005); Ted Jelen, "Political Christianity: A Contextual Analysis," *American Journal of Political Science* 36, no. 3 (1992): 692–714; Ted Jelen and Clyde Wilcox, *Religion and Politics in Comparative Perspective: The One, the Few, and the Many* (New York: Cambridge University Press, 2002); Katherine Meyer, Daniel Tope, and Anne M. Price, "Religion and Support for Democracy: A Cross-national Examination," *Sociological Spectrum* 28 (2008): 625–653; Tim Müller, "Religiosity and Attitudes towards the Involvement of Religious Leaders in Politics: A Multilevel Analysis of 55 Societies," *World Values Research* 2, no. 1 (2009): 1–29; Pippa Norris and Ronald Inglehart, *Sacred and Secular: Religion and Politics Worldwide* (New York: Cambridge University Press, 2004); and H.R. Unruh and R.J. Sider, *Saving Souls, Serving Society: Understanding the Faith Factor in Church-based Ministry* (New York: Oxford University Press, 2005).
2. René Rémond, *Religion et société en Europe: La sécularisation aux XIXe et XXe siècles (1789–2000)* (Paris: Seuil, 2001); René Rémond, *Religion and Society in Modern Europe* (Oxford: Blackwell, 1999); René Rémond, *Le Christianisme en accusation* (Paris: Desclée de Brouwer, 2000); René Rémond, *Le nouvel anti-Christianisme: Entretiens avec Marc Leboucher* (Paris: Desclée de Brouwer, 2005); Paul Valadier, *L'Eglise en procès: Catholicisme et société modern* (Paris: Flammarion, 1999); Paul Valadier, *Agir en politique: Decision morale et pluralisme politique* (Paris: Editions du Cerf, 1980); Paul Valadier *Anarchie des valeurs* (Paris: Albin Michel, 1997); Paul Valadier, *Un Christianisme d'avenir: Pour une nouvelle alliance entre raison et foi* (Paris: Seuil, 1999); Steven Englund, "The Muted Vibrancy of French Catholicism" and "L'Eglise de France: The Church in a Post-Religious Age," *Commonweal: A Review of Religion, Politics and Culture* (May 18, 2001), 12–16.
3. Paul Valadier, *L'Eglise en procès: Catholicisme et société moderne* (Paris: Flammarion, 1999).
4. Gonzalo Villagrán, S.J., "Public Theology in a Foreign Land: A Proposal for Bringing Theology in Public into the Spanish Context" (PhD diss., Boston College School of Theology and Ministry, 2012).

5. Englund, *Commonweal*, May 18, 2001: 12.
6. Carolyn Warner, *Confessions of an Interest Group* (Princeton, NJ: Princeton University Press, 2002), 18.
7. Robert D. Putnam, "The Prosperous Community: Social Capital and Public Life," in *The American Prospect* 13 (Spring 1993), http://epn.org/prospect/13/13putn.html.
8. Philippe Schmitter, "Organized Interests and Democratic Consolidation in Southern Europe," in *The Politics of Democratic Consolidation: Southern Europe in Comparative Perspective*, ed. Richard Gunther, P. Nikiforos Diamandouros, and Hans-Jürgen Puhle, 284–314, 285 (Baltimore: Johns Hopkins University Press). See also Philippe Schmitter, "The Irony of Modern Democracy and the Viability of Efforts to Re-form its Practice," in *Associations and Democracy*, ed. E. O. Wright, 167–183 (London and New York: Verso, 1995).
9. Alfred C. Stepan, *Arguing Comparative Politics* (New York: Oxford University Press, 2001), 216.
10. Robert M. Fishman, "Democratic Practice after the Revolution: The Case of Portugal and Beyond," *Politics & Society* 39, no. 2 (2001): 233–267, 259n6.
11. Archon Fung, "Associations and Democracy: Between Theories, Hopes, and Realities," *Annual Review of Sociology* 29 (2003): 515–539, especially 518–529. See also Archon Fung and Erik Olin Wright, eds., *Deepening Democracy: Institutional Innovations in Empowered Participatory Governance* (London: Verso, 2003).
12. Paul Hirst, *Associative Democracy: New Forms of Economic and Social Governance* (Cambridge, UK: Wiley, 1994), 21.
13. Pazit Ben-Nun Bloom and Gizem Arikan, "Religion and Support for Democracy: A Cross-National Test of the Mediating Mechanisms," *British Journal of Political Science* 43, no. 2 (2013): 375–397, https://doi.org/10.1017/S0007123412000427.
14. José Casanova, "Civil Society and Religion: Retrospective Reflections on Catholicism and Prospective Reflections on Islam Social Research," *Civil Society Revisited* 68, no. 4 (Winter 2001): 1041–1080, 1049. See also José Casanova, *Public Religions in the Modern World* (Chicago: University of Chicago Press, 2011), 229.
15. See İpek Göçmen, "The Role of Faith-Based Organizations in Social Welfare Systems: A comparison of France, Germany, Sweden, and the United Kingdom," *Nonprofit and Voluntary Sector Quarterly* 42, no. 3 (2013): 495–516; Kimberly J. Morgan, "Forging the Frontiers Between State, Church, and Family: Religious Cleavages and the Origins of Early Childhood Education and Care Policies in France, Sweden, and Germany, *Politics & Society* 30, no. 1 (2002): 113–148.

16. See Louella Moore, "Legitimation Issues in the State-Nonprofit Relationship," *Nonprofit and Voluntary Sector Quarterly* 30, no. 4 (2001) 707–719.
17. Moore, "Legitimation Issues," 711.
18. Göçmen, "The Role of Faith-Based Organizations," 509. Other notable faith-based welfare organizations in France include Federation Entraide Protestante and Secours Islamique de France.
19. Willem Adema, Pauline Fron, and Maxime Ladaique, "Is the European Welfare State Really More Expensive?: Indicators on Social Spending, 1980–2012," *OECD Social, Employment and Migration Working Papers* No. 124 (2011), https://www.researchgate.net/publication/241764379_ Is_the_European_Welfare_State_Really_More_Expensive_Indicators_ on_Social_Spending_1980-2012_and_a_Manual_to_the_OECD_Social_ Expenditure_Database_SOCX.
20. S. Bracke, *Journal of Empirical Theology* 25 (2012): 247–248; A. Bäckström and G. Davie, with N. Edgardh and P. Pettersson, *Welfare and Religion in 21st Century Europe: Configuring the Connections (vol. 1)* (Farnham, UK: Ashgate, 2010).
21. A. Bäckström and G. Davie, "A Preliminary Conclusion: Gathering the Threads and Moving On," Chapter 11, in *Welfare and Religion in 21st Century Europe: Configuring the Connections* (vol. 1), ed. A. Bäckström and G. Davie, with N. Edgardh & P. Pettersson (Farnham, UK: Ashgate), 183–199; quote is from page 190.
22. See Frantz-Xavier Kaufmann, *Variations of the Welfare State: Great Britain, Sweden, France and Germany Between Capitalism and Socialism* (Heidelberg: Springer-Verlag, 2013); Ingo Bode, "A New Agenda for European Charity: Catholic Welfare and Organizational Change in France and Germany," *Voluntas: International Journal of Voluntary and Nonprofit Organizations* 14, no. 2 (June 2003) 205–225.
23. Jeffrey Haynes and Anja Henning, *Religious Actors in the Public Square: Means, Objectives and Effects* (New York: Routledge, 2011), 3–5.
24. Pew Research Center, "Size, Projected Growth of Major Religious Groups in Europe, 2010–2050," March 27, 2015, http://www.pewforum.org/2015/04/02/europe/attachment/147/.
25. Pew Research Center, "Largest Religious Group, by Country," June 19, 2015, http://www.pewresearch.org/fact-tank/2015/06/22/what-is-each-countrys-second-largest-religious-group/ft_15-06-12religiousgroups_alargest640px-2/.
26. Ted Jelen and Clyde Wilcox, *Religion and Politics in Comparative Perspective: The One, the Few and the Many* (New York: Cambridge University Press, 2002).
27. Gøsta Esping-Andersen, *The Three Worlds of Welfare* (Princeton, NJ: Princeton University Press, 1990).

PART I

Countries with a Dominant Religious Society

CHAPTER 2

The Entanglement and Disentanglement of Church and State in Irish Social Policy

Michele Dillon

SOCIAL CHANGE IN IRELAND

With a current population size of 4.7 million, the highest since independence (in 1922),[1] the Republic of Ireland has undergone significant demographic and cultural change, especially over the past 30 years. Of particular note is the dramatic change in its religious tenor. Since the 1990s, the proportion reporting no religious affiliation has steadily increased from 2 percent in the 1990s, to 6 percent in 2011, to 10 percent in 2016 (see Fig. 2.1). And maintaining a well-settled and more universal pattern of gender variation in religious attachment, Irish men (11 percent) are more likely than women (9 percent) to be unaffiliated.[2] Non-affiliation in Ireland is low compared to other Western European countries and to the United States, where currently 25 percent have no religious affiliation, more than triple what it was in the 1990s (7 percent). Against this

---

I appreciate Paul Manuel's helpful guiding questions and suggestions, and Emily Mason's research assistance.

M. Dillon (✉)
University of New Hampshire, Durham, NH, USA

© The Author(s) 2019
P. C. Manuel, M. Glatzer (eds.), *Faith-Based Organizations and Social Welfare*, Palgrave Studies in Religion, Politics, and Policy,
https://doi.org/10.1007/978-3-319-77297-4_2

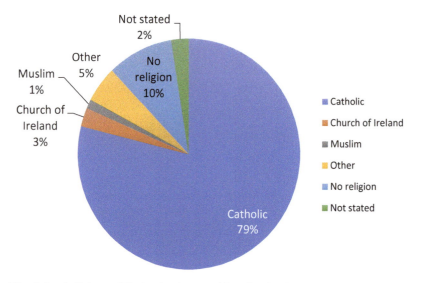

Fig. 2.1 Religious affiliation in the Republic of Ireland, 2016

backdrop, there is a low probability that the trend toward non-affiliation (in both Ireland and the United States) will be reversed owing to the fact that young adults disproportionately account for the unaffiliated. Irish people in their 30s are the least attached to religion, with 12 percent of this group unaffiliated. Given the life-course significance of this age period for family formation (i.e., getting married and having children), it seems likely that the socialization of new birth cohorts will occur in more secular than religious family settings.

The trend toward non-affiliation is largely concurrent with a decline in Catholicism. Today, 79 percent of people in Ireland self-identify as Catholic, a decrease from 84 percent just five years earlier, and from 92 percent in 1991 (see Fig. 2.2).[3] This still represents a high level of attachment to Catholicism. The decline is nonetheless significant, and all the more noteworthy given Catholicism's long historical and cultural dominance in Irish society. For many generations, to be Irish was to be Catholic, notwithstanding the presence of a substantial Protestant minority and a small Jewish population. Today, owing to other intertwined demographic changes, the religious and ethnic composition of the Irish population is more variegated. Among the religiously affiliated, Protestants remain the

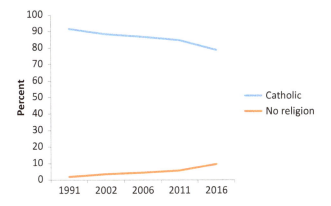

Fig. 2.2 Change in religious affiliation in the Republic of Ireland, 1991–2016

largest minority (3 percent), while Muslims (1.3 percent) and Christian Orthodox (1.3 percent) are growing in number. Further, the Catholic population includes a large number of Poles, Ireland's largest immigrant group.

Indeed, the proportion of non-nationals in Ireland, 12 percent, is also noteworthy. Migration to Ireland visibly increased in the mid-1990s with the rise of the Celtic Tiger (approx. 1995–2005) and peaked in 2007 before the onset of the Great Recession. In-migration stands in contrast to Ireland's history of trans-generational out-migration and diaspora, and it reflects the overall, historically significant improvement in economic and social well-being in Ireland.[4] With the Great Recession, out-migration increased dramatically, especially between 2009 and 2012, and it was mostly well-educated Irish citizens rather than the more recently arrived new immigrants who left.[5] Yet, in-migration has resurged since 2013 with economic recovery. The dynamic nature of migration patterns in Ireland since the early 1990s means that today Ireland's share of foreign-born residents is comparatively high (16 percent).[6] Additionally, many Irish residents have dual citizenship, as Irish-Americans or as Irish-UK and, increasingly, as Irish-Poles.[7]

Other significant demographic patterns include the aging of the population. Currently, 13.4 percent of Irish people are age 65 or older, a notable increase from 11.7 percent just five years earlier. By the same token, there are fewer children and young people; those 25 and younger account for a third of Ireland's population today, a marked contrast to the late 1970s, when they accounted for almost half (48 percent).[8] Related to these patterns is the decline in the Irish total fertility rate, from 3.21 in 1980 to 1.92 in 2016, and decline in the average number of children per family, from 2.0 in 1990 to 1.38 in 2016, though the number of births per 1000 population continues to be comparatively high relative to other Western European countries.[9] Notably too, continuing a long-observed pattern in Ireland, a growing proportion of all births are outside of marriage (36.5 percent), but unlike in the 1970s, they are increasingly not to lone (single) mothers but to cohabiting couples, who account for over a half of all non-marital births.[10]

Economic Fluidity

After years of consumer affluence associated with the Celtic Tiger (approx. 1995–2005), Ireland confronted severe economic austerity in the wake of its collapse exacerbated by the global financial crisis and Great Recession (2007–2008). Banking and financial scandals, the collapse of property prices, government mismanagement, high unemployment, and the more generalized wide-ranging effects of the recession dragged the Irish into a sharp economic downfall. These events also shook people's confidence in political and economic institutions and in their own ability to forge a secure future for themselves and their children. Cuts in employment, wages, welfare benefits and public services, and other government-imposed austerity measures aimed at adjusting to the crisis and rebuilding Ireland's credit rating and EU standing, brought a lot of hardship.[11] Yet, these measures and the resurgent growth in the global economy have resulted in Ireland regaining its economic footing, and have done so in a remarkably short time. In November 2017, its unemployment rate was 6.1 percent, down from 15.9 percent in 2011, household disposable income has steadily increased every year since 2011, and aggregate measures of gross domestic product and gross domestic income are consistently robust.[12]

Poverty and Homelessness

Despite resurging economic growth, however, the at-risk-of-poverty rate (those whose income falls below 60 percent of the country's median household income) has declined only slightly, from 17.2 percent in 2014 to 16.9 percent in 2015. Similarly, the "consistent poverty rate" which takes account of at-risk and those experiencing "enforced [economic] deprivation" was 8.5 percent in 2015, and 8.8 percent in 2014. Women (16.4 percent) are more likely than men (16.1 percent) to be at risk of poverty. As is the case in other Western countries, social welfare benefits are significant buffers against poverty: For example, in 2015, 47.9 percent of women in Ireland and 44.6 percent of men were at risk of poverty before income from pensions and social transfers was taken into account.[13]

Yet, despite welfare assistance, many experience economic and social deprivation, a point underlined by the increasing number of homeless individuals and families in Ireland. In just one year, the number of homeless people increased by 25 percent, from 6525 in July 2016 to 8270 in August 2017, with one in three being homeless children.[14] The assessment of both the nature and extent of homelessness and how to respond to it is politically controversial, and a source of tension between the government and the voluntary philanthropic sector.[15] More generally, housing policy is considered an ongoing crisis issue in Ireland. During the Celtic Tiger, population, economic, and consumer growth accelerated the demand for housing and thus sharply elevated land and house prices as well as personal and mortgage debts. Then, the economy's subsequent crash saw the collapse of property values as well as a decline in owners' ability to pay their mortgages and taxes[16] Housing needs are also complicated by Ireland's openness to accommodating refugees. In 2015, as the refugee crisis and its humanitarian and political implications enveloped the European Union in contentious debate, Ireland committed to take in and resettle 4000 refugees and/or asylum seekers; so far it has accepted 1244 (mostly from Syria and Lebanon). The Irish Refugee Council works to find housing and jobs for the refugees across various towns and counties in Ireland, and thus far resettlement is proceeding relatively smoothly.

The Entanglement of Church and State in Ireland

Any narrative of church–state relations in Ireland must emphasize that while church and state are, and have always been, legally separate institutions, they have a deeply entangled relationship.[17] This is not surprising given the embeddedness of the Catholic Church in Irish society and culture, forging a trajectory that long predates independence and which was cemented during Ireland's long history of subjugation by Britain dating back to the Penal Laws. The Irish Constitution was ratified in 1937. It offers a window into what was widely seen by church and state leaders alike—personified by Dublin Archbishop John Charles McQuaid and the equally devout Prime Minister and Fianna Fail leader Eamon de Valera—as the natural, intertwined compatibility of both church and state in the construal of what was (and ought to be) an essentially "Catholic nation." While recognizing the presence of Ireland's diverse faith traditions, the Constitution affirmed the "special position" of the Catholic Church.

Further in line with Catholic social teaching, it gave special recognition to the family as "indispensable to the welfare of the Nation and the State." It defined it as "the natural primary and fundamental unit group of society ... antecedent and superior to all positive law," and pledged to "guard with special care the institution of Marriage ... and to protect it against attack." Specifically, it declared that "no law shall be enacted providing for the grant of a dissolution of marriage," that is, no divorce. Laws already enacted by de Valera's government prior to the constitution blocked other perceived threats to marriage, the family, and Catholic values. These included the prohibition of the sale and importation of contraceptives, the regulation of dance halls, a tax on foreign newspapers, and the censorship of films and books (including those of famous Irish authors such as Samuel Beckett and James Joyce).

Catholic identity was also embodied in Irish institutions, most notably, in education and in health care and social services; again, this interrelation predated independence. As elaborated by several studies, the interrelation between church and state in Ireland is complex, both historically and today.[18] The church was certainly well able to wield its considerable, and mostly unquestioned, power across all levels and sectors of society, ranging from the regulation of intimate interpersonal relations to setting the parameters of macro-social policy. Yet, its moral monopoly[19] did not derive simply from a unilateral power-grab by the church. Rather, it emerged out of and in relation to a broader mix of political and institutional actors (including upper-class elites in Ireland and England), whose diverse interests and variously shifting interrelational dynamics helped directly and indirectly to advance the church's power at various historical junctures (both under British rule and in post-independence Ireland).

SOCIAL POLICY

As Tony Fahey elaborates, the church's influence on social policy is due not only to the impact of Catholic values and social teaching but also—and perhaps especially—to "a practical influence which arose from the church's role as a major provider of social services."[20] Thus while modern Ireland's social policy has emulated a welfare state system[21] gradually developed and expanded since the 1960s, there is a long history of state—and societal—reliance on the church. Successive government leaders—and with the tacit consent of the local and national community—frequently looked to the church to fulfill roles that in other Western European societies might more appropriately be considered the (welfare) state's responsibility, or as in the United States, considered the remit of a third sector of religious and other non-profit healthcare, social service, and education providers.

In Ireland, the church's provider role includes the ownership of many hospitals and nursing and other care homes (including the now-notorious "mother and baby" homes) by religious orders of nuns.[22] The church's service provider role is also highly visible through an extensive nationwide network of (Catholic-related) voluntary social welfare organizations. These include the St. Vincent de Paul Society, founded in 1844 and currently Ireland's largest voluntary charitable organization; an array of organizations established by the bishops to implement the church's social justice teachings; and additional welfare organizations founded by individual priests and nuns focused on helping the poor, the homeless, and other vulnerable individuals and families: Sister Stan Kennedy who founded Focus Ireland in the mid-1980s to work with homeless people is a case in point; another is the Jesuit Peter McVerry who has also worked with homeless youth for decades.

EDUCATION

There is also a long tradition in Ireland of a national, state system of first-, second-, and third-level education funded and overseen by the Department of Education but under the immediate control of Catholic dioceses and religious orders (of nuns, priests, and brothers). All primary (elementary) schools are state-owned, for example, but (until recently) the school patron and manager was the parish priest (and, in turn, the diocesan bishop) of the parish in which the school is located. "Free" second- and third-level education was introduced by the state in 1968, and prior to then, families paid fees or were awarded scholarships so that their high-achieving children could attend a particular school, with secondary school education mostly organized by single-sex schools owned and controlled by nuns, Christian Brothers, or diocesan priests. Lay-managed (and mixed sex) vocational schools also catered to the educational needs of some, but as their name conveys, they focused on applied vocation-skill development rather than an academic professional track. Additionally, there was and still is a small number of private fee-paying Catholic, Protestant, and non-denominational schools.

College-level education was for many decades dominated by a handful of institutions: the Protestant-controlled Trinity College Dublin, which Catholics were prohibited from attending by Archbishop John McQuaid under pain of mortal sin until 1970; University College Dublin, founded in 1854 under the auspices of the Catholic bishops as the Catholic University of Ireland (with Cardinal John Henry Newman as rector); and University College Cork and University College Galway. The third-level sector greatly expanded in the 1980s and subsequently with the establishment of several regional and national colleges (including, for example, Dublin University Institute, and the University of Limerick).

It is important to note, however, that while education was largely in the hands of the church, the curriculum was highly rigorous and academically driven. Thus, while Catholicism was deeply embedded in the school ethos and calendar and across its various activities, the formal curriculum—other than the specific (relatively short) time allotted for religious education—was heavily secular, including a major focus on languages, literature, writing, music, math, and science. Given the recurring tensions in the United States between conservative Protestant evangelicalism and science, most vivid in debates over the place of evolution in school curricula, it is important to recognize that such tensions tend not to arise in the context of Catholic education. Indeed, debates over "creationism," are largely an American Protestant phenomenon. Notwithstanding the church's infamous disavowal of Galileo, Catholicism's balancing of "faith and reason" has long translated in Catholic education to the embrace of a standardized secular curriculum. A Catholic habitus was certainly inculcated through schools' everyday routine practices (and amplified by home, family, and community habits). Yet, the formal curriculum itself—by advancing the educational achievement of successive cohorts of pupils, and ensuring their readiness for university and professional success, was a secularizing force—and, ironically, one largely facilitated by the church.

The Entanglement of Catholic Teaching with Public Morality

The entanglement of church and state in everyday life in Ireland, and the force it offers against the secularization of that relationship and of Irish society more generally, is encapsulated time and again by episodes that crystallize the intertwining of Catholic teaching and public morality.[23] In the late 1940s, for example, a progressive policy stance by De Valera's government to provide free hospital care to pregnant women and their new-born infants—known as the "Mother and Child" scheme—was forcefully rejected by the bishops.[24] With little opposition to their views, they successfully argued that the proposal was "entirely and directly contrary to Catholic teaching on the rights of the family, [and] the [primacy of the] rights of the Church in education." They pointed out, moreover, that "physical or health education is closely interwoven with important moral questions on which the Catholic Church has definite teaching.... The State has no competence to give instruction in such matters." And as Archbishop McQuaid noted, "The hierarchy cannot approve of any scheme which, by its general tendency, must foster undue control by the State in a sphere so delicate and so intimately concerned with morals."[25]

This was a very different era: a still heavily rural, conservative, and inward-looking society, prior to the economic development and other modernization changes set in motion in the early 1960s. This was the same era in which unmarried mothers and their children were so cruelly treated—dehumanized—by church, state, family, and local people alike. Theologically and institutionally, this was also a very different church, before the changes instituted by Vatican II (1962–1965), including its affirmation of religious freedom, conscience, and church–state differentiation. Neither societal nor church changes however, dramatically altered the "delicate sphere" of moral issues and the conflation of public morality with Catholic morality. In 1974, the Irish Supreme Court ruled that the criminalization of contraception violated the constitutional right to marital privacy, and imposed its expectation on parliament to change the law. Underscoring the cultural hold of Catholicism, the Fine Gael/Labour coalition government's subsequent efforts to decriminalize contraception were thwarted by the moral views of many of its own members, including Fine Gael party leader and Prime Minister Liam Cosgrave, who voted against his own health minister's legislation on grounds of conscience. In other words, a law that would allow married couples to use contraception would be contrary to his adherence to and understanding of Catholic teaching and thus as a Catholic and as a political leader he could not support it.

Ten years later, in 1986, when Fine Gael leader and Prime Minister Garret FitzGerald introduced a proposal to hold a public referendum that sought to modify the constitutional prohibition on divorce, his framing of the issue further amplified the persistence of the church–state–culture entanglement. A Catholic intellectual committed to pluralism (in the tradition of Jacques Maritain), FitzGerald went to great lengths to emphasize that while he himself as a practicing Catholic believed in and was attached to "indissoluble monogamy," he had a sociological duty to recognize that not all individuals believed as he did, and thus they might wish to avail of divorce. Further conveying Ireland's deep-seated Catholic habitus, he acknowledged that members of his own parliamentary party may on grounds of conscience not wish to participate in (their own government-initiated) divorce legalization campaign. He also felt obliged to point out that he and his government colleagues held consultations with leaders of all the churches before finalizing the divorce proposal, and further noted that "some or all of the churches may have different views" regarding the legalization of (what was a highly restrictive) divorce proposal.[26] Given all these affirmations of the facticity of Catholicism in Irish life, it is not surprising perhaps that the divorce proposal was rejected by two-thirds of the electorate. This was so despite the then already-visible prevalence of marital breakdown, despite public opinion support for divorce prior to the referendum debate, and despite the fact that the bishops largely relied on empirical, sociological, and economic reasoning rather than Catholic theology in opposing divorce.

CHURCH AND STATE DIMINISHMENT

Today in Ireland, both the church and the state are somewhat diminished. The church's decline is due to a mix of factors that have accelerated what I have elsewhere called Ireland's compressed secularization.[27] These include the impact of the priest sex-abuse scandals and church leaders' patterned evasion of responsibility as documented in detail in the media and in successive independent reports (e.g., the Murphy Report), the consumer affluence ushered in by the success of the Celtic Tiger, the expansion of the European Union and of study and other travel-abroad experiences that have helped nurture more pluralistic worldviews, and the in-migration of ethnically and religiously diverse people (as noted earlier). The state's diminishment is largely due to its role in abetting the banking and financial malpractices that contributed to Ireland's economic downturn, its loss of financial sovereignty to the EU Commission, the European Central Bank (ECB), and the International Monetary Fund (IMF) in order to bail out the Irish economy, and the subsequent austerity measures it introduced to deal with the enormous financial debt incurred. These events unfolded, moreover, against a series of political scandals pointing to either the incompetence or the malfeasance of several elected politicians.

The intensity of the Celtic Tiger's emphasis on financial capitalism and economic competitiveness reflected a growing political shift since the 1980s in neo-liberal thinking in Irish social policy.[28] Ireland's comparative positioning on such key indicators as the Employment Protection Index and the proportion of GNP allocated to social spending has long pointed to a state driven more by neo-liberal than welfare state ideology.[29] And welfare and taxation policy changes across several domains in the post-Tiger era, including a tax on household water usage and a (temporary) freeze on the minimum wage, further underscore the dominance of neoliberalism. At the same time, there is a long and relatively stable social partnership between the government, employer federations, and trade unions. But the relatively consensual nature of their negotiation of issues of wage protection and employment security tends to allow the state to coopt the unions in policies that undermine the economic and social well-being of low-wage workers and other vulnerable groups.[30]

Poverty and economic inequality were somewhat obscured but nonetheless continued during the Celtic Tiger, and in the wake of its demise, they became foregrounded. Indeed, regressive taxation policies, cutbacks in pensions and other welfare benefits, and the steadily growing increase in homelessness (noted earlier) has prompted some observers to refer to Ireland as "the care-less state."[31] Lynch and colleagues argue that "While there were economic costs for all classes and groups, those who were already impoverished prior to the economic crisis became more impoverished during it. Ireland was and remained a care-less state in the sense that the government disregarded the needs of some of its most vulnerable and powerless citizens during the austerity period, especially if they were unable to be or were not sufficiently resourced, and/or not politically powerful enough to exercise political influence." As Lynch further elaborates, "the market has become the primary producer of cultural logic and cultural value in Irish society."[32]

THE CHALLENGE OF SOCIAL INCLUSION IN NEO-LIBERAL IRELAND

In the context of state "carelessness" and the market-driven cultural turn, the targeting of specific social problems such as poverty, for example, lose priority relative to the goal of asserting Ireland's place as a hub of global capitalism. Its resurging cosmopolitan identity as a vibrant financial destination is vividly conveyed by the impressive redevelopment of the Dublin quays with affluent bars, restaurants, and apartments alongside Google, global finance and consulting companies, and the relocation of established home-grown law practices increasingly well equipped to serve, as they advertise, a global clientele. Against this backdrop, the policy challenges presented by poverty, homelessness, and the health and service needs of under-served, vulnerable groups are not just a financial complication but also a political strain on successive governments. Symbolically, poverty and inequality become euphemized as something else. Thus, the government-funded Combat Poverty Agency, established in 1986, became integrated in 2009 as part of the Social Inclusion Division within the Department of Social and Family Affairs, a Division which a year later was incorporated into the Department of Community, Equality and Gaeltacht Affairs, and since 2011, within the Department of Social Protection (located in Gandon House on Amiens Street, a 15-minute walk from the newly vibrant quays). Euphemization (here, language that reframes poverty more abstractly as social inclusion or as social protection), as Pierre Bourdieu notes, fosters the collective misrecognition of structural inequality and thus reproduces the status quo, leaving intact the inequities that institutional practices, including language, paper over.[33]

Social inclusion, of course, is also the project emphasized by Pope Francis.[34] And he is very clear about what this entails. In *The Joy of the Gospel* (*JG*), issued in November 2013, he identified "an economy of exclusion and inequality" as a fundamental societal ill, and argued that "the inclusion of the poor in society" is "fundamental at this time in history" and to shaping "the future of humanity." In plain-spoken language he argues that attentiveness to the cry of the poor and the oppressed requires a commitment to enacting structural changes. It "means working to eliminate the structural causes of poverty and to promote the integral development of the poor as well as small daily acts of solidarity in meeting the real needs we encounter. The word solidarity is a little worn and at times poorly understood, but it refers to something more than a few sporadic acts of generosity. It presumes the creation of a new mindset that thinks in terms of community and the priority of the life of all over the appropriation of goods by a few."[35] Francis's emphasis is in direct accord with the church's long tradition of social teaching, dating back to the late nineteenth century. Social inclusion is deeply embedded in the Catholic understanding of the common good. As summarized by Jesuit theologian David Hollenbach, its "understanding of justice ... calls for action that goes beyond exclusion to active support for inclusion.... The preservation of human dignity requires positive action in support of those who are vulnerable to de facto conditions of unequal and non-reciprocal interdependence."[36]

The Irish bishops have long shown concern about both national and global poverty establishing, for example, Trocaire in 1973 as a charitable agency sending emergency relief and other help to people in Africa and in Central and South America. In January 2009, the bishops' Commission for Justice and Social Affairs issued a position paper on poverty in Ireland, *In the Wake of the Celtic Tiger: Poverty in Contemporary Ireland*, in which they elaborated on the challenges it poses. They noted that poverty exists "notwithstanding the social gains and economic growth of the Celtic Tiger ... and risks increasing significantly in the current crisis."[37] And they pointed out, "Poverty is not simply about lowness of income.... Poverty denies individuals what they need to flourish and also denies Irish society the gifts of those who never reach their potential. Thus it is both morally reprehensible and economically damaging."[38] More recently, the bishops have rearticulated the moral obligation imposed by poverty and homelessness, calling for the building of "a society where homelessness, and poor housing, which are an affront to human dignity, are eradicated forever."[39] In addition to these verbal nudges, several individual dioceses provide ongoing practical assistance through agencies that cater to the needs of poor and homeless people (as well as help to refugees and other marginal groups).

THE RELIGIOUS DIVESTMENT OF SCHOOLS AND HOSPITALS

Although the problem of homelessness has received widespread attention in recent years, two of the most controversial policy issues have revolved around education and medical care, specifically schools and hospitals. The details of each issue vary but common to both is the entanglement of church and state and the anomalies presented in an increasingly secularized society. The tensions unveiled make clear that a history of cultural and institutional entanglement is not easily set aside.

Schools

Take the case of schools. In a nutshell, baptized Catholic children have priority in admission to state-financed primary schools in Ireland (reflecting policies consonant with the institutionalized patronage/managerial role of the church in education, discussed earlier). Across most of the twentieth century this was not a problem, as Catholics and the small Protestant minority naturally self-sorted to a national school whose respective patron was the local Catholic parish priest or in rarer instances a school under the auspices of the Protestant church. The unspoken (Catholic) denominational nature of Irish state education was taken for granted and only became problematic in the late 1970s when a group of Dublin parents lobbied the state to establish a multidenominational school, a project which after some political wrangling succeeded. Subsequently, "Educate Together" was established (in 1984) as the organizing committee overseeing and lobbying for non-denominational schools. Today, it is patron to 81 national schools across the Republic of Ireland.

This may seem like a culturally resonant solution to the established dominance of the Catholic Church in education. However, as a result of Ireland's growing population and its impact on infrastructure, there is, for the last few years, an insufficient number of school seats available to new cohorts of primary school children, and the vast majority (approx. 90 percent) of schools and seats are under the patronage and control of the church. In this newly competitive societal environment, therefore, a baptized child has an edge over a non-baptized child in access to education. This "baptism barrier" in itself underscores the anomaly whereby the secular state rewards confessional adherence. And the state-bias toward religion/Catholicism is all the more sociologically jarring given that the decrease in religious affiliation, and specifically in Catholic affiliation, coexists in tandem with an increase in non-Catholics and in non-religious individuals.

It would be easy to assume that these anomalies persist owing to the defensively tenacious hold of the church on its otherwise-declining institutional and cultural power. But this inference would be an oversimplification. In fact, the protracted nature of the issue is largely due to the foot-dragging of successive governments who seem unable to devise policies that would facilitate the smooth transition from church to secular patronage—to institute secular control, moreover, of what are institutionally, state-owned, and state-funded schools. This is the case despite frequently voiced openness to the idea from leading Catholic figures such as Dublin Archbishop Diarmuid Martin. Other Catholic voices, such as the Catholic Primary Schools Management Association (CPSMA), express reservations about the loss of a denominational "ethos." Yet such concern—and a broader pattern of what Diarmuid Martin has called "stubborn resistance" within the church[40]—might be allayed by the findings of Catholic-commissioned studies documenting how alternative schooling models and non-denominational curricula attend to religious education and ethical formation.[41] Despite these politically useful resources, and despite lobbying for change by "Educate Together" and other groups and organizations (e.g., "Education Equality," and the Irish Human Rights and Equality Commission), and broad support in public opinion, the government continues to dither on this policy challenge.

Hospitals

The church's presence in Irish medical care is well established. Historically, there has basically been a parallel, complementary structure. This includes state-regulated networks of regional health boards and public hospitals across the country, which since 2005 have been integrated into the newly created Health Services Executive (HSE), a body semi-autonomous of the Department of Health. There are also a significant number of private and public hospitals owned and managed by religious orders of nuns (e.g., including Dublin's Mater and St. Vincent's hospitals) and receiving government funding. The number of church-controlled hospitals has declined in recent years (partly due to the decline in religious vocations), but the financial stake of religious orders is still substantial, estimated at over one billion Euros.[42]

Regardless of whether hospitals are HSE or Catholic (or otherwise privately owned such as the Blackrock Clinic), the Catholic ethos in medical care has long been prevalent, with the historical exception of, for example, the Protestant-controlled Rotunda maternity hospital.[43] The Catholic ethos is especially explicit with respect to maternity care and reproductive issues including sterilization, in vitro fertilization, and, of course, abortion. Abortion has been a contentious policy issue ever since a referendum in 1983 reinforced its already illegal status with a constitutional prohibition (with two-thirds of the electorate voting in favor of what became the constitution's eighth amendment). Currently (January 2018), after several additional constitutional and legal challenges, abortion is legal but highly restrictive (available only if there is a real and substantial risk to the mother's life).

Public support to repeal the eighth amendment and/or to replace it with a more liberal policy will be tested in another referendum on abortion scheduled for summer 2018. The wording of the amendment is not yet published. It's likely, however, that any proposed change, to be accepted by a majority of the electorate, would need to still impose some limits on abortion, thus reflecting current public opinion, which favors legalization in some but not all circumstances. For example, approximately three-quarters or more of the Irish public support abortion in cases of physical (82 percent) and mental (72 percent) health or rape (76 percent). However, fewer support it in cases of severe life-threatening fetal abnormality (67 percent), and far fewer for a less severe abnormality (47 percent). Fewer still—about a fifth—support abortion in cases of economic hardship (21 percent) or for other "on request" circumstantial reasons (23 percent).[44]

The embeddedness of Catholic teaching in medical practice came into sharp public attention in 2012 when a seriously ill pregnant Indian woman who was miscarrying—and who by law was entitled to an abortion—died after being denied one (owing to the presence of a fetal heartbeat) by the hospital affiliated with University College Galway. In thrice denying the request for a termination, the woman and her husband were allegedly told "This is a Catholic country."[45] The incident further galvanized the prochoice movement and more broadly, in light of instances at other hospitals pointing to deficiencies both in maternity and emergency care, highlighted the need for expanded and higher quality hospital services.

The government's response to the infrastructural problem again brought to the fore the entanglement of church and state in Irish life. In proposals issued in 2017, it opted to build a new national maternity hospital on a site owned by a religious order, the Sisters of Charity, who have long been involved in health care provision in Ireland, and because the nuns own the site, they were to be given ownership of the hospital. This was highly controversial within the medical community and among the public at large. A subsequent negotiated agreement gave the hospital's board (which included some sisters) "clinical and operational independence in providing maternity services without religious, ethnic, or other distinction."[46] The nuns' ownership remained problematic, however, and the controversy was eventually resolved when they decided to transfer ownership to a newly formed non-profit company and to have no involvement with the hospital (despite it being on their land). Health Minister Simon Harris welcomed the nuns' decision, describing it as historic, and saying "It directly addresses concerns regarding the question of religious influence … and further illustrates the constructive role of the sisters to facilitate this landmark project."[47]

Can the State Manage the Divestment of Religious Influence?

What is left unsaid is that the sisters did not devise the original building and ownership plan, but that the state did. And it did so, as so often in the past, because the church's resources provided an (apparently) easy and convenient solution that let political leaders off the hook for not being able to envision and realize alternative policies and plans. Thus, the question of religious influence derives its salience as much from the role of the state—and societal collusion—as it does from the church's own interests. In health care, education, and social services, the church is not simply a partner of the state but in practical terms its functionally necessary apparatus. Absent the church's role in all these areas, the state would be confronted with multiple strains on its institutional capacity as well as on its avowed commitment to advancing the economic and social well-being of the Irish people.

For a long time, despite recurring episodic controversies, the church and state had a harmonious and largely consensual relationship. In the current moment, it is remarkably more distant. Indeed, it is ironic, given the close historical alliance of Ireland's mainstream political parties with the church hierarchy that the current leader of Fianna Fail and the current (Fine Gael) health minister have both suggested that the church should surrender its hospital property interests to the state.[48] The strain on church–state relations is exacerbated by a number of interrelated factors. These include the church sex-abuse scandals; the government's official inquiries into them and the shock of their findings on the Irish psyche; the evasive diffusion by both institutions of responsibility for the abuses in state-funded, church-managed schools, detention centers, and mother and baby homes; the state's increased reliance on financial markets and transnational institutions (e.g., the EU, the IMF); and more generally, the increased secular zeitgeist in Irish culture and society.

Yet, notwithstanding these forces, the fact remains that the state is dependent not only on the healthcare, education, and welfare infrastructure controlled by the church but also on the goodwill of church officials to accommodate the increasingly secularized expectations of the state. These same expectations put the state in a bind. They require it to develop a credible, long-term strategic plan showing how it intends to negotiate and manage the new financial, logistical, and broader policy implications entailed by religious divestment in schools, hospitals, and welfare. At the same time, it needs to manage the variegated politics of any such transition given that despite a declining Catholic population, eight in ten Irish people still identify as Catholic. Though further long-term decline is likely with increased secularization, Catholicism will still hold personal salience for many people even if, for example, the "baptism barrier" in access to primary schools is removed.

Religious Freedom

Amid Ireland's changing social reality, there is little discussion of the church's right to religious freedom. This is the case, perhaps, precisely because of its historically dominant presence in Irish public life—its protected special position. (It is interesting to note here that the overwhelming public support in 1972 for the deletion of the church's special recognition in the constitution was largely motivated by efforts to defuse Catholic–Protestant conflicts in the context of the Troubles in Northern Ireland, rather than by a rejection of the church's cultural status per se.) Today, unlike in the United States, where the Catholic bishops have made religious freedom a central issue in their public policy activism,[49] the Irish bishops are relatively reticent about their own and other Catholics' right to religious freedom. This may change as the secularization of civil institutions takes a greater hold. But to date, most of the public discussion, whether regarding schools, hospitals, or public policy more generally, is about the religious freedom of non-religious or minority religious individuals and groups to have their rights protected. There seems to be a generalized assumption that the church should more or less go along with secular changes.

The bishops have long insisted on their (liberal democratic) right to participate in public moral debates and have done so vigorously on divorce, abortion, and same-sex marriage. And their right to do so tends to be conceded, even if grudgingly so by some of their more severe critics. However, few public voices point to the conscience rights of church officials. One exception during the 2017 hospital relocation/building controversy was *Irish Times* religion editor Patsy McGarry. Noting an "unacknowledged element" in the controversy, he argued: "Why should the Sisters of Charity be placed in a position where the State expects they must violate conscience to carry out its will by implementing its laws? … In this Republic, it ought to be realized, accepted, and agreed that they too have a right to live by their beliefs in good conscience and not to do otherwise … as deemed by others."[50] Of further note, rather than defensively making recourse to religious freedom, Archbishop Diarmuid Martin has used the schools' religious divestment issue to emphasize the need for the church to self-critically evaluate how it communicates Catholicism. Indeed, he frequently observes that despite years of Catholic schooling, Irish people greatly lack in Catholic formation.[51]

A New Conscience

The resounding gap between Catholic formation and Catholic identity is crystallized by the Irish vote in favor of the legalization of same-sex marriage. In May 2015, 62 percent of Irish people, a majority in all but one constituency (heavily rural Roscommon–South Leitrim), rejected official church teaching on marriage. Thus, 30 years after two-thirds of the Irish voted against the introduction of divorce, a closely similar majority affirmed gay marriage. Now, the (imagined) Catholic nation had become the first in the world to institute a major social change by popular vote (rather than by a court or parliamentary decision). The vote was the culmination of a gradual but increasingly compressed process of secularization, and the result too of many years of well-organized social movement activism.[52]

While the 1980s projected a tenaciousness in the hold of Catholicism in Irish society (as reflected in the divorce and abortion referenda), the authority of the church had already begun its soon-to-accelerate decline. Public acceptance of "an Irish solution to an Irish problem"—as the (eventual) 1978 legalization of contraception for married couples was dubbed by then Health Minister Charles Haughey—showed an early crack in the church's authority. It represented a half-way solution: a nod to the church's teaching that all sexual activity should occur in marriage, accompanied by simultaneous indifference to its ban on contraception (including within marriage). The subsequent triumph of Catholic teaching on abortion and divorce in the moral debates of the 1980s was not sufficiently robust to buffer the church in light of its own abuses of sexual morality highlighted by priest sex-abuse scandals and the exposure of the sexual affairs of leading clerical figures. And these events unfolded alongside the forcefully coincidental, secularizing impact of the Celtic Tiger. Hence the markers in the path toward increased secularization: The decriminalization of homosexuality (1993), the legalization of divorce (1996), the legalization of same-sex civil unions (2011), the legalization of (restrictive) abortion (2013), and the legalization of gay marriage (2015).

Such cultural change—further reflected in efforts to divest the church from schools and healthcare—is nurtured by and reinforces parallel secular patterns in Catholics' attitudes to sexual morality and in their Mass-going habits. Going to Mass used to be an overarching piece of Irish family and communal life, the focal point of the weekly calendar regardless of other pressing or enticing activities. Those days seem largely over. In 1990, 85 percent reported going to weekly Mass, and in 2008, 43 percent did so. Estimates in 2017, including those by church officials, suggest that it's about 25 percent, with minimal attendance in several working-class Dublin parishes.[53] In rural Ireland, where there is a somewhat greater persistence of Catholic liturgical life, decline in commitment and the severe shortage of priests means that church closures and parish mergers are now commonplace. Going to Mass still matters to many Irish people, but it's clearly less salient and a less frequent event than in pre-Tiger days. Other forms of spirituality also still matter, as underlined by the continuing popularity of, for example, pilgrimages to Knock, Lough Derg, and Lourdes. Yet, given that the Mass and the Eucharist are core to Catholic theology and obligatory to personal and communal Catholic identity, the decline in weekly attendance is a significant marker of secularization and specifically of the church's diminished relevance.

Against the backdrop of the church's declining religious and cultural authority, there is some ambivalence apparent among the hierarchy about their aims for the church and how they envision their current and future role. Diarmuid Martin takes the high road, pointing to the need to deal with the new reality and to focus on "fostering faith" rather than condemning secularization.[54] Yet, he seems at a loss in articulating a path forward. Eamon Martin, the Archbishop of Armagh and Primate of all

Ireland, strikes a more defensive posture. He criticizes what he portrays as the current "almost compulsory [secular] consensus on controversial issues," and which caricatures and essentially denies religious voices a critical role in critiquing public culture.[55] Invoking Vatican II, both bishops talk of a more lay-engaged church. But the deep clericalism in Irish society, which persisted despite the changes articulated by Vatican II, makes that goal quite challenging. Unlike in the United States, for example, where Catholics who disagree with church teachings simultaneously exercise a deeply felt sense of ownership of Catholicism, their Irish counterparts appear more indifferent.[56] And the impasse in Ireland is exacerbated by a wedge between priests and bishops; in particular, the bishops maintain a distant relationship with the Association of Catholic Priests (ACP), an organization representing about a third of Irish priests, and they have been hesitant in accepting their invitation to dialogue.[57]

The decline of the church does not mean that Ireland is absent a moral conscience.[58] Secular voices are well capable of articulating a vision of a just society, a theme which has had political salience in Ireland since the 1970s, though blinkered by the Celtic Tiger. The challenge today is to ensure that the secular articulation of justice avoids being diluted to a narrow focus on individual rights alone and instead maintains appreciation for the fact that the individual is always situated in community, and increasingly in multiple intersecting communities with varied needs and vulnerabilities.

Social movements too can mobilize collective action, as underscored by the Marriage Equality Movement, for example. Similarly, local Catholic-related (e.g., the St. Vincent de Paul Society) and secular (e.g., the Lions Club) charitable organizations have a well-regarded public role, and this is unlikely to change even as more Irish people may disaffiliate from religion. In a sense, charity work (while clearly not sufficient to supplant the state) is secularized, that is, woven into everyday local life in ways that are largely independent of the church (despite its institutional involvement). Critical voices from academia and the press also matter, as exemplified by Irish sociologist Kathleen Lynch who is guided, as she states, "by the belief that the purpose of scholarship and research is not just to understand the world, but to change it for the good of humanity."[59] Thus individual and organizational voices in dialogue with one another and with political and religious leaders can steer Ireland on a path toward greater pluralism, justice, and equality, and one which, by definition, affirms the rights of all, including the church, to enrich the public sphere and the articulation of social policy.

Notes

1. Cormac Halpin, "A Growing Nation—Older, More Connected, Less Religious, and More of Us Living Under Each Roof," *Irish Independent*, April 7, 2017, 27.
2. "Statistical Yearbook of Ireland 2017," Central Statistics Office, last modified 2017, http://www.cso.ie.
3. "Statistical Yearbook of Ireland 2017."
4. Tony Fahey, "Population," in *Contemporary Ireland: A Sociological Map*, ed. Sara O'Sullivan, 13–29 (Dublin: UCD Press, 2007); and Tony Fahey, Helen Russell, and Christopher T. Whelan, "Quality of Life after the Boom," in *Quality of Life in Ireland: Social Impact of Economic Boom*, ed. Tony Fahey, Helen Russell, and Christopher T. Whelan, 1–10 (Dordrecht, Netherlands: Springer, 2008).
5. Irial Glynn and Philip O'Connell, "Migration," in *Austerity & Recovery in Ireland*, ed. William Roche, Philip O'Connell, and Andrea Prothero, 304–5 (New York: Oxford University Press, 2017), 290.
6. "OECD 2017," *International Migration Outlook 2017*, 2017, https://data.oecd.org/migration/foreign-born-population.htm.
7. Halpin, "A Growing Nation," 27.
8. Central Statistics Office, "Statistical Yearbook."
9. Central Statistics Office, "Statistical Yearbook;" Eurostat, "Statistics," http://ec.europa.ed/Eurostat.
10. John Fitzgerald, "Changing Pattern of Family Formation," *Irish Times*, January 26, 2016, http://www.irishtimes.com.
11. William Roche, Philip O'Connell, and Andrea Prothero, eds., *Austerity and Recovery in Ireland*, eds. (New York: Oxford University Press, 2017).
12. "Statistical Yearbook of Ireland 2017."
13. "Statistical Yearbook." For a detailed analysis of poverty and inequality in post-Celtic Tiger Ireland, see Kathleen Lynch, Sara Cantillon, and Margaret Crean, "Inequality," in *Austerity and Recovery in Ireland*, ed. William Roche, Philip O'Connell, and Andrea Prothero, 252–71 (New York: Oxford University Press, 2017).
14. *Focus Ireland*, last modified 2017, http://www.focusireland.ie.
15. Vivienne Clarke, "Housing Agency says Homelessness is 'Dreadful' but 'Normal,'" *Irish Times*, November 13, 2017, http://www.irishtimes.com.
16. Rob Kitchin, Rory Hearne, and Cian O'Callaghan, "Housing," in *Austerity and Recovery in Ireland*, ed. William Roche, Philip O'Connell, and Andrea Prothero, 272–89 (New York: Oxford University Press, 2017).
17. These two paragraphs draw on Michele Dillon, *Debating Divorce: Moral Conflict in Ireland* (Kentucky: University Press of Kentucky, 1993).

18. Tony Fahey, "The Catholic Church and Social Policy," in *Values, Catholic Social Thought, and Public Policy*, ed. Brigid Reynolds and Sean Healy, 143–63 (Dublin: Conference of Religious of Ireland, 2007); Tom Inglis, *Moral Monopoly: The Catholic Church in Modern Irish Society* (Dublin: Gill and Macmillan, 1998); Joe Moran, "From Catholic Church Dominance to Social Partnership Promise and Now Economic Crisis, Little Changes in Irish Social Policy," *Irish Journal of Public Policy* 2, no. 1 (July 2010), http://www.ijpp@ucc.ie; Michel Peillon, *Welfare in Ireland: Actors, Resources, and Institutions* (Westport, CT: Praeger, 2001); and John H. Whyte, *Church and State in Modern Ireland* (Dublin: Gill & Macmillan, 1980).
19. Inglis, *Moral Monopoly*.
20. Fahey, "The Catholic Church," 143.
21. Peillon, *Welfare in Ireland*.
22. Dan Barry, "The Lost Children of Tuam," *New York Times*, October 28, 2017, http://www.nytimes.com.
23. These three paragraphs draw on Dillon, *Debating Divorce*, 24–5.
24. Whyte, *Church and State*.
25. Dillon, *Debating Divorce*, 24–5.
26. Dillon, *Debating Divorce*, 33–43.
27. Michele Dillon, "Secularization, Generational Change, and Ireland's Post-Secular Opportunity," in *The Catholic Church in Ireland Today*, ed. David Cochran and John Waldmeir (Lanham, MD: Lexington Books, 2015), 45–64.
28. Kieran Allen, "The Irish Political Elite," in *Are the Irish Different?*, ed. Tom Inglis, 54–64 (Manchester: Manchester University Press, 2014).
29. Sean O'Riain, *The Rise and Fall of Ireland's Celtic Tiger* (New York: Cambridge University Press, 2014).
30. Allen, "The Irish Political Elite," 54–64; Lynch et al., "Inequality," 252–71; and Moran, "From Catholic Church Dominance."
31. Kathleen Lynch, "The Care-less Irish State" (paper presented at the International Workshop on "*Are the Irish Different?*" Dublin, Ireland, September 2012).
32. Lynch, "The Care-less Irish State," 260.
33. Pierre Bourdieu, *Practical Reason: On the Theory of Action* (Stanford, CA: Stanford University Press, 1991).
34. Michele Dillon, *Postsecular Catholicism: Relevance and Renewal* (New York: Oxford University Press, 2018).
35. Pope Francis, "The Joy of the Gospel (Evangelii Gaudium): Apostolic Exhortation," *Origins* 43, no. 28 (December 5, 2013), 53, 185, 188.
36. David Hollenbach, *The Common Good and Christian Ethics* (Cambridge: Cambridge University Press, 2002), 226.

37. Irish Commission for Justice and Social Affairs (ICJSA), *In the Wake of the Celtic Tiger: Poverty in Contemporary Ireland* (Dublin: Veritas, 2009).
38. ICJSA, *In the Wake of the Celtic Tiger*, 5.
39. Patsy McGarry, "'Homelessness an Affront to Human Dignity,' Catholic Bishops Say," *Irish Times*, December 8, 2016, http://www.irishtimes.com.
40. Diarmuid Martin, "The Challenge for the Church in the 21st Century" (presentation, St. Killian's Lecture, Wurzburg, Germany, July 7, 2017), http://www.dublindiocese.ie.
41. Merike Darmody and Emer Smyth, *Education about Religions and Beliefs (ERB) and Ethics* (Dublin: Economic and Social Research Institute, 2017).
42. Paul Cullen, "How Much Power has the Church in Today's Healthcare System?," *Irish Times*, March 20, 2017, 2.
43. Paul Cullen, "Religious Orders Own Hospitals Worth Over Euro1bn," *Irish Times*, March 20, 2017, 2.
44. Pat Leahy, "Opinion Poll Shows Voters Cautious on Abortion," *Irish Times*, May 27, 2017, http://www.irishtimes.com.
45. Kitty Holland, "Woman 'Denied a Termination' Dies in Hospital," *Irish Times*, November 14, 2012, http://www.irishtimes.com.
46. Comment, "Maternity Hospital Delay Frustrating," *Sunday Independent*, April 23, 2017.
47. Paul Cullen, "Minister Welcomes 'Historic Decision' by Nuns to End Role in Maternity Hospital," *Irish Times*, May 29, 2017, http://www.irishtimes.com.
48. Cullen, "Religious Orders," 2.
49. Dillon, *Postsecular Catholicism*.
50. Patsy McGarry, "Sisters of Charity Must Be Allowed Exercise Their Conscience Too," *Irish Times*, May 20, 2017, http://www.irishtimes.com.
51. Diarmuid Martin, "The Challenge for the Church in the 21st Century."
52. Grainne Healy, *Crossing the Threshold: The Story of the Marriage Equality Movement* (Newbridge, Ireland: Merrion Press, 2017).
53. Diarmuid Martin, "The Challenge for the Church in the 21st Century."
54. Martin, "The Challenge for the Church in the 21st Century."
55. Eamon Martin, "The Church in the Public Sphere—A Perspective from Ireland" (presentation, The 2017 Newman Lecture, University of East Anglia, Norwich, England, 2017), http://www.armagharchdiocese.org.
56. Dillon, *Postsecular Catholicism*.
57. Sarah McDonald, "Jesuit Theologian Fr. Gerry O'Hanlon Argues that a Synodal Form of Church at All Levels is Urgently Needed to Salvage the Catholic Faith in Ireland," *National Catholic Reporter*, January 24, 2017, http://www.ncronline.org.

58. Liam Ryan, "Church and Politics: The Last Twenty-Five Years," *The Furrow* 30, no. 1 (January 1979): 3–18.
59. Lynch, "List of Contributors, in *Austerity and Recovery in Ireland*, ed. William Roche, Philip O'Connell, and Andrea Prothero (New York: Oxford University Press, 2017), xxi.

CHAPTER 3

Religiously Oriented Welfare Organizations in Italy Before and After the Great Recession: Toward a More Relevant Role in the Provision of Social Services?

Ugo Ascoli and Marco Arlotti

INTRODUCTION

As is well known, Italy is a paradigmatic example of the so-called Southern European welfare model.[1] The main features of this model concern a highly fragmented and categorical system of protection in the case of risks like unemployment and retirement from the labor market, while health care is delivered through a universalist approach. Social services are structurally residual, and this implies that the support for subjects in need is mainly delegated—according to the principle of subsidiarity—to the family and intergenerational solidarities.[2] Moreover, in a general context

U. Ascoli (✉)
Università Politecnica delle Marche, Ancona, Italy

M. Arlotti
Politecnico di Milano, Milan, Italy

characterized by increasing demand and diffusion of new social risks,[3] the Italian welfare state has been not able to adapt its arrangements, while retrenchment of social policies has been particularly significant.[4]

The literature has extensively analyzed the socio-economic and socio-political factors behind the specific trajectory of development of the Italian welfare state,[5] considering also the role played by socio-cultural factors, including the Catholic religion and religious organizations.[6] Indeed, as in other Mediterranean countries,[7] the role of religion in terms of actors providing welfare services, values, and beliefs among the population seems to have been crucial in shaping welfare institutions, as well as in the formulation and identification of the main goals related to the development of social policies. Based on these premises, this chapter investigates the role played by religious organizations—that is, Catholic organizations—within the Italian welfare system, focusing on a specific policy field: social services. This role will be analyzed from a long-term perspective focusing also on recent years characterized by the impact of the great economic recession.

Our hypothesis is that, from a long-term perspective, the role played by Catholic organizations has been crucial as far as the specific trajectory of development taken by the Italian system of social services. Moreover, over the past decades, this relevance seems to have increased due to specific institutional reforms, which have strongly supported a process of "subsidiarization" of social policies,[8] as well as the impact of the current economic recession with the related increase in terms of demand for social services. However, given the fact that this relevance has arisen in a context of welfare state retrenchment and inertia of decision makers, a potential risk for Catholic organizations is that of playing a more substitutive role (rather than a complementary one) in the delivery of social services, thus exacerbating the overall degree of territorial fragmentation and inequalities existing within Italian society.

After this general introduction, the section "The Italian Context: The Emergence of New Social Risks in a (Still) Predominantly Catholic Society" provides a general analysis of the Italian case, focusing on the main socio-economic and socio-demographic trends, including changing religious affiliation, while the section "The Italian Welfare State in Comparative Perspective" highlights the main structural traits of the Italian welfare state. The section "Church and State Relations in the Social Policy Field: A Historical Perspective" focuses on the historical path of church–state relationships in Italy, considering the role played by the Catholic organizations in the development of social services, while the section "The Role of Catholic Organizations in the Field of Social Services: Before and After the Great Recession" takes into account in particular the past decades (before and after the great economic recession). The final section summarizes and discusses the main findings.

THE ITALIAN CONTEXT: THE EMERGENCE OF NEW SOCIAL RISKS IN A (STILL) PREDOMINANTLY CATHOLIC SOCIETY

Over the past decades, Italian society has undergone growing and deep transformations in the socio-demographic sphere as well as in the labor market. Regarding the first dimension, it is important to note that in a context of decreasing fertility coupled with a progressive increase in the life expectancy, the outcome has been population aging. In 2016, life expectancy at birth was 80.6 years for men and 85.1 for women. Older people (aged 65 years and over) were over 13.5 million—22 percent of the total population, while potential frail elderly people (i.e., aged 80 years and over) were 6.1 million—6.8 percent of the total population.[9] In 2016 the value of the old-age dependency ratio, which measures the percentage of population 65 and over as a share of those of working age (i.e., 15–64 years), was the highest (34.3 percent) in the European Union (European average of 28 countries was 29.3 percent).[10]

Another important socio-demographic process is the growth in the foreign-born population. In 2016 there were about 5 million foreign-born people in Italy, or 8.3 percent of the country's population.[11] This growth has been sustained by several factors, such as second-generation births and the increase in migratory fluxes, seen for instance with the expansion of the European Union and, more recently, in the wake of geopolitical instabilities in Middle East and Africa.

Parallel to socio-demographic changes, other relevant transformations have affected the socio-economic dimension. A massive recourse to flexible contracts since the mid-1990s has undermined stable employment conditions, particularly for young workers entering the labor market for the first time. Intergenerational solidarities and reciprocity networks have mainly mitigated this new condition of risk.[12] However, Italian families have also been increasingly weakened by changing family arrangements (such as a growing number of single households, divorced families, lone parents) and by growing care needs related to population aging. Moreover, during the last decade, the impact and the prolonged duration of the Great Recession have stressed the economic conditions of Italian families, resulting in an increase in the level of poverty among specific social groups (large families with minors, or with blue-collar workers as head of family) and within the most traditionally deprived and poorer territorial areas (i.e., southern regions).[13]

Overall, these changes suggest the emergence of new social risks that, however, have not been matched by a recalibration of the welfare state, as discussed in the section "The Italian Welfare State in Comparative Perspective." In this context, a growing and crucial role in providing social services at the territorial level has been played by third sector organizations, including the Catholic ones. Indeed, the Italian Catholic Church can rely on resources and on an organizational system that is among the most developed in Europe.[14] In 2009 (according to the latest data available), a total of 14,246 health and social services managed by affiliated Catholic Church organizations were working, with a total of 420,000 persons involved, most of them volunteers and lay persons.[15] This strong relevance of the Catholic Church is embedded in a society in which persons declaring themselves as belonging to Catholic religion are still a large majority of the Italian population (see Figs. 3.1 and 3.2).

At the same time, over the years and in the wake of the process of secularization, the attitude of the Italian people toward Catholicism has changed, with a decrease in the number of regular churchgoers (see Fig. 3.3) as well as of persons baptized or getting married in a religious ceremony.

It is important to notice that these trends tend to be differentiated according to the generational cohort of reference (secularization is stronger among the young cohorts than among the older ones) and at the territorial level (in southern regions religious attitude is higher).[16] In more general terms, according to Cartocci, an analysis of the religious composition of Italian society can be sketched in four main groups as follows: a first "central" group in terms of religiosity (about 10 percent of the Italian population) is constituted by persons strongly involved in Catholic organizations and as volunteers in parish activities; a second group, called "Catholicism of minority" (about 20 percent of the Italian population), is constituted by persons who are regular churchgoers; the third group is the most numerous one in Italy (about 50 percent of the total population, called "Catholicism of majority"), including people who attend religious

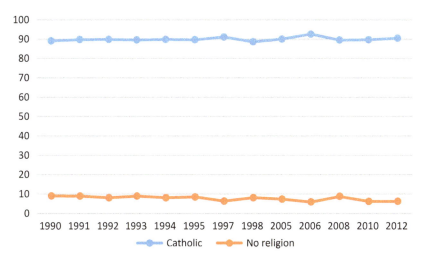

Fig. 3.1 Change in religious affiliation in Italy, 1990–2012. Source: Data calculated by Andrea Parma (Polytechnic of Milan) on Eurobarometer microdata, several waves

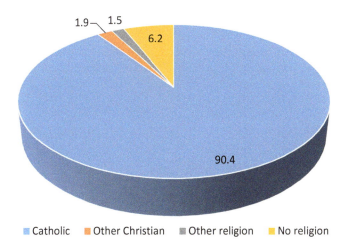

Fig. 3.2 Religious affiliation in Italy, 2012. Source: Data calculated by Andrea Parma (Polytechnic of Milan) on Eurobarometer microdata, several waves

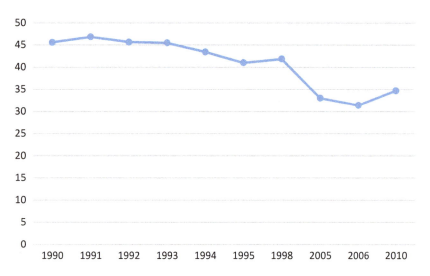

Fig. 3.3 Changes in the number of regular churchgoers (only Catholics) in Italy, 1990–2010. Note: "Regular churchgoers" includes those attending religious services (apart from weddings or funerals) more than once and once a week. *1996–1997; 1999–2004; 2007; 2009; 2010–2012: data not available.* Source: Data calculated by Andrea Parma (Polytechnic of Milan) on Eurobarometer microdata, several waves

ceremonies only for special events (for instance Christmas Mass); the remaining 20 percent of the Italian population is equally divided among those who are not regular churchgoers, but who have a certain degree of trust in the Catholic Church (for instance they provide the so called "Otto per mille"[17]—eight per thousand—to the Catholic Church or they opt for the hour of religion—that is, Catholic religion—in their children's school curriculum); and those totally disinterested in the Catholic religion (including also persons affiliated to other religions).[18]

To sum up, this reconstruction of the religious composition of Italian society shows that if on the one hand the level of religiosity is still very high among the population (the first three groups cover 80 percent of the Italian population), on the other hand it seems that for a large portion of the Italian people (the so-called Catholicism of majority) the affiliation with the Catholic Church tends to be more a cultural trait than a spiritual one.

The Italian Welfare State in Comparative Perspective

The Italian welfare system certainly cannot be numbered among those historically the most prepared to meet the new scenarios produced by the industrial revolution. For the entire nineteenth century, the new social demand was met in Italy, albeit partially, by institutions and organizations linked to the Catholic Church, principally the so-called *opere pie*, church charities, and by the predominantly secular forms of self-organization that involved workers, peasants, and artisans (Workers' Mutual Aid Societies).

During the first 20 years of the 1900s in Italy, as in the largest European countries, compulsory social insurance systems came into being, covering accidents at work, old age, and unemployment, even though participation was quite low. The social policies of the Fascist period significantly enlarged the welfare system, which was founded on a strictly sectoral and corporate criterion, the basic aim of which was social control and the broadening of support for the regime.[19] It is important to underline that in the 20 years of Fascism (see also the next section), there was a close collaboration pact between the state and the Catholic Church whereby the church was entrusted with providing the main services for the poor, the sick, the elderly, or the weak, whom the regime did not consider capable of contributing positively to economic development. At the same time, the Workers' Mutual Aid Societies were dealt a blow in that they were considered essentially places of anti-regime socialization and political education.

In the 1950s Italian welfare was still to be found almost last in the rankings of countries in Europe for its ability to meet principal social needs. Only later during the "Glorious Thirty" was there notable development in social policies that led to pension and health care coverage for almost the entire population. The personal social services system, on the other hand, remained firmly the same as in the past for another 20 years.[20] At the beginning of the 1970s, having come up in the European rankings, Italy was within the average as regards the level of coverage (in other words, the number of insured people) in the working population[21]: "It now falls fully within the so-called continental pattern: together with Belgium, France, Luxemburg, and Holland, it is part of that group of countries in which there is a great prevalence of monetary transfers. This is very different from the social democracies of Northern Europe and Great Britain which are distinguished by what has been defined the 'Scandinavian pattern' in which the supply of public services appears considerably more important."[22]

At this point any "universal footprint" is still missing with the exception of education policies that were completely reorganized with the 1962 reform. The majority of personal services were in the hands of religious organizations. It should also be pointed out that "already at the end of the 60s … the first experiments that offered an alternative to residential care had already got under way in some important towns of the Centre North (Milan, Bologna, and Florence). These included home care and the opening of the first municipal nursery schools"[23] and are proof of a push by the local authorities toward the modernization of the public services system. However, it was only in the 1970s that a new service culture took shape. At the same time, there was a move toward universalistic policies that placed people center stage. These range from the introduction of the municipal nursery schools (1971) to the psychiatric reform (1978), to the National Health Service (1978) that took the place of the Health Insurance Schemes (Casse Mutue) set up by the Fascist regime 50 years earlier, or rather of a system of welfare differentiated by work sector. In the same period, national legislation brought in the divorce law (1970) and the voluntary interruption of pregnancy (1978). State-run personal social services began to spread throughout the country alongside the still significant number of private, mainly church-run services, delivered through the so-called *opere pie*. However, it is important to note that the development of a public system of social services, managed by local authorities, has been undermined over the years. It has been affected by structural territorial fragmentation as well by the missed definition by the central state of a national framework law on social services (see the section "Church and State Relations in the Social Policy Field: A Historical Perspective"), which is in part related to the political conflict that arose around the dissolution of the *opere pie* and the transfer of functions and resources of them to local authorities.[24]

In more general terms, the 1980s and 1990s saw the start of a new phase of the principal welfare systems where very soon the need to tackle the "new social risks"[25] and problems of public finance fostered the adoption of neo-liberal policies. These were aimed at radically reducing the sphere of public intervention,[26] even though the real cuts have been introduced in more recent years, gaining particular momentum with the austerity policies set in motion by the 2008 crisis.[27] There was talk of explicit retrenchment accompanied by policies of hidden retrenchment, with programs that reduced the overall capacity to cover the population against important risks, failing to provide an adequate response to the changes that had taken place.[28] In some cases, we have witnessed the reorganization of policies aimed at taking on the new challenges, the so-called recalibration measures.[29] There have been very few steps taken toward "social investment," that is, toward policies that put "human capital" at the hub of the entire supply chain of knowledge and education (early childhood education and care, education and lifelong training), and help to make efficient use of human capital (through policies supporting women's and single parents' employment, through active labor market policies, but also through specific forms of labor market regulation and social protection institutions that promote flexible security), while fostering greater social inclusion (notably by facilitating access to the labor market for groups that have traditionally been excluded).[30] In any case, the resilience of the welfare systems to change and cutbacks seems to be strong for two reasons: first, because of the opposition of those who fear that the outcome of the reforms would be against their interest; and second, due to path dependency in which past decisions and the institutions set up as a result appear able to bind current and future policies to a given system.

The Italian case is a clear example of the evident prevalence of cutback policies when set against the few areas in which there has been an attempt to reorganize and reshape policies.[31] The severe recession (2008–2016) accentuated the crisis and fostered the adoption of austerity stratagems that have caused a further push toward measures of retrenchment. In this scenario, the move toward a new period of the public supply of services has been brusquely interrupted. Italy is now ranked among the lowest when compared with the most important European countries in terms of employment services, personal social services, education services, and those covering social health and social care. There has been an increased shift toward the privatization of social services. Families have become encumbered with the growing burden of meeting their social needs (a real return to familism) (see "The Italian Context: The Emergence of New Social Risks in a (Still) Predominantly Catholic Society" above) at a time when they are much less able to be "welfare agencies" than during the "Glorious Thirty" given the change in their size, market trends, and social, demographic, and cultural changes. Services linked to employment status and not to citizens' rights, ranging from pensions to health, are on the rise. Thus the firm seems to increasingly assume a more central role and become a mini-welfare state.[32] Occupational welfare in firms appears to be growing significantly,[33] as is happening or has happened in many European countries.[34]

Church and State Relations in the Social Policy Field: A Historical Perspective

As described in the section "The Italian Welfare State in Comparative Perspective," for a long time after unification (1861), public intervention for social purposes was very limited, and response to the principal social needs came from organizations closely linked to the Catholic Church or from largely secular mutual benefit societies. The very important role played by the church in the social policy field was mainly through two types of organization: church charities and rural banks.

The church charities or *opere pie* were private welfare and/or charitable bodies that were primarily Catholic. As the 1890 reform law stated, they took it upon themselves to "help the poor, both in health and sickness, to provide education, instruction, the training for some profession, art or trade, or to aid in any other way their moral or economic improvement."[35] The roots of these charities go back to the Middle Ages. They developed strongly in the sixteenth century and over time became the means by which the Catholic Church expanded its work in support of the most vulnerable.

Following the unification of Italy (1861), the first survey shows that "there were more than 17,000 Church charities whose assets were valued as being much higher than the state revenue (more than double) and equal to half of the entire public debt. When the number of Church charities is calculated with respect to population, the Neapolitan provinces and Sicily take first place with 11,567 Church charities for around nine million inhabitants. In second place, come Lombardy/Veneto with 3,617 Church charities for five and a half million inhabitants."[36]

However, when considering the robustness of the assets, a severe imbalance in favor of the Northern regions becomes evident: "The value of real estate owned by the charitable bodies in Northern Italy was around 1,126 million lire, against 341 and 430 million for central Italy and Southern Italy respectively."[37] Based on the data furnished later by Parliamentary Commissions, the 1880 census documents show over 21,000 church charities with a territorial distribution that demonstrates a severe imbalance in favor of the provincial capitals, urban centers, and northern regions. In 1900 their number had grown to 23,272.[38] In order to fully assess the role and importance of the charities in Italy at the end of the nineteenth century, it is worth reflecting upon the extent of their activities bearing in mind that this was a period before the establishment of an Italian welfare system and when Bismarck was planning the first compulsory health insurance program.

The church charity activities included the following: charitable donations and charity, child care, care for the disabled, education, care for prisoners and ex-prisoners, measures in support of the poor, hospitals for the sick and chronically ill, and care of widows. The needs of the nascent industrial society were already evident. The ascent of the Italian economy, which historians place at the beginning of the twentieth century, made social demand—a demand that charities and mutual aid societies tried to address—even more complex. Leaving aside the introduction of compulsory schooling in 1877, the law on child labor in 1886, and the first laws on maternity protection in 1911, the first organized state response in terms of services only materialized in the second half of the 1920s, when the Fascist regime was at its height. The next leap forward occurred in the new Italian Republic only after the 1960s.[39]

There was a significant number of church charity-run hospitals (over 2000 in 1880): "even at the end of the century, the hospitals are more like shelters for the chronically ill and the poor. Admission and aid are closely governed by the regulations of the Church charities and the municipal authorities who often use them to control the poorest and most dangerous classes/elements of society. Those who seek refuge in these hospitals are mainly old people, orphans and young servant girls who stay on much longer than a simple health issue would require. In the urban centers of the North, however, they also start taking in members of the new working and productive classes who are now exposed to dangers and growing causes of disease; therefore, farm workers as 'patients' also begin to increase."[40]

The first legislation brought in by the Italian state made it obvious that it did not want to enter into conflict with the church that ran and controlled the charities. In Law 753/1862, "with regards to Church charities, the role of state power is in reality limited to the exercise of a merely technical-formal control by the peripheral authorities."[41] The prevailing attitude toward social problems was aimed at impeding direct public commitment. Until the end of the century, the dominant idea seems to have been that "the Church charity system offers so much potentiality that it could continue and exonerate the State of any financial commitment on the social front"; at the same time there was an awareness that it was necessary "to take the road of modernization and rationalization."[42]

In order to accomplish this, the law of 1890 was passed, in which the government demonstrated its wish to control the church charities and make them more efficient, entrusting to a public body (the administrative provincial council) duties relating to the analysis of the budget and balance sheet as well as control of the resolutions regarding both staff and modifications of assets. There was a need to remedy the bad management of the charitable institutions and the equally bad surveillance of them carried out by the public authorities. Thus, we witness the full "nationalization" of the church charities that were transformed into IPAB (Istituzioni pubbliche di assistenza e beneficenza/Public Institutions of Welfare and Charity) in that they were given public legal personality. The functions performed by the ex-church charities however were not affected: the Crispi government "leaves most of the healthcare for the poor to the Church charities, now the IPAB."[43] The new law clearly made a great step forward by recognizing the goals of the charitable institutions as public aims; however, the law seems to be "still marked by paternalism and social control of the beneficiaries with very limited scope in the overall set-up of the system."[44] We are faced with "a phase of regulation without financial commitment from the State,"[45] a formula that effectively sums up the relationship between state and church concerning social services through the first decades of the twentieth century. Only after World War I did the Italian State for the first time assume direct responsibility for the delivery of specific services in this field, for "the care and support of disabled war veterans, orphans and some categories of war casualties."[46]

Later, during the 20 years of Fascism, in the very first phase of the regime, methods of control over the church charity system were intensified. But from the 1926 laws onwards, considerable autonomy was returned to these organizations, even greater than that established in the 1890 legislation.[47] Among the first provisions of the regime appear donations to the church, concessions of privileges that had been limited or abolished for 30 years, and not least the reform of the laws on church charities, which so gladdened Pope Pius XI. Following these measures, with the 1929 Lateran Pacts, the new marriage law and the law on ecclesiastical bodies, there was a return to the jurisdiction of the church both over the education of the family and charity and welfare. The signing of the Lateran Pacts in 1929, which was an agreement of mutual recognition between the Kingdom of Italy and the Holy See, was one more step in the acknowledgment of the church's role in social matters. It meant the establishment of regular bilateral relations between church and state and "secured" the sphere of social work performed by the religious charitable and welfare institutions. With the signing of the Concordat, which defined civil and religious relations in Italy between the church and the government, the Pacts guaranteed the recognition of Catholicism as the state religion of Italy. This had important consequences on the state school system, which became the institution that taught the Catholic religion.

A kind of "division of work" in the social field came into being: public charity had to provide for the old, those unfit for work, and the poor and needy, an area covered mainly by the church charitable bodies. Protection and care of the healthy and those who could make an active contribution to economic development, with particular emphasis on childhood and the young, fell to the Fascist state and its social policies, which were high on the government agenda. The Italian welfare system established after World War II and during the "Glorious Thirty" was based on the system of social services inherited from the Fascist period. This was firmly anchored in a series of national public bodies and in the strong central role played by individuals and organizations closely linked to the Catholic Church, such as the IPAB.

As already pointed out in the previous section, it was only in the 1970s, and particularly toward the end of that decade, that a new public commitment toward social services took shape, through a gradual dissolution of national public bodies and a decentralization of their functions and responsibilities to subnational government levels. However, such decentralization was undermined by the failed dissolution and transfer of the IPAB to Regions and Municipalities, which should have guaranteed the construction of a more organic system of social services at the territorial level. Indeed, the strong opposition of religious institutions, supported also by the centrality and strength of the great Catholic party, Christian Democracy (DC),[48] for many years inhibited the approval of a national framework law on social services aimed to frame the process of decentralization by defining guiding principles and minimum standards to be guaranteed by Regions and municipalities.[49] The national framework law on social services was passed only at the end of 1990s (see the next section), and this long gap stimulated a fragmented and chaotic development of social services at the territorial level, coupled with a growing increase in territorial disparities, in particular among the richer regions in the north and center of Italy, which had a more generous and extensive system of social services than the residual and poorer system of social protection in the southern regions.[50]

When considering the church's important role in the social policy field, it is important to remember, alongside the church charities, the Rural Banks, which were actual credit cooperatives for small farmers. They began to spread at the end of the nineteenth century. The first Rural Bank was established in 1883 in Loreggia in the province of Padua, founded by the economist and philanthropist Leone Wollemborg. It was based on the German model of Friedrich Wilhelm Reiffeisen and aimed to "reproduce in Italy that beneficial expansion of rural credit that in those years was occurring in the countryside of many European countries. In Germany, in 1888, there were 900 operational Rural Banks, which provided very active support to small and medium-sized farmers. Ten years later, in Austria, Hungary, and Belgium, the spread of these banks also led to concrete and positive outcomes."[51] The Rural Bank project was backed mainly by country parish priests who knew only too well the enormous difficulties encountered by small landowners, tenant farmers, and sharecroppers looking for credit, albeit modest, to overcome the financial difficulties of the farm or for unexpected family needs: "against the background of widespread illiteracy in our countryside, right from the establishment of the first Rural Bank of Wollemborg, it was the priests who were essential to their operation, due to the trust that they knew how to instill in their parishioners and the ability to carry out the formal requirements laid down by the law."[52] The overriding need to make credit available to the weakest players in the agricultural sector coupled with the simplicity of the organization of the Rural Banks led to their enjoying broad support. However, they were only successful when economic pressures combined with the Catholic movement that had gained strength after the publication of *Rerum Novarum*. This encyclical, promulgated on May 15, 1891, by Pope Leo XIII, stated views on social questions and laid down the modern social doctrine of the church.[53]

The deep-seated hostility toward the unitary liberal state as a result of its fiscal policies, the extension of compulsory conscription, the inflexibility in conceding personal and political liberty, as well as the insensibility toward social questions contributed to strengthening the ecclesiastical presence in the country areas. This led to the founding of the first Catholic Rural Bank in 1892:

"From then on, expansion was both significant and swift, much more dynamic than that of the secular or 'neutral' banks in which the idealistic driving force was less vibrant as it lacked the cohesive element that marked the Catholic banks that grew up around a parish, always involved a priest to manage them and led to the setting up of dairy cooperatives, soup kitchens, consumer cooperatives and itinerant teachers of agriculture. The Catholic Mutual Aid Society quickly discovered that in the Rural Banks lay its greatest support and expansion, imagination and penetration, always adding new ways of taking action in the social sphere ... they offered personal and family help which did not always just consist of giving agricultural credit, but rather assistance that went as far as friendly actions for its members like the dowry for a daughter or the building of a house."[54]

In 1897, the Catholic Rural Banks already numbered "more than 86% of all the Italian Rural Banks, an overwhelming numerical superiority which they maintained even in the 1900s."[55] Through the first years of the twentieth century, more than three-quarters (75.9 percent) of the Banks were situated in the north of Italy. Later they began to spread to other areas, yet even in 1915, half of the Italian Rural Banks operated in the northern regions.

THE ROLE OF CATHOLIC ORGANIZATIONS IN THE FIELD OF SOCIAL SERVICES: BEFORE AND AFTER THE GREAT RECESSION

As we saw in the previous section, the role of the Catholic Church and religious organizations has traditionally been crucial in Italy as far as the specific trajectory of development of the system of social services is concerned. At the beginning of the 1990s, the propensity of Catholic organizations to be involved in this policy field remained prominent.[56] Given these premises, in this section we will analyze the role of Catholic organizations from the 1990s onwards, considering two main phases: a first phase covering the approximate period from the 1990s up to the years just before the advent of the Great Recession; and a second phase that covers the subsequent years.

Before the Crisis: Growing Catholic Volunteerism and the Affirmation of the Principle of Subsidiarity

Despite the collapse of the Christian Democracy (DC) party at the beginning of the 1990s, the social and political activisms of the Catholic Church and related organizations did not disappear. Rather, the absence of a direct political affiliation led the Catholic Church to change its political strategy, in particular through a more direct involvement in the public and political debate aimed to defend "non-negotiable" Catholic values against the forces of secularization.[57] Thus, in addition to traditional fields (for instance, anti-abortion and anti-contraception advocacy), the activism of the Catholic Church has widened to new fields, such as the defense and promotion of the traditional family in contrast to new forms of family arrangements and gay marriage or the opposition to new forms of assisted reproduction and practices of euthanasia.[58] Moreover, following a consolidated historical legacy, a policy field central to Catholic activism has been social assistance, especially in the wake of a growing expansion of Catholic volunteerism during the 1990s.

The increasing involvement of Catholics in volunteer activities was related to the emerging and progressive diffusion of new social risks in Italian society, but it was also strongly supported by the Catholic Church, in particular starting from the condemnation by Pope John Paul II in his 1991 encyclical *Centesimus Annus* (hundredth year), about the faults of the welfare state, dominated by bureaucratic functioning and unable to involve and value the contribution of the civil society to the welfare of the society.[59] Thus, Catholic volunteering and the attempt to support wider recognition of the principle of subsidiarity in Italian law have been two key strategies pursued by the Catholic Church to promote a new civil society able to pursue a more general function of solidarity and charity in the Italian society.[60]

In this context, the expansion of Catholic volunteering as well as the influence of the principle of subsidiarity has played a crucial role in the case of social services.[61] For instance, it is worth noting that in 2009 more than two-thirds (65 percent) of social services provided by Catholic organizations (based, to a large extent, on the involvement of volunteers) started their activities just during the 1990s.[62] This process has been stimulated by many factors, such as the growing privatization and externalization of welfare services, which took place in Italy beginning in the 1990s in a context of increasing budgetary constraints,[63] but also crucial was the spread of subsidiarity and participatory rhetoric about the need to widen the range of actors involved in social services in order to improve their efficacy and effectiveness.[64]

Indeed in 2000, after many years of debate and strong political conflicts, the national framework law on the integrated system of social services (Law 328/00) was passed by the Italian Parliament. This law contained an extended subsidiarization of social policies, both between the state, regions, and local authorities and between public and private (non-profit and for-profit) actors.[65] In accordance with the principle of "vertical" subsidiarity the national framework law planned a wide delegation of competencies to the authorities closest to citizens (i.e., regions and in particular local authorities). While following the principle of "horizontal" subsidiarity the role of non-profit and for-profit organizations was extensively acknowledged not only in the management of social services, but also in planning, co-definition of goals, and design of these services.[66] Thus, in this frame, the cooperation and collaboration between public and private actors acquired a strategic relevance.[67] The subsidiarization of social policies was also confirmed in 2001 by a second important institutional reform, that is, constitutional reform (Law 3/2001), which recognized at the constitutional level the principle of "horizontal" subsidiarity (art. 118) and increased the degree of "vertical" subsidiarity attributing to the regions also an exclusive legislative competence for social services (art. 117). The role of the central state was, instead, limited only to the definition of the essential levels in this sector (*livelli essenziali di assistenza sociale* [essential levels of social assistance]) aimed to guarantee a minimum social citizenship standard across the country.

During and After the Crisis: A Renewed Involvement of Catholic Organizations?

In the European context, Italy has been among the countries most severely and extensively affected by the impact of the great economic recession, which began in late 2007.[68] As a consequence, there has been a structural increase in poverty and deprivation: for instance, during the period 2007 and 2014, the number of individuals under the absolute poverty threshold more than doubled from 1.7 million to 4.1 million.[69] The expansion of poverty and social exclusion has been related not only to the persistence of the crisis, but also reinforced by the specific structure of the system of social protection (first, the lack of a general minimum income scheme, set up at the national level only in 2017) as well as by very ineffective antipoverty measures implemented amid the crisis.[70]

Moreover, severe austerity measures implemented during the crisis due to the Eurozone parameters and the need to contain a huge national debt have implied draconian reductions in financial transfers from the state to local authorities, which bear the responsibility to provide social services.[71] For instance, the national fund for social policies established in 1998 as the main institutional tool for the financing of social services has been affected by a drastic reduction of the yearly resources allocated, from almost 1.8 billion in 2007 to 343.8 million in 2013.[72] Consequently, local social expenditure has also dropped significantly in particular since 2010 (−5 percent during the period 2010–2013).[73]

In addition to austerity and to the inefficacy of anti-poverty policies, it is important to note that the overall capacity of the Italian social assistance system to provide an adequate response to social needs, in particular through social services at the territorial level, was already weakened before the advent of the Great Recession. Indeed, although the central state was endowed (according to the national framework law 328/00 and the constitutional reform approved in 2001) with the responsibility to set up the essential levels for social provisions (see above), these levels have been only vaguely defined (basically, only listing a set of measures to be provided from cash to in-kind measures), without any precise definition in terms of standard (such as eligibility criteria, amount, duration, professions involved) and, in particular, without any financial resources covering them.[74] Thus, the implementation of the essential levels has never taken place. As a result, public regulation has been undermined, and the structural gaps in the provision of social services between center-northern and southern Italy increased over the years.[75] In this context of growing inadequacy of the public intervention in providing support to people in need, third sector organizations, including religious ones, have become crucial in filling the gaps of the welfare state.[76] In particular, Catholic organizations have played a key role both as political actors and as providers of social services.[77]

Regarding the first dimension, it is important to mention the central role played by Caritas (the pastoral organization of the Italian Bishop's Conference), which increasingly pressed the national government in order to introduce a universal minimum income scheme aimed to cope with the structural expansion of poverty and deprivation in Italy since the advent of the economic crisis. In 2013, Caritas and Acli (the Christian Associations of Italian Workers) promoted a more intense mobilization on this topic, forming the Alleanza contro la povertà (Alliance against poverty),[78] a wide political platform in which more than 30 (religious and non-religious) organizations engaged in the field of poverty and social exclusion (including also the main trade unions and the Conference of the Italian regions) were involved. Two of its main goals were to raise public awareness and to develop a technical proposal to introduce a new universal minimum income scheme, called REIS—Reddito di inclusione sociale (income for social inclusion).

According to this technical proposal, the REIS is an income benefit scheme managed by local authorities and integrated with social and labor market programs in cooperation with third sector organizations and aimed at supporting the activation and social re-insertion of the beneficiaries. It was presented and discussed at several events. It is important to note that the design of the REIS has been finally (partly) considered also by the central government, which since December 2017 has introduced a new national minimum income scheme against poverty (Reddito di inclusione [the inclusion income] or REI). In May 2017, the central government and the Alleanza contro la povertà also signed a specific memorandum regarding the main steps for the implementation of this new public measure.

Many factors can explain this important political activism of Catholic organizations on a national scale.[79] First, the advent and the duration of the crisis have structurally increased the number of poor and deprived people as well as changed the traditional profiles of poverty including, for instance, impoverished middle-class households and non-standard employees. These changes suggest a growing functional pressure at the territorial level as well as for Catholic organizations traditionally involved in the field of poverty and social exclusion; thus, there is a related need for a broader intervention of social solidarity at a national scale. Second, the proposal advanced by the Alleanza contro la povertà and, in particular, the need to combine income benefits with activation programs aimed at supporting the re-insertion of the beneficiaries—which has also been introduced by the central government within the Reddito di inclusione (inclusion income, REI)—can be framed as a "strategic" step coherent with the principle of "horizontal" subsidiarity in recognizing the role of third sector organizations, including the religious ones, in the co-definition of goals and the design and implementation of public programs. Finally, another important factor has been the election of Pope Francis, who has supported and stimulated a stronger involvement of Catholics on the social issues in Italy, defining a change in the political strategy of the Catholic Church and widening the goals for political mobilization compared to the traditional "non-negotiable values."

In addition to political action, Catholic organizations have taken on a growing role in filling the gaps of the Italian welfare state during the economic crisis at the territorial level as well, where they function as providers of social services through a widespread set of activities aimed to support people in need. Here it is possible to identify two main branches of activities.[80] The first refers to new types of interventions—in addition to the traditional ones (such as dorms, canteens)—implemented by parishes, dioceses, and organizations affiliated with the Catholic Church and specifically aimed at coping with the emerging of new poverty conditions due to the economic crisis. The overall number of these interventions has almost doubled during the last years, passing from 577 in 2010 to 1.148 in 2013.[81] These interventions include micro-credit initiatives for households and enterprises; non-refundable loans funded through specific solidarity funds established by the dioceses in order to support people in extreme need; innovative practices for food distribution (through ethical stores or through specific prepaid cards); and projects of orientation and support for work and housing issues. The second branch of activities refers, instead, to the projects proposed by the dioceses, coordinated by Caritas and funded (in addition to Caritas's own resources) through financial resources allocated yearly by the state according to the "Otto per mille" (see below). These projects cover a wide range of potential needs, ranging from households in critical conditions, minors, immigrants and asylum seekers, prisoners, frail elderly people, homeless, and drug-addicted people.

Table 3.1 below shows some data about the implementation of the "Otto per mille" projects during the last years. There has been an increase in the number of dioceses involved in these projects. Moreover, during the period 2009–2012 with the peak of the economic crisis, the number of projects as well as the financial resources implemented has significantly grown (both about +30 percent) while it decreased in 2015 though reaching levels still higher than in 2009.

At the same time, a closer look at the territorial distribution of the resources allocated through the "Otto per mille" projects (see Table 3.2) shows some important critical features that might negatively affect this intervention by Catholic organizations. For instance, comparing the territorial allocation of the resources for the "Otto per mille" projects with the territorial distribution of poor people—who are, of course, one of the main targets of these projects—a sort of reverse distribution of the resources emerges, which penalizes in particular the southern regions. Indeed, in 2015, 37.6 percent of the total budget was allocated to these regions, but at the same time they represented more than 45 percent of poor people in Italy. One of the factors behind this mismatch in the allocation of resources may be also related to the territorial imbalances

Table 3.1 "Otto per mille" projects, 2009; 2012; 2015

	2009	2012	2015
% of dioceses involved	51.6	53.6	61.9
Number of projects	195	258	213
Total expenditure (mil. Euro, values rounded up)	20.8	28.5	24.2

Source: Author's elaboration on Caritas data. Caritas, *Rapporto Annuale 2009*, http://www.caritasitaliana. it/home_page_archivio/pubblicazioni/00001943_Rapporto_annuale_2009.html; Caritas, *Rapporto annuale 2012*, 2012, http://www.caritasitaliana.it/home_page_archivio/pubblicazioni/00003335_Rapporto_annuale_2012_.html; and Caritas, *False ripartenze. Rapporto 2014 sulla povertà e l'esclusione sociale*, 2015, http://www.caritasitaliana.it/home_page/area_stampa/00004776_False_partenze___Rapporto_Caritas_Italiana_2014_su_poverta_e_esclusione_sociale_in_Italia.html

Table 3.2 A comparison between the territorial allocation of the "Otto per mille" resources and the territorial distribution of poor people, 2015

	Total expenditure "Otto per mille" projects: territorial allocation (%)	Total poor people territorial distribution (%)
North	42.4	40.1
Center	20.0	14.6
South	37.6	45.3

Source: Author's elaboration on Caritas, *Rapporto 2016 sulla povertà e l'esclusione sociale*, 2016, http://www.caritasitaliana.it/home_page/area_stampa/00006623_Rapporto_2016_sulla_poverta_e_l_esclusione_sociale.htmland; and Istat, *La povertà in Italia* (Roma, 2016), https://www.istat.it/it/archivio/189188

affecting at the subnational level the role and the relevance of Catholic organizations in the field of social services. Indeed, according to the last census in 2009 on the interventions and social services provided by Catholic organizations, they were more developed in the northern and central regions than in the southern ones.[82]

CONCLUSION

In this chapter we have seen how Catholic organizations' role has been crucial in shaping the specific trajectory of development of the Italian system of social services. Moreover, during the past decades, this relevance has increased due to the subsidiarization of social policies and the impact and persistence of the current economic recession, which have strongly increased the demand for social services while local governments—that is, the main institutional actors endowed with responsibilities for social services—have been constrained by austerity measures and cuts in public transfers. In this context, the Catholic Church appears destined to become increasingly important in providing services. A public welfare that is both inadequate and in retreat, faced with an ever-growing heterogeneous social demand stemming from rising poverty and the turbulent growth in migratory flows, will increasingly accentuate the importance of the Italian welfare mix. At least in the short term, greater pressure is foreseeable on voluntary organizations, associations, social cooperatives, foundations, charitable trusts, and ecclesiastical bodies linked more or less directly to the church and parishes. In this sense, considering the "what if" counterfactual question, the non-contribution of these actors, including Catholic organizations, would most likely lead to a barely sustainable pressure on the welfare state in a context of rigid budgetary constraints. However, at the same time, it is important to note that the crucial role played by Catholic organizations in the delivery of many different welfare services is also affected by specific critical features. Indeed, in a context in which the welfare state is under retreat, these organizations risk playing more or a "substitutive" role rather than a complementary one in the delivery of social services. They may further increase processes of dualization and differentiation existing in social protection systems at the subnational level (in particular between northern and southern regions), given a limited capacity for intervention and the uneven territorial distribution of Catholic organizations both in terms of activities and resources mobilized.

NOTES

1. Maurizio Ferrera, "The Southern Model of Welfare in Social Europe," *Journal of European Social Policy* 6 (1996): 17–37; Ugo Ascoli and Emmanuele Pavolini, eds., *The Italian Welfare State in a European Perspective* (Bristol, UK: Policy Press, 2015).
2. Manuela Naldini and Chiara Saraceno, "Social and Family Policies in Italy: Not Totally Frozen but Far from Structural Reforms," *Social Policy and Administration* 42, no. 7 (2008): 733–48.
3. Peter Taylor-Gooby, ed., *New Risks, New Welfare: The Transformation of the European Welfare State* (Oxford: Oxford University Press, 2004).
4. Ascoli and Pavolini, *Italian Welfare State*.

5. Maurizio Ferrera, Valeria Fargion, and Matteo Jessoula, *Alle radici del welfare state all'italiana* (Padua, Italy: Marsilio, 2012); Ascoli and Pavolini, *Italian Welfare State*.
 6. Massimo Paci, *Pubblico e privato nei moderni sistemi di welfare* (Naples: Liguori, 1989); Ivo Colozzi, "Religione, valori e welfare state: il caso italiano," *Sociologia e Politiche Sociali* 3 (2012): 45–73.
 7. John Gall, "Is There an Extended Family of Mediterranean Welfare States?," *Journal of European Social Policy* 20, no. 4 (2010): 283–300.
 8. Yuri Kazepov, "The Subsidiarization of Social Policies: Actors, Processes and Impacts. Some Reflections on the Italian Case from a European Perspective," *European Societies* 10, no. 2 (2008): 247–73.
 9. Istat, *Rapporto annuale 2017* (Rome, 2017), https://www.istat.it/it/archivio/199318.
10. Eurostat online database, http://ec.europa.eu/eurostat/data/database.
11. Istat, *Rapporto annuale 2017*.
12. Costanzo Ranci and Mauro Migliavacca, "Everything Needs to Change, So Everything Can Stay the Same: Italian Welfare State Facing New Social Risks," in *The Italian Welfare State in a European Perspective*, eds. U. Ascoli and E. Pavolini, 21–47 (Bristol, UK: Policy Press, 2015).
13. Chiara Saraceno, "Simmetrie perverse: I paradossi delle politiche di contrasto alla povertà negli anni della crisi in Italia" [Perverse symmetries: The paradoxes of policies to combat poverty in the years of crisis in Italy], *Politiche Sociali/Social policies* 1 (2014): 27–40.
14. Franco Garelli, "The Public Relevance of the Church and Catholicism in Italy," *Journal of Modern Italian Studies* 12, no. 1 (2007): 8–36.
15. Cenosa (Consulta ecclesiale nazionale degli organismi socio-assistenziali [National ecclesial consultation of social-welfare organizations]), *Rilevazione delle opere sanitarie e sociali ecclesiali in Italia*, [Detection of ecclesial health and social works in Italy] Sintesi, 2012, http://www.caritasitaliana.it/caritasitaliana/allegati/2758/Censimento%20-%20SINTESI.pdf.
16. Roberto Cartocci, *Geografia dell'Italia cattolica* (Bologna: Il Mulino, 2011); Guido Formigoni, "L'Italia cattolica e la secolarizzazione," *Il Mulino* 5 (2011): 769–78.
17. In Italian fiscal law, the "Otto per mille"/eight per thousand is a compulsory part of the annual income tax that citizens can decide to devolve for social aims to the Catholic Church or to the state or to other religions.
18. Cartocci, *Geografia dell'Italia cattolica*. Also see Marcin Lisak, Review of Roberto Cartocci, *Geografia dell'Italia cattolica* (Bologna: Il Mulino, 2011), in *Oikonomia* 2 (June 2012): 70–71, http://www.oikonomia.it/index.php/it/oikonomia-2012/giugno-2012/274-roberto-cartocci-geografia-dell-italia-cattolica-il-mulino-bologna-2011-pp-179.

19. M. Ferrera, *Il Welfare State in Italia* (Bologna: il Mulino, 1984); V. Fargion, *Geografia della cittadinanza sociale in Italia* (Bologna: il Mulino, 1997).
20. Patrizia David, "Il sistema assistenziale in Italia," in *Welfare State all'italiana*, ed. U.Ascoli, 185–205 (Rome; Bari: Laterza, 1984).
21. Peter Flora and Arnold Joseph Heidenheimer, *The Historical Core and Changing Boundaries of the Welfare State*, in *The Development of Welfare States in Europe and America*, 185–205 (New Brunswick, NJ: Transaction Books, 1981); Jens Alber, "Le origini del Welfare State: teorie, ipotesi ed analisi empirica" [The origins of the Welfare State: theories, hypotheses and empirical analysis], *Rivista Italiana di Scienza Politica* 3 (1982) 361–421; U. Ascoli, ed., *Welfare State all'italiana* (Rome; Bari: Laterza, 1984), 20–22.
22. Ascoli, *Welfare State all'italiana*, 20–22.
23. David, "Il sistema assistenziale in Italia."
24. Fargion, *Geografia della cittadinanza sociale in Italia*; Ilaria Madama, *Le politiche di assistenza sociale* [Social assistance policies] (Bologna: Il Mulino, 2010); Ilaria Madama and M. Ferrera, "Le politiche di assistenza sociale" [Social assistance policies], in *Le politiche sociali. L'Italia in prospettiva comparata*, ed. M. Ferrera, 227–80 (Bologna: Il Mulino, 2006).
25. Peter Taylor-Gooby, ed., *New Risks, New Welfare: The Transformation of the European Welfare State* (Oxford: Oxford University Press, 2004).
26. P. Pierson, ed., *The New Politics of the Welfare State* (Oxford: Oxford University Press, 2001).
27. W. Korpi and J. Palme, "New Politics and Class Politics in the Context of Austerity and Globalization: Welfare State Regress in 18 Countries, 1975–1995," *American Political Science Review* 97, no. 3 (2003): 425–46; P. Starke, *Radical Welfare State Retrenchment: A Comparative Analysis* (Basingstoke, UK: Palgrave Macmillan, 2008); G. Bonoli and D. Natali, eds., *The Politics of the New Welfare State* (Oxford: Oxford University Press, 2012); F. Garelli, *Religione all'italiana* (Bologna: Il Mulino, 2011).
28. J.S. Hacker, "Privatizing Risk without Privatizing the Welfare State," *American Political Science Review* 98, no. 2 (2004): 243–60; J.S. Hacker, *The Great Risk Shift* (Oxford: Oxford University Press, 2006); W. Streeck and K. Thelen, eds., *Beyond Continuity: Institutional Change in Advanced Political Economies* (Oxford: Oxford University Press, 2005); P. Taylor-Gooby, *New Risks, New Welfare* (Oxford: Oxford University Press, 2004).
29. M. Ferrera, A. Hemerijck, and M. Rhodes, *The Future of Social Europe: Recasting Work and Welfare in the New Economy* (Oeiras, Portugal: Celta, 2000).

30. N. Morel, B. Palier, and J. Palme eds., *Towards a Social Investment Welfare State?* (Bristol, UK: Policy Press, 2012), 2.
31. U. Ascoli and E. Pavolini, eds., *The Italian Welfare State in a European Perspective* (Bristol, UK: Policy Press, 2015).
32. J.S. Hacker, *The Great Risk Shift*.
33. Emmanuele Pavolini, Ugo Ascoli, and Maria Luisa Mirabile, *Tempi Moderni. Il welfare nelle aziende in Italia* (Bologna: Il Mulino, 2013); M. Arlotti, U. Ascoli, and E. Pavolini (2017), "Fondi sanitari e policy drift. Una trasformazione strutturale nel sistema sanitario nazionale italiano?," *La rivista delle politiche sociali*, 2 (2017): 77–92.
34. David Natali, Emmanuele Pavolini, and Bart Vanhercke eds., *Occupational Welfare in Europe* (Brussels: European Social Observatory, 2017).
35. Law no. 6972, July 17, 1890.
36. G. Vicarelli, *Alle radici della politica sanitaria in Italia* (Bologna: Il Mulino, 1997), 102.
37. Fargion, *Geografia della cittadinanza sociale in* Italia, 71.
38. Madama and Ferrera, "Le politiche di assistenza sociale," 253.
39. David, "Il sistema assistenziale in Italia"; Ferrera, *Il Welfare State in Italia*; Fargion, *Geografia della cittadinanza sociale in Italia*; Vicarelli, *Alle radici della politica sanitaria in Italia*; Madama, *Le politiche di assistenza sociale*.
40. Vicarelli, *Alle radici della politica sanitaria in Italia*, 105 (our translation).
41. Fargion, *Geografia della cittadinanza sociale in Italia*, 74.
42. Fargion, *Geografia della cittadinanza sociale in Italia*, 75.
43. Vicarelli, *Alle radici della politica sanitaria in Italia*, 111.
44. Madama and Ferrera, "Le politiche di assistenza sociale," 253.
45. *Geografia della cittadinanza sociale in Italia*, 77.
46. *Geografia della cittadinanza sociale in Italia*, 77–78.
47. A totally different fate befell the over 6000 Workers Mutual Aid Societies (6535 in 1904, a million members with respect to the around three-and-a-half million industrial workers), disbanded by the Fascist regime around the mid-1920s because their activity was considered openly in contrast with the nationalist aims set out by the government. The loans, particularly those offered by the factories, represented a form of self-organization which Fascism could not tolerate since it was the imperative of the regime to pursue their aim of absolute social control, especially over the proletarian classes.
48. Madama and Ferrera, "Le politiche di assistenza sociale."
49. Fargion, *Geografia della cittadinanza sociale in* Italia; Madama, *Le politiche di assistenza sociale*.

50. Fargion, *Geografia della cittadinanza sociale in* Italia; Kazepov, "The Subsidiarization of Social Policies."
51. L. Gheza Fabbri, *Solidarismo in Italia fra XIX e XX secolo* (Turin, Italy: Giappichelli, 1996), 125.
52. Gheza Fabbri, *Solidarismo in Italia*, 131.
53. Pope Leo XIII, Encyclical *Rerum Novarum* [of revolutionary change] or the Rights and Duties of Capital and Labor, May 15, 1891, http://w2.vatican.va/content/leoxiii/en/encyclicals/documents/hf_l-xiii_enc_15051891_rerum-novarum.html.
54. Gheza Fabbri, *Solidarismo in Italia*, 133, 177.
55. G. Tamagnini, *Le Casse Rurali (principi, storia, legislazione)* [The Rural Funds (principles, history, legislation] (Rome: Edizioni de La Rivista della Cooperazione, 1952), 106.
56. At the end of the 1990s, the IPAB still "covered 40% of beds available in the residential care facilities both public and private ... we are talking about over 4500 IPAB (4680) that employ 107,000 workers and offer care to over 412,000 people, 90% of which are the elderly." C. Ranci, *Oltre il Welfare State*, [Beyond the Welfare State] (Bologna: Il Mulino, 1999), 179–80. After the approval in 2000 of the new national framework law on social services (Law 328/00), the IPAB have been dissolved and transformed in public companies for welfare services or in private associations/foundations.
57. T. Bailey and M. Driessen, "Mapping Contemporary Catholic Politics in Italy," *Journal of Modern Italian Studies* 21, no. 3 (2016): 419–25.
58. R. Cartocci, *Geografia dell'Italia cattolica* (Bologna: Il Mulino, 2011); Garelli, *Religione all'italiana*.
59. John Paul II, Encyclical Letter *Centesimus Annus* [Hundredth year], 1999, http://w2.vatican.va/content/john-paul-ii/en/encyclicals/documents/hf_jp-ii_enc_01051991_centesimus-annus.html. See also, Ivo Colozzi, ed., *Dal vecchio al nuovo welfare percorsi di una morfogenesi* [rom the old to the new welfare pathways of a morphogenesis] (Milan: Franco Angeli, 2012).
60. I. Colozzi, *Religione, valori e welfare state: il caso italiano*, Sociologia e Politiche Sociali, 3 (2012): 45–73.
61. F. Bolzonar, "A Christian Democratization of Politics? The New Influence of Catholicism on Italian Politics since the Demise of the Democrazia Cristiana," *Journal of Modern Italian Studies* 21, no. 3 (2016): 445–63.
62. Cenosa, *Rilevazione delle opere sanitarie*.
63. Ascoli and Pavolini, eds., *The Italian Welfare State*.
64. Kazepov, "The Subsidiarization of Social Policies."
65. Kazepov, "The Subsidiarization of Social Policies."
66. Kazepov, "The Subsidiarization of Social Policies."

67. F. Bolzonar, "A Christian Democratization of Politics?"
68. Enzo Valentini, Marco Arlotti, Fabiano Compagnucci, Andrea Gentili, Fabrizio Muratore, and Mauro Gallegati, "Technical Change, Sectoral Dislocation and Barriers to Labor Mobility: Factors behind the Great Recession," *Journal of Economic Dynamics and Control* 81, no. C (2017): 187–215.
69. Istat, *La povertà in Italia* (Rome, 2015), http://www.istat.it/it/archivio/164869.
70. Saraceno, "Simmetrie perverse."
71. A. Simonazzi, "Back to the Mediterranean Model? Italy's Reopening Gap with the European Social Model," *Economia e Lavoro* [Economy and Work] 2 (2014): 109–22.
72. Ascoli and Pavolini, eds., *The Italian Welfare State*.
73. L. Pelliccia, *Spesa per il welfare locale: un bilancio dei cambiamenti nell'epoca di rigore finanziario* [Spending on local welfare: a balance of changes in the era of financial rigor], 2017, https://welforum.it/spesa-welfare-locale-bilancio-cambiamenti-epoca-rigore-finanziario/.
74. M. Leon and E. Pavolini, "Social Investment or Back to Familism: The Impact of the Economic Crisis on Family and Care Policies in Italy and Spain," *South European Society and Politics* 19, no. 3 (2014): 353–69.
75. Y. Kazepov, "Italian Social Assistance in the European Context: Residual Innovation and Uncertain Futures," in *The Italian Welfare State in a European Perspective*, ed. U Ascoli and E. Pavolini, 101–31 (Bristol, UK: Policy Press, 2015).
76. M. Bassi, "The Christian Support Networks for Immigrants in Palermo," *Partecipazione e Conflitto* 7, no. 1 (2014): 58–82.
77. X. Itçaina, "*Catholicism, Social Economy and Local Welfare in Times of Crisis: Comparing Spanish and Italian Territories* (Florence: EUI Working papers, 2014).
78. Further information about the Alleanza and the proposal advanced of income for social inclusion can be found at http://www.redditoinclusione.it/.
79. I. Madama and M. Jessoula, "Alleanza contro la povertà e reddito minimo. Perchè può essere la volta buona," in *Rapporto Caritas 2015—Politiche contro la povertà in Italia*, ed. Caritas, 91–104 (Rome: 2015), http://s2ew.caritasitaliana.it/materiali/Pubblicazioni/libri_2015/Rapporto_politiche_poverta/Caritas_rapporto_politiche_poverta2015.pdf; Bailey and Driessen, "Mapping Contemporary Catholic Politics in Italy."
80. Caritas, *Povertà in Italia: dati e politiche* (Rome, 2013), http://www.caritasitaliana.it/home_page_archivio/pubblicazioni/00003426_Poverta_in_Italia__dati_e_politiche.html; Caritas, *Rapporto Annuale 2009* (Rome, 2010), http://www.caritasitaliana.it/home_page_archivio/

pubblicazioni/00001943_Rapporto_annuale_2009.html, Caritas, *Rapporto annuale* (Rome, 2012), http://www.caritasitaliana. it/home_page_archivio/pubblicazioni/00003335_Rapporto_annuale_2012_.html.
81. Caritas, *False ripartenze. Rapporto 2014 sulla povertà e l'esclusione sociale* (Rome, 2015), http://www.caritasitaliana.it/home_page/area_stampa/00004776_False_partenze___Rapporto_Caritas_Italiana_2014_su_poverta_e_esclusione_sociale_in_Italia.html.
82. Cenosa, *Rilevazione delle opere sanitarie.*

CHAPTER 4

Muted Vibrancy and the Invisible Politics of Religion: Catholic Third Sector, Economic Crisis, and Territorial Welfare in Spain

Xabier Itçaina

Interactions between politics and religion are frequently reduced to highly publicized and politicized ethical, political, or "purely religious" issues. Focusing instead on what faith-based religious actors (in the case of Spain, mostly Catholic) are actually doing in the social economy and welfare at the national and local levels, this chapter aims to highlight the discrete—though effective and not necessarily conflictive—interplay between religion, policy, and politics. More specifically, the involvement of religious actors in welfare, beyond their charity-oriented activity, extends to the solidarity economy and the empowerment of the most vulnerable populations. These articulations between charity and solidarity tend to deepen connections among civil sectors as they generate new interactions between religious organizations, social movements, and policy makers.

X. Itçaina (✉)
University of Bordeaux, Sciences Po Bordeaux, CNRS,
Centre Emile Durkheim, Bordeaux, France

For Catholic organizations in Spain, the 2008 economic crisis constituted both an opportunity (for the legitimation of their ethical views on the regulation of capitalism) and a constraint (with a decrease in public and private resources). Far from being relegated to the private sphere, as the classic approach to secularization would assume, religious organizations were assigned a new role—frequently by default—in local welfare regimes, thus anticipating and substituting for public authorities.

This chapter will address the changing role of the Spanish Catholic Church along the lines proposed by the editors of this volume, who themselves follow the analytical scheme proposed by Haynes and Hennig on the political role of religious actors in the public sphere.[1] The first section ("path development") outlines the structure of the religious marketplace in Spain and the transformations of the church–state model inherited from the democratic transition; the second section ("objectives") analyzes what faith-based (mostly Catholic) actors try to achieve in the public arena, with a brief historical survey since the democratic transition of the 1970s; the third section ("means and strategies") focuses specifically on the way Catholic actors operate in the welfare services arena in Spain, with particular attention on the 2008 economic crisis; the fourth section ("effects") addresses the implications of this involvement for interactions between religious actors and the welfare state; and, finally, the concluding section ("public perceptions") contextualizes the perceptions of this social involvement of Catholic actors within broader perceptions of religion and politics. Both the third and fourth sections also highlight the internal pluralism displayed by the complex web of Catholicism. The chapter deals with Spain as a whole, with specific references to a local case-study conducted in the Spanish Basque Country, a region characterized by the strong presence of social capital, a highly decentralized welfare system, a highly secularized society, and a particular "muted vibrancy" characteristic of the Catholic networks working in the social field.

PATH DEVELOPMENT: THE RELIGIOUS AND INSTITUTIONAL CONTEXTS

The first section outlines both the religious and institutional contexts of the welfare action of the Spanish Catholic Church. It first briefly reviews the current religious composition of Spanish society, before addressing the path of church–state relations in this country. Both aspects provide an essential background to the social action of the church.

A Country Where Practicing Catholics Are in the Minority

Spain has undergone a rapid process of secularization since the democratic transition. Taking a historical view, sociologist Pérez-Agote has spoken of the "third wave of secularization"[2] experienced by Spanish society since the beginning of the 1990s. This third wave made itself felt by a change in religious self-definitions. Practicing and non-practicing Catholics were transformed into individuals with positions more distanced from religion: the number of agnostics and those indifferent to religion increased to a non-negligible extent and that of atheists even more. This phenomenon was particularly significant in the Autonomous Communities in the Basque Country, Catalonia, and Madrid, where in 2005 the largest group of respondents was made up of those indifferent or agnostic. In these three regions, two-thirds of young people between 15 and 24 years of age were atheist, indifferent, or agnostic, while in Andalusia, Castile and Leon, Galicia, and Valencia, the largest group of respondents remained that of non-practicing Catholics, indicating that the second wave was still prevalent.[3] The third wave thus made itself felt both through a crisis in the church *and* in religion itself. Adopting Hervieu-Léger's categories, Pérez-Agote makes it clear that this was no longer the stage of "decatholicization" or "mix and match" that marked the second wave but was now a phase of "exculturation" during which culture gradually lost its Catholic roots.[4] This process was particularly marked in the Basque Country where, as Pérez-Agote has stressed, politics and the national question somehow took the place of religion as newly central social questions.[5] As a result of this process, the religious portrait of Spain in recent years, roughly from 2015 to 2017, offers the image of a half-full/half-empty glass; that is, even though 71 percent of Spaniards self-identified as Roman Catholic in 2015 (half-full), other surveys continue to evidence a continuing decrease in the numbers of people defining themselves as Catholics, together with increasing numbers of non-believers, atheists, and believers in other religions (half-empty).[6] (See Fig. 4.1.)

A more recent survey confirms this statistical decline. According to a July 2017 CIS survey, 68.8 percent of those surveyed defined themselves as "Catholics," 2.3 percent as "believing in another religion," 15.7 percent as non-believers, and 10.2 percent as atheists.[7] At the same time, the ratio of Christian to civil marriages flipped: in 1996, there were 148,950 Catholic marriages and 44,780 civil marriages, but in 2014, there were 50,540 Catholic marriages and 107,820 civil marriages.[8]

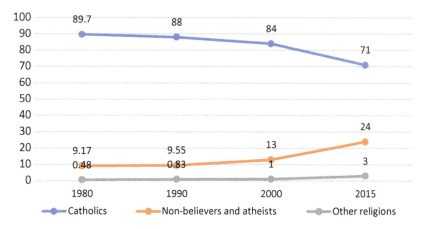

Fig. 4.1 Religious self-definition in Spain. Source: Adapted from J. Marirrodriga, "España no va a misa pero reza al santo. El número de practicantes desciende, pero los españoles se siguen considerando mayoritariamente católicos," *El País*, June 2, 2016. Based on CIS data

Religious participation is another classic indicator of the vibrancy of a faith-based community. In 2015, among declared Catholics, only 14.3 percent attended Mass almost every Sunday and Saint's Day, not including special ceremonies such as marriages, communions, and funerals, and 58.9 percent of Catholics rarely attended Church services.[9] As a result, Spain, like Portugal, could be considered a country where practicing Catholics are in the minority.[10]

There are yet signs of life for Catholicism in Spain. This decrease in rates of regular church attendance contrast sharply with a renewal of interest and participation in popular and festive religiosity, which has been widely reported by anthropologists.[11] This renewal of folk religiosity has to do with its very local character, and to the linkages between popular devotions and local identities. This new interest in local religion also relates to the de-institutionalization of Catholicism, to "religious bricolage" and to a major distancing on the part of believers with respect to the church hierarchy.[12] This apparent paradox was summed up by columnist from *El País* as "[a] country that doesn't go to Mass, but that prays to its Saint."[13]

There has also been an increase in the number of believers in other religions in Spain, though this remains very low—less than 3 percent in 2015. This increase is related to Spain's transformation, since the early

1980s, from a country of emigration to a country of immigration. That is, the new immigrants bring their religious beliefs with them to Spain. As in other European countries, there is a sharp contrast between low rates of religious participation and the highly politicized controversies surrounding minority religions, in particular Islam. (See Fig. 4.2.)

The Church–State Relationship: A Flexible Separation Regime

The mode of church–state relations is not necessarily of central importance in models explaining the welfare role of the church. Nonetheless, Catholic social action takes place within regimes regulating church–state relations, regimes that constitute a set of constraints and resources bearing down upon actors.

Unlike European countries with a Protestant culture where the principle of confessionality, or elite pluralism, holds sway, Catholic countries tend to follow a regime of egalitarian separation and pluralism.[14] This Catholic regime is characterized by two major principles: first, the state has no part in the organization of churches, and second, there is equality between confessions as regards their respective rights and duties. Separation

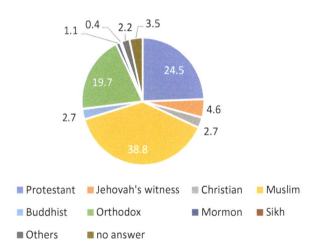

Fig. 4.2 Believers in religions other than Catholicism in Spain. Source: Adapted from CIS, *Estudio no. 3123. Encuesta social general española (ESGE) 2015*, pregunta 79ª, p. 82. (Protestant" refers to Evangelist, Anglican, Baptist, Methodist, Lutheran)

regimes have two principle variants. In a flexible separation regime, which holds sway in northern and central Europe—including Germany, Austria, and Holland—and with distinct arrangements in post-Franco Spain and post-Fascist Italy, the separation of church and state is accompanied by cooperation agreements between church and state. In contrast, a rigid separation regime characterized French secularism after 1905, Spain under the Second Republic (1930–1939) and the Italy of the *Risorgimento*.

A feature of a flexible separation regime is that it gives rise to a specific funding system for the Catholic Church. This regime has itself undergone institutional transformations at the margins, following changes to structures of political opportunity and ideological preferences in governmental majorities. Several attempts to reform the legal standing of the Catholic Church gave rise to a great deal of politicization in Spain during the Socialist Party's last two periods in office (2004–2011). These controversies over the system of political regulation of the church focused around the issue of the church's funding. The current Spanish system is based on the 1979 agreements between the state and the Holy See which reformed the 1953 Concordat and provided that the state would set the level of an annual grant to the Catholic Church. Felipe Gonzalez's Socialist government had established transition arrangements in 1988 with an allocation to the church of the 0.52 percent of income tax which taxpayers had chosen to earmark for the Catholic Church. The contribution from the state was in theory supposed to be added to this 0.52 percent for a transitional period of three years. However, since 1988, the state's contribution to the church has always been greater than the amount collected by this tax, with the proportion of taxpayers choosing to contribute to the church stabilizing around 33 percent. In addition to this allocation from taxation, which some within the church, arguing from the Italian example, would like to see raised from 0.5 percent to 0.8 percent, the Catholic Church also benefits from fiscal exemptions. The Zapatero government hesitated for some time between a minimal position where the government would go no further in its funding of the church, and a desire for reform without being outflanked on the left.

An agreement signed in September 2006 between the Conference of Spanish Bishops (CEE) and the government was intended to put an end to this uncertainty through a compromise solution. The percentage of the assignment from Personal Income Tax (IRPF)[15] to the Catholic Church would rise from 0.52 percent to 0.7 percent, but the annual additional budgetary amount would no longer be paid to the church and the CEE would have to account for the use made of the assignment from taxation on an annual basis. Finally, the agreement marked the end of exemption from Value Added Tax (VAT), thus complying with a European requirement. Judged "moderately satisfactory" by the Catholic Church,[16] the agreement was greeted in lukewarm terms by minority religions. According to the principal Protestant Federation FEREDE[17] and the Islamic Commission, while the new system brought greater clarity by ending supplementary contributions from the state, it nevertheless continued a considerable advantage for the Catholic Church by funding it through taxation. For its part, the CEE constructed an argument stressing the savings made by the state due to the work of the Catholic Church in social matters.[18] Since this 2006 reform, according to data published by the CEE, the number of taxpayers earmarking a proportion of their IRPF for the Catholic Church has risen, reaching 34.87 percent of those declaring a tax return in 2013.[19] This public debate on church funding should not conceal the fact that a large number of church-related social organizations may also receive direct or indirect public funding as non-profit organizations.

The regime of church–state relations thus helps to define an institutional framework inside which collective Catholic action can take place. Simultaneously constraining and empowering actors, this moving institutional framework locates Catholic mediation within a dual public debate, not only about the sectors concerned by Catholic social action but also about the status of churches within the public sphere. In Spain, the state is thus experiencing a tension between the desire to reduce the advantages, and particularly the fiscal advantages, enjoyed by the Catholic Church compared to other denominations and non-religious civil society, while handling the church carefully because of the social activities which it undertakes.

Objectives: What Do Religious Actors Intend to Achieve in the Public Arena?

This dual sociological and legal-constitutional context provides an action framework through which the Spanish Catholic Church gains access to the public arena. Before focusing on the role played by the Catholic Church as regards welfare, we need to frame more globally the church's attitude toward the Spanish public arena.

Since the democratic transition, the Spanish Church has never renounced active participation in public debate, whether related to its own sector-based interests (such as on church–state relations or education) or to broader public issues (notably on ethically laden issues such as divorce, abortion, marriage, etc., as well as issues of immigration, the territorial unity of Spain, and welfare). In this respect, the Spanish case can be analyzed in light of the "deprivatization" of public religions argument developed by Casanova.[20] The deprivatization of religion can be explained by looking at three instances. First, religions may enter the public sphere to protect not only their own freedom and rights, but also the "very rights of a democratic civil society to exist against an absolutist, authoritarian state."[21] In Spain, the church played a key role in democratization after the end of the dictatorship. Second, religion may enter the public sphere "to question and contest the absolute lawful autonomy of the secular spheres and their claims to be organized in accordance with principles of functional differentiation without regard to extraneous ethical or moral considerations."[22] The recession provided an opportunity for the church to publicize its message on social justice and its critical approach to neoliberalism. Third, religion may enter the public sphere "to protect the traditional life-world from administrative or juridical state penetration. … public mobilization of the so-called Moral Majority and the Catholic public stand on abortion in support of the 'right to life' are examples of this instance."[23] The recession also provided an opportunity for the church hierarchy to renew its protectionist discourse on family-related issues and link them to the socioeconomic situation.[24]

Since the first Socialist governments (1982–1996), the church has intervened critically on moral issues and on political corruption. But the church's interventionism was rejected by public opinion, including among Catholic groups, which ended up accepting the proposed reforms, such as divorce or contraception.[25] The restorationist turn taken by the Vatican under John Paul II reinforced public and societal detachment from the church, while stifling dissenting voices within it. Subsequent political changes in power were more (with the Popular Party 1996–2004) or less (Socialist Party 2004–2011) favorable to the sectoral claims of the church, but they did not fundamentally alter this process of detaching public opinion from the political involvement of the church.

However, and against all expectations, the political involvement of the Spanish Church was renewed in the mid-2000s, when the Socialist governments (2004–2011) undertook a series of reforms on ethically laden issues. Unlike in other European countries, the church did not remain passive with respect to this detachment. Since the mid-2000s, the church has taken a more offensive stance on public issues related to highly sensitive policies such as the 2004 education reform, same-sex marriage reform in June 2005, and the new abortion law eventually passed in December 2009.[26] These protests occurred mainly under José Luis Rodríguez Zapatero's Socialist rule (2004–2011) and were characterized "by the visible presence of the SCC which, in alliance with social and partisan forces, has acted as a political contender."[27] This renewed involvement of the church had political consequences, as political leaders also re-introduced debates related to secular education, divorce, and abortion not only during the 1980s but also more recently from 2004 to 2011. As a result, religiosity remained a key element for understanding Spanish electoral behavior, especially in those elections where the political elite had focused the debate on moral issues.[28]

In this respect and at first glance, the Spanish case would appear to go against the "strategic silence" approach as proposed by the editors of this volume. For Paul Christopher Manuel and Miguel Glatzer, "interestingly in some of our cases, the Catholic Church has been remarkably muted on national debates over abortion and same-sex marriage. We wonder if this represents a sort of 'strategic silence' on behalf of the religious groupings to de-emphasize politically divisive social issues in favour of the important work of meeting basic human needs—to spread the gospel by actions and not by words."[29] In the Spanish case, from the mid-2000s, the church, or more exactly, specific sectors of the church, namely the Spanish Episcopal Conference, conservative catholic movements such as Opus Dei or the Legionaries of Christ, took the lead in an openly political strategy of public presence. They were seconded and supported by conservative associations (on family issues, for instance), and by some groups within conservative political parties. In contrast, church voices were less audible on welfare and socioeconomic issues, despite their discreet but structuring role in this respect. To put this another way, "strategic silence" was to be found among *some* sectors of the church. This was especially the case for welfare services, on which the next sections will now focus.

Means and Strategies: How Do Religious Actors Operate in the Arena of Welfare Services?

The role of the Spanish Catholic Church in providing welfare services was particularly important during the economic crisis that hit Spain after 2008. Spain was one of the Eurozone countries hardest hit by the crisis. The austerity policies implemented by the state, under European pressure, paved the way for the current strong presence of the third sector, and particularly the Catholic one.

Even if Catholic welfare action is far from being monopolistic, Cáritas Española, as the official social organization of the church, deserves special attention. On one hand, Caritas appears to be the church's frontline actor working for the provision of basic welfare services and highlighting new areas of need. In addition to its organizational primacy, Caritas has a major role in coordinating Catholic organizations working in the social field and the institutional proximity of Caritas to diocesan hierarchies reinforces its legitimacy. During and after the economic crisis, Caritas developed a three-pronged action of analysis, operational action, and political advocacy. Published in 2017, the *Cáritas en la última década* (Caritas in the Last Decade) document synthesized these three dimensions.[30]

The analysis was carried out in particular through the Observatorio de la realidad social (Observatory of Social Reality) set up by Caritas and by the FOESSA Fomento de Estudios Sociales y de Sociología Aplicada Foundation. Caritas focused on the structural causes of the crisis, seen as the accumulation of social risks during the period of economic growth (2000–2007). During this period, the social integration model had shown its precariousness: 51 percent of the population was affected by at least one indicator of social exclusion.[31] These trends worsened during the crisis: between 2008 and 2016, median income decreased by 2 percent, while the Consumer Price Index rose by 12.5 percent. Poverty rates increased from 19.8 percent in 2008 to 22.3 percent in 2016. Consequently, the number of people assisted by Caritas increased: 40,000 homeless people per year, 4000 detainees or ex-detainees, 3500 seasonal workers in agriculture, and 3000 people in situations of prostitution and/or human trafficking. In the first years of the crisis, Caritas looked after 400,000 people in its reception and assistance centers. This number had increased to more than one million in 2012. The crisis caused an overall increase in social inequality, a high level of intergenerational transmission of poverty, and an increase in precariousness. In 2008, 11.7 percent of working people lived below the poverty line. In 2016, this rate increased to 14.1 percent. The quality of employment became an issue: those sectors which usually generate employment in Spain (such as services and the construction sector) proved to have little added value, to be very sensitive to changes in economic cycles, while they experienced a high degree of precariousness. Caritas and FOESSA also stressed that, even if the economic situation had eased slightly since 2015, this improvement was very slow: 70 percent of households had not felt the effects of the economic recovery. The savings capacity of households deteriorated: 60 percent of households were living with a level of savings so low that they could not hold out for more than one or two months without additional income.

In response to this situation, Caritas began to develop its own solidarity initiatives in order to reduce situations of both great poverty and precariousness. Although, in the past, the family had proved its role as a safety net in times of crisis, that was no longer the case: the number of households where members were unemployed and whose only income came from the retirement pensions of a person aged over 65 had increased threefold over the last decade.[32] This situation led Caritas to spend 200 million Euros on its family programs. Additionally, Caritas promoted an Income Guarantee System, an idea which originated in the 1990s. Caritas made special efforts in many directions, especially with its employment program. Apart from employment, basic rights (housing, health, basic needs) were under threat during the crisis. In 2007, 16 percent of Spaniards were affected by social exclusion; this figure rose to 25 percent in 2013. In this respect, Caritas provided comprehensive assistance including housing, family help, health, and legal assistance. Caritas invested 200 million Euros in 2007 and 358 million Euros in 2016. There was also increased solidarity: the number of Caritas volunteers rose from 56,400 in 2007 to 84,500 in 2016.[33]

Caritas complemented its welfare action by constant political advocacy. On the one hand, Caritas criticized recent policy reforms for having generated a high level of risk for the most vulnerable categories and for weakening essential safety nets related to human rights. Caritas has criticized the lack of state policy guaranteeing a minimal income, at a time when there are more than 700,000 households with no income. At the same time, there is no policy guaranteeing the right to be housed, although in 2010 there were more than 93,000 foreclosures.

Specifically, Caritas criticized the loss of human rights related to summary seizures of household goods (related to the Ley de Seguridad Ciudadana, the Citizens' Security Law). Additionally, Caritas pays special attention to the relationship with countries of the South, in two respects. First, Caritas denounced a fall in official Development Aid to 0.12 percent of gross domestic product (GDP) (well below the initial objective of 0.17 percent). Second, Caritas led a political campaign in favor of the dignity of migrants, focusing on legislation on foreigners, internment centers for aliens, and the reception of migrants and refugees. Caritas has extended its analysis of social exclusion to political and institutional disaffiliation. According to a FOESSA-Caritas survey, 83.4 percent of the population living below the poverty line see no value in voting,[34] 66.3 percent think that it is pointless to form or join associations, and 71.1 percent find political campaigns to be useless. As such, social exclusion may lead to political marginalization, a weakening of social capital, and perhaps even to democratic breakdown. These concerns led Caritas to set their dual definition of participation, through public services and through community organizations:

> Caritas, during all these years, has stressed the importance of public services, and has always promoted their pivotal role as guarantors of rights. But at the same time, Caritas supported the participation of the whole community, on the premise that bearing witness, active commitment and change are the best remedies for apathy and abdication of responsibility.[35]

More fundamentally, Caritas argues that, in the collective representation, the crisis did not lead to a radical questioning of the model of growth, while the causes of the crisis are structural. The crisis did nothing but consolidate two images: first, the market is seen as the only place where needs are satisfied, and second, every individual must be the guarantor of his or her own well-being. In response, Caritas has developed a two-pronged approach based on adopting gift-giving practices and the active role of the community. Concrete initiatives based on these principles were promoted, most of them drawing on the solidarity-based economy: social integration companies, cooperatives, special job centers, ethical finance, and fair trade, among others.[36] By promoting the solidarity-based economy, Caritas refuses to be restricted to its purely charitable role, but instead promotes personal empowerment and a more structural criticism both of the retrenchment of the welfare state and the neo-liberal turn of economic policies.

Effects: Religious Actors' Involvement and the Welfare State

This section analyzes the intended and unintended consequences of the religious actors' involvement in the transformations of the Spanish welfare state. In this respect, it is first necessary to emphasize the decisive role of the Catholic third sector in the making of the Spanish welfare regime. The Catholic third sector benefits from an extensive territorial coverage. In addition to the education sector, the presence of Catholic or Catholic-related organizations in the welfare sector is measurable through their weight in social and parochial centers, hospitals, child care centers, civic associations, foundations, and institutes of religious organizations, among other entities. Significant studies, such as the one conducted in Catalonia, have emphasized this complementary, yet subsidiary, role of the Catholic third sector in the delivering of social services, alongside state services, especially in times of crisis.[37] With a local focus, Belzunegui and colleagues have proposed a network analysis of the various branches of the social organizations of the diocese of Tarragona, again in Catalonia.[38] Elander, Daavelar, and Walliser have compared the role of faith-based organizations in the local welfare regimes in two urban configurations, Madrid and Barcelona.[39] Obviously, and as it has been noted in Portugal, significant pressure would be placed on the Spanish welfare state if these groups did not operate and if these services were stopped overnight.[40] This would be particularly true concerning the emergency care (food, clothing, and health) to the most vulnerable populations, but also in the case of social activation programs for people remote from the labor market.

This sort of "dependence" by the secular welfare state on Catholic third sector organizations creates an ambivalent situation in times of crisis, when tensions over the public expenditure force the state and the social organizations to reconsider their mutual relationship. Together with the Red Cross, Caritas is the largest Spanish voluntary organization, and as such, it receives the most support from the state.[41] However, this financial support is considerably less than the funding received by the organization from private donations. Caritas therefore intends to maintain its financial independence from the state. The recession has accentuated this situation with budgetary cuts forcing the organization to seek alternative resources. In 2008, 38.3 percent of its funding came from public funds and 61.7 percent from private funds. The relative share of public funding fell to 27.07

percent in 2014. But in absolute terms, public funding remained stable between 2008 and 2014, while private funding increased by 66 percent over the same period.[42] Due to its increased social assistance initiatives, Caritas had to spend substantially more on its programs (+40 percent between 2008 and 2014) in Spain and abroad.[43]

The question of resources opens a wider debate over the structural changes of the welfare state demonstrated by the importance of the Catholic third sector in welfare policies. In this respect, as Pettersson has emphasized, the key to understanding these interactions between the welfare state and the religious third sector lies more in the welfare governance style implemented in the territories rather than in national models for church–state relationships.[44] In that respect, despite an apparent paradox, the strong presence of religious organizations in the welfare should not be surprising in a very secularized society such as the Spanish one, given that this presence is the consequence of the increasing outsourcing of care services to third sector organizations.[45]

Spain, as a Mediterranean welfare state, is characterized by the relevance of religious actors in private action in support of the family and the poor.[46] The increase in state welfare over the last decades has relegated the charitable action of the Catholic Church to an important but complementary role.[47] At the same time, however, welfare in Southern European countries has in recent times experienced a pattern of liberalization in the delivery of welfare services, which has had the effect of "a certain extension of free market morals, in the proliferation of "non-profit making"— but characteristically subsidized—NGOs and other providers within the third sector, and the reinforcement of welfare privatization."[48]

At the most basic level, it was the liberalization of welfare services, and most particularly the outsourcing of certain welfare services, including personal services, that brought religious organizations to the fore, at the same time weakening family policy resources. León and Pavolini, following Moreno and Marí-Klose, stress the lower impact in Spain than in Italy of the church's positions on family policy at a time of crisis.[49] However, the return of these organizations took place on the basis of their identity as third sector organizations and not so much on the basis of their religious identity. In a sense, the liberalization of welfare—and particularly the outsourcing of care services—has brought religious organizations back to the front line, this time as third sector organizations, reversing the sidelining which the secularization of welfare had produced.

In Spain, this general trend was rendered more complex by an asymmetrical decentralization, which led to the consolidation of regional welfare regimes.[50] As an illustration, the public welfare system was significantly better in the Basque Country and in Navarra than in many other regions, because of their greater institutional and fiscal capacities arising from their respective Statutes of Autonomy.[51] In the case of these two regions, the benefits arising from policy innovation by regional governments with a degree of fiscal autonomy exceeded the advantages of uniformity.[52] Basque welfare was also characterized by well-established cooperation between the regional government and the third sector, including the Catholic third sector. In this case, the policy influence of Catholic organizations has extended far beyond their function as data and service providers. In the Basque Country, a highly decentralized region, Catholic organizations have made legislative proposals whose outcomes could be expected to impact on regional institutions. During the industrial crisis of the 1980s, Caritas had already played a pioneering role in the Basque Parliament in the preparation of Law 2/1990 of May 3, 1990, that introduced, on the French model, a minimum wage for the socially excluded. Additionally, as a result of the political work carried out by Caritas together with other organizations, a draft bill was approved by the Basque Parliament in 2007—before the crisis—forcing public administrations to include a social clause in public tenders, to the advantage of social businesses and social cooperatives.

This role played by public institutions and by Catholic and secular associations prevented the 2008 crisis from being as destructive in the Basque Country as it was in many other Spanish regions. However, austerity policies were to be implemented here as well, although somewhat later and despite resistance by the Basque government, especially on health care expenditure. In December 2011, the Basque authorities tightened the criteria for entitlement to the minimum wage benefit,[53] particularly as regards the time period during which migrants had to officially register as residents. In this context, the social work carried out by Catholic organizations became more important than ever. In addition, the Harresiak apurtuz[54] campaign in favor of migrants' health rights had a positive outcome when the Basque government, led first by a socialist majority (2009–2012) and then by the PNV Basque nationalists (since 2012), decided to override injunctions from the Spanish Ministry of Health in order to maintain a universal health care system in the Basque Country.[55] It is worth pointing out that this consolidated partnership occurred in one of the most secularized regions of Spain,[56] but with a long tradition of Catholic voluntary associations. Elander, Daavelar, and Walliser have also described the local welfare regimes in Madrid and Barcelona as allowing "FBOs [faith-based organizations] to participate more or less in the debate, design and implementation of policies, ranging from a very inclusive (with the whole third sector) Barcelona, to a much more market-led Madrid."[57]

To sum up, it is undeniable that the Catholic third sector has played and still plays a crucial role in the Spanish welfare mix, even with regional variations due to the decentralization of welfare. This role has less to do with the intensity of religious belief in these regions than with the institutional arrangements on the delivery and outsourcing of welfare services. In this context, the Catholic organizations do not limit their role to service provision, but they also play a role as a data provider and as a social whistleblower. Thanks to their unique territorial networking, Caritas can generate fine-grained data, which is collected by field operators in local and regional reception centers. These data contribute greatly toward the framing of the problem of social exclusion by policy makers. Additionally, Caritas and other Catholic organizations try to impact on policy making on welfare issues, both at the state and regional scales.

Contrasted Public Perceptions

In this section, I will make a distinction between how this social involvement of the church is perceived by the Spanish society as a whole and the internal debate *within* Catholicism with respect to the role of the church in the changing Spanish welfare mix.

Public Perception in Society

We might think that the role of the church should be perceived under a positive light with respect to its action in welfare. However, surveys show a more contrasted picture, as evidenced by this CIS survey conducted in 2008, at the onset of the economic crisis (see Table 4.1).

These results should be treated with caution. Negative perception of the church's "responses" are important, but so are also the lack of knowledge and opinion about the positions of the church. On the issues of "AIDS in the Third World" and "scientific research," the "don't know" answer receives higher results than the "yes" item. Nonetheless, the fight against poverty ranks first among the positive evaluations of the church action.

Table 4.1 Public perceptions of the Catholic Church in Spain

	Yes	No	Don't know	No answer	(N)
The spiritual needs of the people	32.8	52.5	13.9	0.8	(1774)
Problems related to the family life	26.2	61.0	12.0	0.8	(1774)
Problems of overpopulation in developing countries	23.2	58.5	17.3	1.0	(1774)
Problems related to scientific research (biotechnologies, genetic engineering, etc.)	12.2	64.5	22.1	1.2	(1774)
The problem of the development of AIDS in the Third World	18.0	62.3	18.8	0.8	(1774)
Violent conflicts in the world	20.8	62.3	15.9	1.0	(1774)
Difficulties experimented by the immigrant population	29.4	51.2	18.4	1.0	(1774)
Problems related to poverty	37.6	49.4	11.9	1.1	(1774)

Q (only for respondents having only Spanish nationality): *In general, do you think that the Catholic Church is providing adequate responses to … ?*

Source: CIS, "Religiosidad," Estudio no. 2752, *Monografías CIS* 276, Fuera de colección CIS 49, question 40, February 8, 2008 (our translation)

As a consequence of the 2008 recession, the church suffered from the general decrease in institutional trust. Looking at the 2009 and 2011 European Social Surveys, Stathopoulou and Kostaki observe a significant decrease of institutional trust in Spain and in Greece in relation to the recession, followed by an increase of interpersonal trust.[58] Moreover, according to a CIS survey in April 2014 measuring trust in Spanish institutions, the church was ranked only 7th out of 16 entities, after the Guardia Civil (ranked first), the police, the army, and the monarchy, but before Parliament and the government.[59] The church was perceived as a component of a globally challenged institutional order. But here again, this global perception needs to be qualified according to the segment of the Catholic Church, which is under scrutiny. According to a 2012 *Metroscopia-El País* survey, the action of the Catholic Church as a whole was seen in a positive light by only 38 percent of the respondents. At the same time, the social work of the church was regarded positively (75 percent of positive opinions), as was the work of the local parishes (49 percent), unlike the way bishops fulfill their functions (16 percent of the respondents). It should also be noted that the church still ranked above Parliament, the banks, and the political parties. (See Table 4.2.)

Table 4.2 Public perceptions of the institutions

In percent	Agree	Disagree
Doctors	93	6
Scientists	90	6
Public school teachers	88	10
Social care bodies of the church (Caritas)	75	22
Parish priests	49	44
Catholic Church	38	58
Bishops	16	76
Parliament	16	81
Banks	11	88
Political parties	9	88

Q: *Do you approve of the way [name of the institution] fulfills its function?*
Source: adapted from *Metroscopia-El País* survey, José Juan Toharia, "Los españoles y las instituciones. 3. La Iglesia. De influente a casi irrelevante," *El País*, August 18, 2012

Internal Pluralism: Two Catholic Approaches to Subsidiarity

The church's welfare activity is also perceived in a pluralistic fashion within the Catholic organizations, with contrasting perceptions of the subsidiarity relations between the welfare state and the social organizations of the church. At least two positions can be contrasted in this respect. On the one side, some organizations maintain an approach of subsidiarity that is closer to the neo-liberal agenda. This position is notably defended in Spain by Catholic movements and organizations such as Opus Dei, which is present both in the social field and in the private for-profit economy. Here, the free market is seen as the essential principle regulating society, as are the conditions of economic growth, personal liberty, and a guarantee of equal opportunities. The state's role is perceived as at best residual. In an instructive comparison between two Catholic movements, Opus Dei and Communion and Liberation, Colonomos sees in both the expression of Catholicism's "conservative modernization" in the economic and political field.[60] Statism is seen as a threat to free enterprise and initiatives from civil society. Non-profit activities are presented through a discourse intended to make them consistent with the discourse of entrepreneurship, and they fulfill a series of functions not covered by public authorities.[61] In this view, the economic recession is seen not so much as a threat but rather as an opportunity to liberate civil society from state control.

By contrast, another Catholic approach maintains a conception of subsidiarity and relations with government, which is noticeably different from the first school of thought. Subsidiarity, in this instance, means not *less* state involvement but *better* state involvement. With a strong presence in social matters, the organizations concerned are badly hit by budgetary restrictions on social policies, restrictions that weaken both those being aided and the organizations themselves. Consequently, far from magnifying the retreat of public authorities from regulation of social matters, this withdrawal is perceived more as an abandonment of responsibility by government. Subsidiarity means neither substitution, nor confusion: the role of public authorities also consists of guaranteeing the quality and efficiency of services, which involves a control dimension. This is especially true in the case of third sector organizations based on volunteering, themselves often precarious and at risk of failing to comply with legal requirements.

This position is to be found among the organizations of the church that are most involved in welfare and social action. In the Basque Country, this was particularly sensitive for Caritas, but also for the social sector of the Jesuits,[62] some social foundations related to religious orders (like the Itaka foundation, related to the Piarists); and basic ecclesial communities such as the Bidari community. Such a critical approach to subsidiarity led these social Catholic organizations to political advocacy, especially in times of recession when the retrenchment of the state became obvious. Catholic organizations campaigned on sociopolitical issues, either alongside other social movements, or on their own and *as* Catholic organizations.

Joining broader coalitions alongside other social movements constituted a further step away from the traditional charity-based and depoliticized attitude of the church. The religious dimension, in these cases, becomes more discrete and fades away into the background of the tight coalition formed around the common cause. In Bilbao, Catholic organizations campaigned long before the crisis alongside social movements on specific issues such as migration. The economic crisis, however, broadened the scope of campaigning to cover the new social categories hit by the economic difficulties.

Catholic social organizations also conducted campaigns in their own name, stressing their religious identity. In Bilbao in 2011, a group of Catholic social organizations from Bizkaia[63] decided to come together to better address social needs and to form new partnerships with the secular third sector and with public administration bodies.[64] On June 11, 2012, the collective issued a manifesto, *Bizkaiko Elizaren gizarte erakundeen manifestua* (*Manifesto of the Social Organizations of the Church of Bizkaia*), signed by 21 Catholic organizations. Their diagnosis of the crisis laid stress on three aspects[65]: first, an attachment to the European model of the welfare state; second, concerns about a recent policy shift that weakened vulnerable populations (in the Basque Country, a reform of the requirements for minimum income benefit and changes in requirements for receiving special assistance for social inclusion, and, at the Spanish level, labor market reform and Executive Order 16/2012 that abolished the right of foreigners to receive health assistance without a legal residence permit); and third, a growing collective imagination, conveyed by media and political discourse, that tended to make disadvantaged people the guilty party.[66] The manifesto identified four requirements:

- a need to take up a proactive attitude in order to defend the social model against the restrictions of the system and increasing individualism;
- a reaffirmation of personal, community-based, and institutional commitment to the most vulnerable on the part of church organizations;
- the duty of public administrations to guarantee rights and fair redistribution of goods on behalf of the most vulnerable; and
- the obligation of every member of society to "live simply so that others can simply live."[67]

In addition, the Ellacuria Centre, a Jesuit organization, went public in campaigns calling for religious freedom and the rights of religious minorities. These campaigns concerned the Basque regional law on cults and urban planning in Bilbao as regards places of worship. The Ellacuria Centre also joined the Spanish campaign led by the Jesuit[68] Service for Migration and the Jesuit NGO Pueblos unidos asking for effective regulation of internment centers for foreigners. Additionally, in March 2016, a collective constituted by Spanish Catholic organization working with migrants and refugees (Cáritas Española, CONFER [Conferencia española de religiosos], the Justice and Peace Commission, and the social sector of the Company of Jesus) went public to denounce the agreement between the European Union and Turkey concerning the removal of refugees to Turkey.[69] Other campaigns had negative outcomes, such as that seeking changes in the minimum wage in Euskadi. Moreover, in April

2013 the national campaign in favor of a citizens' initiative law against house evictions failed because of the opposition of the Popular Party.[70] Even these failed campaigns, however, provided an opportunity to voice claims and to disseminate data among social and political milieus lacking basic knowledge about social exclusion. Additionally, the transnational dimension of the church opened new arenas for social Catholic advocacy. The Caritas network monitors and lobbies European institutions. Hit severely as they were by the crisis, national delegations from Southern European Caritas (Italy, Spain, Portugal, Greece) and Ireland released in 2013 a common document on this issue, expressing a closely argued criticism of the inefficiency of the austerity policies adopted in this countries under pressure from the European Union.[71]

Catholic associations in these instances campaigned *as* religious organizations by offering their own specific readings of the crisis. In other terms, and as a counterpoint to what "identity-affirming Catholics"[72] might argue, for these "open Catholics," mobilizing alongside secular social movements did not mean abandoning their religious identity: quite the contrary. Establishing solid partnerships with public authorities did not prevent Catholic organizations from engaging in advocacy from a more prophetic perspective, either alongside other social movements or acting alone.

To sum up, the perception of the social work of the Catholic Church can be observed through two prisms. In public opinion, the image of the church has suffered from the general degradation of the legitimacy of Spanish institutions during and after the recession. At the same time, the social work undertaken by specific sectors of the church is considered in a more positive light. Within the Catholic Church, however, significant debates have arisen about the role of the church in the changing Spanish welfare mix. At least two approaches clashed: a liberal conception of subsidiarity and a solidarity-oriented one—with its own variants, notably a "radical-prophetical" trend.[73] The recession, while reactivating the social dimension of the church, also gave new salience to its internal cleavages.

Conclusion: Strategic Silence Versus Politicization?

Emphasizing the internal pluralism of the Spanish Catholic Church leads us to address in a qualified manner the "strategic silence" approach proposed by the editors of this volume. Relying on Warner's approach to the Catholic Church as an interest group, the editors point out that the church made some effort to influence public policies to ensure that health and welfare benefits are available to those in need.[74] In Spain, social sectors of the church effectively maintained this sort of "strategic silence" in order to de-emphasize politically divisive issues in favor of the important work of meeting basic human needs. Significantly, in 2013 the Foundation Compromiso y Transparencia (Commitment and Transparency) published an article titled "The Social Contribution of the Church: A Silent Revolution,"[75] insisting on the discrete social work undertaken by the Catholic Church in Spain. The church developed an expertise in social exclusion, an expertise that was acknowledged by policy makers and that did not necessarily imply a strong politicized statement of the definition of exclusion as a public problem.

However, this attempt at de-politicization of religious agency was doubly challenged. On the one hand, the Spanish Church hierarchy in the mid-2000s voiced its claims in national debates over abortion, same-sex marriage, and ethical-laden issues, a strategy of politicization not necessarily shared by all the Catholic welfare organizations. On the other hand, the 2008 economic recession urged the socially most-committed sectors of the church to reinforce their political work against the dismantling of the welfare state and against the austerity policies. Thus, the radical-prophetic segments of the church found themselves close to anti-austerity social movements in defending basic social rights, vulnerable populations, migrants, and so forth. Politics, in other words, came back to the fore, which rendered the interplay between Catholicism and the Spanish public sphere more complex than ever.

Acknowledgments The author thanks Paul Christopher Manuel and Miguel Glatzer for their invitation, and Mike Fay, Paul Christopher Manuel, and Heather Dubnick for their help in translating this chapter. Part of this work originated in a two-year stay at the European University Institute in Florence (2012–2013), with the support of the European Commission under a Marie Curie Intra-European Fellowship.

NOTES

1. Jeffrey Haynes and Anja Hennig, "Introduction," in *Religious Actors in the Public Sphere: Means, Objectives and Effects*, ed. Jeffrey Haynes and Anja Hennig, 1–13 (Abingdon, UK: Routledge, 2011).

2. Alfonso Pérez-Agote, "Les trois logiques de la religion en Espagne," in *Catholicisme en tensions*, ed. Céline Béraud, Frédéric Gugelot, and Isabelle Saint Martin, 37–49 (Paris: Éd. de l'EHESS, 2012). For Pérez-Agote, the *first wave of secularization* of consciences in Spain goes back to historical sequences preceding the Civil War, when intellectual and political currents generated secularizing forces. These movements were faced by a Catholic Church, which had scarcely experienced any moves toward internal secularization. This first wave was brutally interrupted by the Civil War. The *second wave of secularization* stemmed from the boom in economic development and the coming of the consumer society from the 1960s to the end of the 1980s. Frontal opposition to the Church gave way to a gradual distancing, without there necessarily being any conflict with institutional religion.
 3. Pérez-Agote, "Les trois logiques," 41.
 4. See Danièle Hervieu-Léger, *Le pèlerin et le converti, la religion en mouvement* (Paris: Flammarion, 1999).
 5. Alfonso Pérez-Agote, *Los lugares sociales de la religión: la secularización de la vida en el País Vasco* (Madrid: CIS, 1990).
 6. Adapted from Jorge Marirrodriga, "España no va a misa pero reza al santo. El número de practicantes desciende, pero los españoles se siguen considerando mayoritariamente católicos," *El País*, June 2, 2016, https://politica.elpais.com/politica/2016/06/01/actualidad/1464802794_896104.html. Based on CIS data.
 7. CIS, Estudio no. 3183. Barómetro de julio 2017, p. 21, http://www.cis.es/cis/export/sites/default/-Archivos/Marginales/3180_3199/3183/es3183mar.pdf.
 8. Marirrodriga, "España no va a misa" (data compiled from INE, *El País*, and Radiografía de España).
 9. Church attendance among Catholics: "hardly ever": 58.9 percent, "several times a year": 15.2 percent, "a few times a month": 8.2 percent; "Almost every Sunday and Saint's Day": 14.3 percent; "several times a week": 1.8 percent (Marirrodriga, "España no va a misa").
10. Paul Christopher Manuel, "The Catholic Question in Contemporary Portuguese Society: A Case of Muted Vibrancy?," Open Forum CES Paper Series, no. 14 (Center for European Studies at Harvard University, 2012).
11. See, among others, Antoinette Molinié, *La Passion selon Séville* (Paris: CNRS Editions, 2016).
12. Hervieu-Léger, *Le pèlerin et le converti*.
13. Marirrodriga, "España no va a misa."
14. Philippe Portier, "Le mouvement catholique en France au XXe siècle. Retour sur un processus de dérégulation," in *Le mouvement catholique français à l'épreuve de la pluralité: enquêtes autour d'une militance éclatée*, ed. Jean Baudouin and Philippe Portier, 17–47 (Rennes, France: Presses universitaires de Rennes, 2002).

15. Impuesta sobre la Renta de las Personas Físicas, Personal Income Tax.
16. Agencias, "El Gobierno anuncia un acuerdo con la Iglesia que eleva al 0.7% la aportación voluntariadel IRPF," *El País*, September 22, 2006, https://elpais.com/sociedad/2006/09/22/actualidad/1158876004_850215.html.
17. Federación de Entidades Religiosas Evangélicas de España.
18. Fernando Giménez Barriocanal, *La financiación de la Iglesia católica en España* (Madrid: Editorial EDICE/Conferencia Episcopal Española, 2007).
19. Fiscal Exercise 2013, on IRPF 2012 (CEE, "Declaración de la renta 2013," Madrid, February 20, 2014, http://www.conferenciaepiscopal.es/index.php/irpf/2012.html).
20. José Casanova, *Public Religions in the Modern World* (Chicago: University of Chicago Press, 1994).
21. Casanova, *Public Religions*, 57.
22. Casanova, *Public Religions*.
23. Casanova, *Public Religions*.
24. Xabier Itçaina, "The Spanish Catholic Church, the Public Sphere, and the Economic Recession: Rival Legitimacies," *Journal of Contemporary Religion* (forthcoming, 2018).
25. Casanova, *Public Religions*, 88–9.
26. Susana Aguilar Fernández, "Fighting against the Moral Agenda of Zapatero's Socialist government (2004–2011): The Spanish Catholic Church as a Political Contender," *Politics and Religion* 5 (2012): 671–94.
27. Aguilar Fernández, "Fighting against the Moral Agenda," 691.
28. Guillermo Cordero, "La activación del voto religioso en España (1979–2011)," *Revista española de investigaciones sociológicas* 147 (2014): 3–20.
29. Paul Christopher Manuel and Miguel Glatzer, "'Use Words Only If Necessary': The Strategic Silence of Organized Religion in Contemporary Europe," introduction to this volume.
30. Cáritas Española, "Cáritas en la última década" [Cáritas in the last decade], Cáritas report (Madrid: Cáritas Española, 2017), http://www.caritas.es/Memorias.aspx?Id=456.
31. Cáritas Española, "Cáritas en la última década," 1.
32. Cáritas Española, "Cáritas en la última década," 8.
33. For an account of the solidarity initiatives taken by the church in the Basque region, in comparison with the Italian province of Forlì, see Xabier Itçaina, "The Crisis as a Constrained Opportunity? Catholic Organizations and Territorial Welfare in the Basque Country and Emilia-Romagna," *Religion, State and Society* 43, no. 2 (2015): 118–32.
34. Caritas Española, "Cáritas en la última década," 10.
35. Caritas Española, "Cáritas en la última década," our translation.

36. Caritas Española, "Cáritas en la última década," 11.
37. Rosa Coscolla and Marina Aguilar *L'acció social en les entitats socials d'església* [Social Action and Church-Affiliated Social Entities] (Barcelona: Ed. Claret, 2014).
38. Angel Belzunegui, Ignasi Brunet, and Carme Panadès, *L'acció social de l'Església. Estudi sobre l'acció social de l'Església en l'àmbit territorial de l'Arxidiòcesi de Tarragona* (Tarragona: Anàlisi Social i Administrativa/ Universitat Rovira i Virgili, 2011).
39. Ingemar Elander, Maarten Davelaar, and Andrés Walliser, "Faith-based Organisations, Urban Governance and Welfare State Retrenchment," in *Faith-Based Organisations and Exclusion in European Cities*, ed. Justin Beaumont and Paul Cloke, 81–103 (Bristol, UK: The Policy Press, 2012).
40. Manuel, "The Catholic Question," 12.
41. Teresa Montagut, "Assessing the Welfare Mix: Public and Private in the Realm of Social Welfare," in *The Spanish Welfare State in European Context*, ed. Ana Marta Guillén and Margarita León, 111 (Farnham, UK: Ashgate, 2011).
42. Cáritas Española, *Resumen Memoria 2014* (Madrid: Cáritas, 2015).
43. Cáritas Española, *Resumen Memoria 2014*, 10.
44. Per Pettersson, "Majority Churches as Agents of European Welfare: A Sociological Approach," in *Welfare and Religion in 21st Century Europe: Volume 2: Gendered, Religious and Social Change*, ed. Anders Bäckström, Grace Davie et al., 15–59 (Farnham, UK: Ashgate, 2011).
45. See Itçaina "The Crisis as a Constrained Opportunity?" and "The Spanish Catholic Church."
46. John Gal, "Is There an Extended Family of Mediterranean Welfare States?" *Journal of European Social Policy* 20, no. 4 (2010): 283–300.
47. Luis Moreno, "The Model of Social Protection in Southern Europe: Enduring Characteristics?," *Revue française des affaires sociales* 5, no. 5 (2006): 74.
48. Moreno, "The Model of Social Protection," 77; Itçaina, "The Crisis as a Constrained Opportunity?"
49. Margarita León and Emmanuele Pavolini, "'Social Investment' or Back to 'Familialism': The Impact of the Economic Crisis on Family and Care Policies in Italy and Spain," *South European Society and Politics* 19, no. 3 (2014): 363; Luis Moreno and Pau Marí-Klose, "Youth, Family Change and Welfare Arrangements. Is the South Still So Different?," *European Societies* 15, no. 4 (2014): 493–513.
50. Raquel Gallego and Joan Subirats, "Regional Welfare Regimes and Multi-Level Governance," in *The Spanish Welfare State in European Context*, ed. Ana Marta Guillén and Margarita León, 97–118 (Farnham, UK: Ashgate, 2011).

51. See Itçaina, "The Crisis as a Constrained Opportunity?"
52. Moreno, "The Model of Social Protection in Southern Europe."
53. *Publico.es*, "Euskadi endurecerà el accesso a la renta mínima," September 13, 2011, http://www.publico.es/espana/euskadi-endurecera-acceso-renta-minima.html.
54. A pro-immigrant advocacy coalition integrated by secular and religious bodies in the Basque Country.
55. *El País*, "El Tribunal Constitucional avala la atención sanitaria a los sin papeles," December 17, 2012.
56. Alfonso Pérez-Agote, *Los lugares sociales de la religión*.
57. Ingemar Elander, Maarten Davelaar, and Andrés Walliser, "Faith-Based Organisation," 91.
58. Theoni Stathopoulou and Anastasia Kostaki, "Religiosity, Trust and Tolerance in Times of Recession. The Cases of Spain and Greece," in *The Debt Crisis in the Eurozone. Social impacts*, ed. Nikos Petropoulos, George O. Tsobanoglou, 251–80 (Newcastle, UK: Cambridge Scholars Publishing, 2014). However, "the more religious the respondents declare themselves and the more frequent church-goers they are, the more they trust institutions in both countries" (262). While in Greece, religiosity has had a negative impact on tolerance and social trust, this correlation was less obvious in Spain.
59. CIS, *Barometro de abril 2014. Estudio no. 3021, Avance de resultados*, http://datos.cis.es/pdf/Es3021mar_A.pdf.
60. Ariel Colonomos, *Églises en réseaux: Trajectoires politiques entre Europe et Amérique* (Paris: Presses de Sciences Po, 2000).
61. This approach brings to mind the philanthropic conception of the third sector in which a company makes a distinction between economic activity, which may operate in accordance with a capitalist accumulation regime, and its "social arm," acting through a social foundation, trust, association, or cooperative. Andrea Muehlebach, on the basis of a study of the third sector in the Italian region of Lombardy, talks of the "Catholicization of neo-liberalism" to designate the way in which Communion and Liberation and the *Compagnia delle opere* are said to turn to the third sector and volunteering to legitimize government's retreat from territorial welfare. Andrea Muehlebach, *The Moral Neoliberal. Welfare and Citizenship in Italy* (Chicago: Chicago University Press, 2012).
62. In Bilbao, the Jesuit social presence was based on a revised formulation of Liberation Theology, following the teaching of Ignacio Ellacuría, a Biscayan Jesuit priest killed in San Salvador in 1989, who gave priority to the agency of "popular majorities." All these experiments were close to the "open Catholicism" paradigm in condemning the excesses of economic

neo-liberalism, collaborating with the secular third sector, and showing a distanced relation to the church hierarchy. Philippe Portier, "Le mouvement catholique en France au xxe siècle. Retour sur un processus de dérégulation," *Le mouvement catholique français à l'épreuve de la pluralité: enquêtes autour d'une militance éclatée* in Jean Baudouin and Philippe Portier, 17–47 (Rennes, France: Presses universitaires de Rennes, 2002).
63. Caritas diocesana, Fundación EDE, Fundación Gizakia, Fundación Lagungo, Asociación Bidesari.
64. Manu Moreno, "Grupo de entidades sociales de Iglesia," *Papiro* 195 (2012): 40–1.
65. *Bizkaiko elizaren gizarte erakundeen manifestua*, Bilbao, June 11, 2012, http://bizkaia.hitza.eus/2012/06/29/bizkaiko-elizaren-gizarte-erakundeen-manifestua/.
66. *Bizkaiko elizaren gizarte erakundeen manifestua.*
67. *Bizkaiko elizaren gizarte erakundeen manifestua.*
68. Intellectual foundations of this Catholic social thinking can be found in the *Revista de fomento social*, which was born under the auspices of the Society of Jesus (see among others, vols. 283–84 (2016), Special Issue "For a Just Global Economy").
69. Cáritas, CONFER, Justicia y Paz, Sector Social de la Compañía de Jesús, "Las entidades de acción social de la Iglesia en España rechazan el acuerdo suscrito entre la U.E. y Turquía para devolver a todos los refugiados," Press release, March 8, 2016.
70. *El Mundo*, "Los promotores de la iniciativa popular sobre desahucios la retiran del Congreso," April 18, 2013, http://www.elmundo.es/elmundo/2013/04/18/espana/1366279340.html.
71. Caritas Europa, *The Impact of the European Crisis. A Study of the Impact of the Crisis and Austerity on People, With a Special Focus on Greece, Ireland, Italy, Portugal and Spain* (Brussels: Caritas Europa, 2013).
72. For Portier ("Le mouvement catholique en France"), identity-affirming Catholics oppose relativism, rejecting modernity and asserting the supremacy of papal doctrine and the visibility of religion. Open Catholics, by contrast, call for more distanced relations with the hierarchy, advocate freedom of conscience on moral and ethical issues, and condemn the excesses of economic neo-liberalism while also promoting solidarity and social rights. For the French context, see also Steven Englund, "L'Église de France. The church in a postreligious age," *Commonweal*, May 18, 2001, 2–16 on the distinctions between "classical-liberal" and "neo-classical" Catholics; and Yann Raison du Cleuziou, *Qui sont les cathos aujourd'hui? Sociologie d'un monde divisé* (Paris: Desclée de Brouwer, 2014) on intra-Catholic pluralism.

73. Gonzalo Villagrán Medina, "Teología pública: una propuesta para hablar teológicamente de temas sociales a la sociedad pluralista española," *Revista de Fomento Social* 67 (2012): 637.
74. Carolyn Warner, *Confessions of an Interest Group: The Catholic Church and Political Parties in Europe* (Princeton, NJ: Princeton University Press, 2000).
75. Javier M. Cavanna, "La contribución social de la Iglesia: una revolución silenciosa," *Compromiso empresarial*, February 28, 2013, https://www.compromisoempresarial.com/tercersector/ong/2013/02/la-contribucion-social-de-la-iglesia-una-revolucion-silenciosa/.

CHAPTER 5

The State, Religious Institutions, and Welfare Delivery: The Case of Portugal

Paul Christopher Manuel and Miguel Glatzer

This chapter examines the role and function of religious-based organizations in the delivery of social services and the strengthening of associational life in Portugal.[1] It asks whether the concept of muted vibrancy provides a theoretical understanding of the role of Catholicism in contemporary Portuguese society. That is, how might a church in a newly consolidated democratic regime, in a time of economic crisis, with a past relationship to a fascist regime, that has lost high-visibility battles on divorce, gay marriage, and abortion, and whose numbers of adherents is declining, contribute to the deepening of democracy? The Portuguese case is complicated by the path of development of its civil society: independent interest organizations have historically been weak, and in the place of other civic associations, the Roman Catholic Church—and especially its many charitable organizations—has traditionally been viewed as the embodiment of Portuguese civil society. In light of the fact that the

P. C. Manuel (✉)
American University, Washington, DC, USA

M. Glatzer
La Salle University, Philadelphia, PA, USA

© The Author(s) 2019
P. C. Manuel, M. Glatzer (Eds.), *Faith-Based Organizations and Social Welfare*, Palgrave Studies in Religion, Politics, and Policy,
https://Doi.org/10.1007/978-3-319-77297-4_5

Catholic Church has been experiencing a drop of adherents over the past 30 years, this chapter also examines an apparent contradiction facing contemporary Portugal: since there are decreasing numbers of Catholics available to perform needed social services, what kinds of pressures would be placed on the secular welfare state if the Catholic associations were someday to close? Are Catholic third sector organizations indications of a muted vibrancy of Portuguese Catholicism, and do they contribute to a robust associational life in Portugal?

Five Key Questions

This chapter will proceed by an examination of the following five key questions, three of which were developed by Jeffrey Haynes and Anja Henning.[2] *Grosso modo*, they seek to identify the historical path, objectives, means, strategies, effects, and public perception of Catholic civic organizations in Portuguese society.

- *Path Development*: What is the path of the church–state relationship in Portugal?
- *Objectives*: What do Portuguese religious actors intend to achieve in their public actions?
- *Means and Strategies*: How do religious actors operate in the Portuguese public square?
- *Effects*: What are the consequences (intended or unintended) of religious actors' political/public involvement?
- *Public Perception*: How is Catholicism viewed by the Portuguese population?

Question One: Path Development

The path development of the Portuguese "religious marketplace," following the concept developed by Ted Jelen and Clyde Wilcox,[3] has been dominated by a single religious tradition for the last 800 years. The issuance of the papal bull *Manifestis Probatum* started this historical path, when Pope Alexander III recognized Afonso Henriques as the first King of Portugal in 1179. This papal bull followed a string of military victories against the occupying Moorish forces who had ruled Portugal since 711, ultimately leading to the complete reconquest of the national territory— known in Portugal as the Reconquista.

Manifestis Probatum was arguably the start of a close and formal relationship between Roman Catholicism and the Portuguese nation-state. Over the subsequent 800 years, church–state relations have revolved around the fact that the pope named the first king. Some Portuguese like that fact, and others do not. This path set the terms of many subsequent problems for those interested in democratizing society and separating church and state, usually referred to as the clerical/anti-clerical divide. The Portuguese church–state cleavage may thus be traced to the very founding moment of the nation; this cleavage served as an important dividing line between Enlightenment-era reformers (younger, well-educated aristocrats) who promoted secular forms of political and societal authority relations, and the defenders of traditional forms of authority (the crown, the military, the aristocracy, and the Roman Catholic Church) who adhered to the divine right of rule. Centuries later, Pope Pius IX issued the *Syllabus of Errors* in 1864, which condemned the modern project and called on good Catholics to resist. The battle lines were thus drawn and would subsequently define church–state relations in twentieth-century Portugal. Accordingly, over the last 100 years, there have been periods of clericalism and anti-clericalism; pro-church legislation and anti-church legislation; an embrace of church teachings and a rejection of the same; and a devotion to, and rejection of, Catholic rituals, saints, and teachings.

Since the first Portuguese republic was declared in 1910, Portugal has experienced three distinct phases of church–state relations. The anti-clerical Republican regime (1910–1926) sought to remove the church from the public square; the pro-clerical fascist and corporatist Salazar regime (1926–1974) reintegrated the church into society but always kept it at arm's length from political power; and, in the time since the April 25, 1974, revolution (1974–present), contemporary Portugal has undergone a dramatic political, economic, and cultural transformation. The new democratic regime has sought to regularize its relationship with the church and to support its good works, where possible.

Throughout all of this—democracy and Fascism, war in Europe and with its African colonies, isolation from Europe and integration into Europe, clericalism, and anti-clericalism—the legacy of *Manifestis Probatum* has arguably remained ingrained in the societal fabric of Portuguese society. This religious legacy functions as a sort of cognitive lock for many Portuguese, who cannot even envision a non-Catholic Portugal. It also serves as an ongoing source of ontological sustenance and continuity with the past. In addition, a fidelity to the Gospel and to the vision of Queen Leonor perhaps still fuels an ongoing societal mission to help those in need, predicated on corporal works of mercy.[4]

Changing Patterns of Religious Devotion in Portugal

The Centro de Estudos e Sondagens de Opinião at the Universidade Católica Portuguesa completed a survey in 2011 (in the midst of the austerity crisis) on devotional patterns and belief systems in Portugal.[5] The results have identified a significant change in religious devotion patterns among the Portuguese. Whereas Roman Catholicism accounted for well over 90 percent of the total population at the start of the twentieth century, these new results suggest that the population of Portugal is not as Catholic as it used to be.[6] Both Table 5.1 and Fig. 5.1 indicate that although Portugal remains a Roman Catholic-majority country, there is marked diversity in its contemporary religious marketplace. Of note, some 14 percent of the respondents indicated that they had no organized religion or were indifferent, agnostic, or atheist.

Table 5.1 Religious affiliation in Portugal, 2011

Questions	% of population
Belief in God, but without a religion	4.6
Indifferent	3.2
Agnostic	2.2
Atheist	4.1
Roman Catholic	79.5
Evangelical Christian	2.2
Other protestant	0.2
Orthodox Christian	0.5
Muslim	0.3
Jehovah's witnesses	1.3
Other Christian	0.3
Other non-Christian (including Jewish)	0.4 (Jewish 0.1)
No response/don't know	0.6

Source: Centro de Estudos e Sondagens de Opinião and Centro de Estudos de Religiões e Culturas, "Identidades Religiosas em Portugal: Representações, Valores e Práticas," ed. Alfredo Teixeira, 2011 (summary of paper presented at the Plenary Assembly of the Conferência Episcopal Portuguesa, Fátima, April 16–19, 2012, Universidade Católica Portuguesa Com o patrocínio da Conferência Episcopal Portuguesa), Table 4, p. 3, http://www.esb.ucp.pt/sites/default/files/images/inquerito_2011_resumo.pdf

THE STATE, RELIGIOUS INSTITUTIONS, AND WELFARE DELIVERY... 107

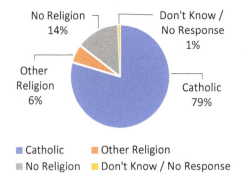

Fig. 5.1 Religious affiliation in Portugal, 2011. Source: Centro de Estudos e Sondagens de Opinião and Centro de Estudos de Religiões e Culturas, "Identidades Religiosas em Portugal: Representações, Valores e Práticas," ed. Alfredo Teixeira, 2011 (summary of paper presented at the Plenary Assembly of the Conferência Episcopal Portuguesa, Fátima, April 16–19, 2012, Universidade Católica Portuguesa Com o patrocínio da Conferência Episcopal Portuguesa), Table 4, p. 3, http://www.esb.ucp.pt/sites/default/files/images/inquerito_2011_resumo.pdf

Table 5.2 and Fig. 5.2 show some movement away from Roman Catholicism in Portugal. Since 1999, those self-identifying as Roman Catholic have dropped by 7 percent, and those self-identifying as without religion have increased by almost the same percentage. One could deduce from these results that those leaving the Catholic faith are not joining another confession, and that they simply consider themselves as persons without religion.

Table 5.3 focuses on the 79.5 percent of the Portuguese population self-identifying as Roman Catholic (reported in Table 5.1) in terms of how they practice their faith, by region. The results show that nationally, 49.2 percent of Roman Catholics regularly practice their faith, 40.6 percent do so occasionally, and 20 percent never do so. In other words, out of a population of approximately 10 million people, about 7.9 million claim Catholicism; according to our calculations, about 4 million Portuguese are irregular or non-practicing Catholics who are hedging their spiritual bets, so to speak; and around 3.9 million Portuguese regularly practice their Catholic faith.

Table 5.3 also shows some significant regional distinctions in the practice of Portuguese Catholicism: regular religious practice is stronger in the north (56 percent regular participation) and in the center (56.2 percent)

Table 5.2 Categories of religious positions among believers (in percentages)

Categories	1999	2011	Change
Roman Catholic	86.9	79.5	−7.4
Other religions	2.7	5.7	+3.0
Without religion	8.2	14.2	+6.0
Don't know/no response	2.2	0.6	−1.6
Total	100	100	

Source: Centro de Estudos e Sondagens de Opinião and Centro de Estudos de Religiões e Culturas, "Identidades Religiosas em Portugal: Representações, Valores e Práticas," ed. Alfredo Teixeira, 2011 (summary of paper presented at the Plenary Assembly of the Conferência Episcopal Portuguesa, Fátima, April 16–19, 2012, Universidade Católica Portuguesa Com o patrocínio da Conferência Episcopal Portuguesa), Table 4, p. 3, http://www.esb.ucp.pt/sites/default/files/images/inquerito_2011_resumo.pdf

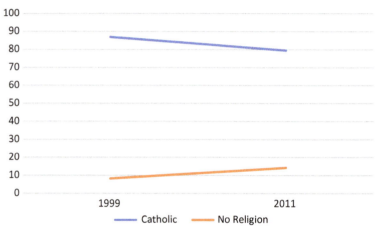

Fig. 5.2 Change in religious affiliation in Portugal, 1999–2011. Source: Centro de Estudos e Sondagens de Opinião and Centro de Estudos de Religiões e Culturas, "Identidades Religiosas em Portugal: Representações, Valores e Práticas," ed. Alfredo Teixeira, 2011 (summary of paper presented at the Plenary Assembly of the Conferência Episcopal Portuguesa, Fátima, April 16–19, 2012, Universidade Católica Portuguesa Com o patrocínio da Conferência Episcopal Portuguesa), Table 4, p. 3, http://www.esb.ucp.pt/sites/default/files/images/inquerito_2011_resumo.pdf

Table 5.3 Religious practices of Roman Catholics in Portugal, 2011 (in percentages)

Catholics, according to practice (aggregate data based on question "How often do you attend Mass")	North	Center	Lisbon and environs	Alentejo	Algarve	National total
1. Nominal Catholic (never)	8.9	6.9	13.3	11.9	20.0	20
2. Occasionally practicing Catholic (1–2 times per year)	22.2	19.8	32.0	27.8	36.0	25.2
3. Irregularly practicing Catholic (up to 11 times per year)	12.9	17.1	17.7	16.6	18.0	15.4
4. Regularly practicing Catholic (1–2 times per month)	14.8	16.7	12.9	15.9	7.0	14.5
5. Observant Catholic (all Sundays and holy days, more than once per week)	29.0	28.0	15.1	17.9	10.0	23.7
6. Devout Catholic (deeply involved in the life of the parish)	12.2	11.5	9.0	9.9	9.0	11.0

Source: Centro de Estudos e Sondagens de Opinião and Centro de Estudos de Religiões e Culturas, "Identidades Religiosas em Portugal: Representações, Valores e Práticas," ed. Alfredo Teixeira, 2011 (summary of paper presented at the Plenary Assembly of the Conferência Episcopal Portuguesa, Fátima, April 16–19, 2012, Universidade Católica Portuguesa Com o patrocínio da Conferência Episcopal Portuguesa), http://www.esb.ucp.pt/sites/default/files/images/inquerito_2011_resumo.pdf

than in the south, in Alentejo (43.7 percent) and the Algarve (26 percent). Thirty-seven percent of those living in the urban area of Lisbon and its environs regularly practice their Catholic faith.

Although national numbers indicate that Portugal remains a Catholic-majority country, they also reveal Portugal to be a Catholic-minority practicing country. Summing up the findings:

- A significant majority of Portuguese (79 percent) self-identify as Roman Catholic, but this number has been dropping over the last 30 years.
- A significant minority of Portuguese regularly practice their faith (approximately 3.9 million people).
- Portuguese Catholicism is practiced with greater frequency in the center and northern parts of the country than in the south or in the greater Lisbon metropolitan areas.

These numbers suggest that the Catholic Church in Portugal is not the religious monopoly it used to be; they also suggest that the impression that the Catholic Church is in rapid decline in Portuguese society may be overstated. There is a decline in the overall numbers, but the fact that four million people regularly practice their faith suggests an ongoing vibrancy of Portuguese Catholicism. To that point, the Jesuit priest Hermínio Rico argues that many young people in Portugal regularly attend Mass, "not in every parish, of course, but in many—those which adapt to a younger audience." In Rico's view, Catholicism in Portugal is more vibrant than elsewhere in Europe, including Spain.[7]

The Complicated Historical Path of the Santa Casa da Misericórdia de Lisboa

One province where one can see a *vibrantly muted* Catholic life in Portugal is in the many charitable organizations. Father Lino Maia, president of the Confederação Nacional das Instituições de Solidariedade—CNIS (National Confederation of Solidarity Institutions), states that the CNIS has about 2850 associated institutions nationally, including Misericórdias and Mutualidades.[8] Arguably, the most visible Catholic-inspired charitable organization in Portugal is the Santa Casa da Misericórdia de Lisboa. Other Santa Casa da Misericórdia institutions were subsequently created throughout the Portuguese-speaking world. More recently, Portuguese immigrants in France founded the Santa Casa de Misericórdia de Paris in 1994. The unifying and trans-historical mission of the Santa Casa da Misericórdia—and indeed of all the Catholic charitable organizations—is predicated in the Christian Gospel: namely, to provide needed assistance to the vulnerable and the marginalized and to improve individual lives, social relations, institutions, and collective projects. Or, in theological terms, believers are required to perform corporal works of mercy to those in need.[9]

However, the close church–state relationship during much of Portugal's history complicates efforts today to separate Catholic-associated charitable societies from secular state-run ones. The Portuguese state—in the person of Queen Leonor—created the non-profit in 1498, which causes much confusion today.[10] That is, Queen Leonor combined what we now would differentiate as state services and religious services into one entity with the creation of the Santa Casa da Misericórdia de Lisboa in 1498 (the same year Vasco da Gama reached India). What may have made sense under a

late fifteenth-century Catholic monarch creates conceptual confusion under a twenty-first-century secular democratic regime: the Misericórdia de Lisboa has been on a twisted and complicated church–state institutional path for the last 500 years, fraught with definitional problems.
Let's start with definitions. To be classified as a religious organization, a group ordinarily needs to function as an independent agency from the government. If an organization relies on state funding, one can reasonably ask where the public/private boundaries lie. In Portugal, most of the private groups have cooperation agreements with the government, normally under the statute of Instituições Particulares de Solidariedade Social— IPSS (Private Institutions of Social Solidarity). Religious-based organizations are classified as Pessoas Colectivas Religiosas (Register of Legal Religious Persons), as established by Decreto-Lei no. 134/2003.[11]

What is the Misericórdia, exactly? Is it a third sector organization, a governmental one, or some unique combination that only makes sense in a Portuguese historical context? It could certainly be argued that the Santa Casa da Misericórdia de Lisboa is not a third sector institution, because it is not fully private and independent of government. The Santa Casa da Misericórdia de Lisboa is independent from the rest of the Misericórdias and is funded by the state lottery. To this point, Lino Maia explains:

> The Misericórdia of Lisbon is not the third sector, but it is in an institutional relationship (it is state-owned). Beyond the Misericórdia of Lisbon there are over 380 Misericórdias nationally. Between 1500 and the present, there has been a widespread idea among the Portuguese that in every county (and city), there should be a Misericórdia. All these Misericórdias in Portugal are canonical structures linked to the Catholic Church (under the Cardinal of Lisbon) and thus are the third sector.[12]

Rui Branco, following the seminal 1979 article on corporatism by Collier and Collier, suggests that one could argue the Santa Casa da Misericórdia de Lisboa is a strange form of a third sector organization. That is, in their article, Collier and Collier nuance state–civil society relations based on a continuum that extends from full autonomy (not the case of the Santa Casa da Misericórdia de Lisboa) to some sort of "corporatism" within the framework of inducements and constraints (closer to the case of the Misericórdia de Lisboa).[13] As a semi-public body, it is not fully independent from government for its governance, but still maintains a religious-based, and not a secular, mission.[14] A quick glance at its website (under mission and values) reveals its commitment to corporal works of mercy—not something the secular government usually talks about.[15] So, at the very least, one could say that the Santa Casa da Misericórdia de Lisboa is a Catholic historical residue in a secular state—not unlike the enigma of a Christian cross sitting atop the secular state-owned Panthéon in Paris.[16]

The twisted path of church–state relations in Portugal has led to the current situation, in which the functions of the state and the Misericórdia have overlapped and continue to be obfuscated by historical traditions and other factors. The Santa Casa da Misericórdia de Lisboa is a singular case: it has delegated public functions, enjoys a semi-public status, and receives almost the full amount of the national lottery to fund its activities. Silvia Ferreira argues that:

> The Misericórdia de Lisboa is a special type of organization, distinguishable from other Misericórdias. It has a semi-public status (the board includes members of the public sector, and the provedor (director) is chosen by the government). It receives almost the full amount of the national lottery and it has delegated public functions. With that money it is in charge of social assistance in the region of Lisbon and it makes agreements with other non-profits for the delivery of social services. It plays in Lisbon the role that the social security administration has in the remaining parts of the country. This special status corresponds to the framework these kinds of organizations had before the Portuguese revolution, and is almost unique.[17]

Likewise, Hermínio Rico points out that "[t]here are many IPSS in Portugal. Misericórdias are just one kind—the older ones—but they all work through contracts with the State Social Security, in which they receive from the state (the welfare system) a certain amount for the services they provide each of their beneficiaries. Thus, the state finances private providers of social services. In the end, it's only the management of the funds that is private, not the source of the funds."[18]

Indeed, all the Misericórdias claim a mission based in corporal works of mercy—which are at the foundation of twentieth-century Catholic social teaching. The desire to help those in need harmonizes with the core objectives of the secular welfare state, but these are still two distinct institutions. The Santa Casa da Misericórdia de Lisboa is the oldest one, and the one most closely associated with the government. The União das Misericórdias—responsible for the rest of the country—is significantly more independent of the government, but still relies on state support.

Setting aside the question of whether the Santa Casa da Misericórdia de Lisboa is a third sector organization, we can identify many other social service organizations in Portugal. Loosely following the useful categories developed by Andres Walliser and Sara Villanueva, we can identify three main types of Christian-based third sector organizations in Portugal.

- First, the *policy implementation sector* describes those legal organizations operating under a state-granted formal statute. In this category, the IPSS status formally recognizes and supports the work of the organization in a specific area of need. This describes the Santa Casa da Misericórdia de Lisboa (Lisbon Holy House of Mercy) as well as the União das Misericórdias Portuguesa (Portuguese Union of Houses of Mercy); the Confederação Nacional das Instituições de Solidariedade Social—CNIS (National Confederation of Social Solidarity Institutions); the Associações de Solidariedade Social (Social Solidarity Associations); the União das Mutualidades Portuguesas (Union of Portuguese Mutual Societies); the Associações de Socorro Mútuo (League of Mutual Aid Associations); and the Centros Sociais e Paroquiais de Bem-Estar Social (Parochial Social Centers of Social Well-Being). Lino Maia reports that "relations between the leaders of the CNIS and the *Misericórdias* are very good, with regular meetings setting common strategy."[19]
- Second, the *community sector* describes those Catholic and other Christian organizations which are motivated by scripture to work directly with the most vulnerable, ordinarily outside of the state. These groups include Cáritas Portuguesa, Sociedade de São Vicente de Paulo (SSVP), and the Legião da Boa Vontade (Good Will Legion).
- Third, the *philanthropic associations sector*, which has a policy-specific focus, has clear social aims, does not engage in economic activity, and is very reliant on donations. These groups—sometimes in conjunction with the state—seek to provide needed services and improve efficiencies in the delivery of goods in specific policy areas (including refugees, poverty, prisons, and many others). They include O Serviço Jesuíta aos Refugiados—JRS (Jesuit Refugee Service); Obra Católica Portuguesa das Migrações (Portuguese Catholic Work for Migrants); Coordenação Nacional da Pastoral Penitenciária (National Coordination for Prison Ministry); Obra Nacional da Pastoral dos Ciganos (National Pastoral Work for Gypsies); Ajuda à Igreja que Sofre (Help to a Suffering Church); Terra dos Sonhos (Field of Dreams, for children suffering from incurable diseases); and many others.

These three categories show the complexity of faith-based third sector work in Portugal. Sónia Sousa has importantly observed that if the inquiry is limited to the Misericórdias, a substantial portion of social services institutions would be left out. In her view, "faith-based and privately-owned not-for-profit organizations account for the bulk of the social services in Portugal, more so than the Misericórdias. For example, there are about 2,500 institutions which are members of CNIS and another 1,800 non-CNIS members outside the sphere of Misericórdias."[20] Arguably, the long and twisted path of the church–state relationship in Portugal has led to the development of this wide array of social service third sector organizations, many of which are founded upon the principles of corporal works of mercy.

Question Two: Objectives

Let us now consider their objective: What do Catholic civic organizations hope to accomplish in the public square? This question brings us to what J. Von Essen has referred to as "the problem of goodness"—that is, determining whether these organizations are being altruistic for its own sake, or in expectation of some form of payment.[21] At first glance, one form of "payment"—for lack of a better word—for religious-motivated people is eternal salvation, rooted in the corporal works of mercy. Theologically, performing good works alone does not replace a belief in Christ, but such actions do put into practice a love of Christ. There are several scriptural bases for this work. Consider, for example, John 10:3 37–38:

> If I do not perform my Father's works, do not believe me; but if I perform them, even if you do not believe me, believe the works, so that you may realize (and understand) that the Father is in me and I am in the Father.

And again, in James 2:26:

> For just as a body without a spirit is dead, so also faith without works is dead.

Scriptural passages such as these motivated Queen Leonor to launch the Santa Casa da Misericórdia de Lisboa in 1498. Simply put, corporal works of mercy—which are the center of Roman Catholic understanding of intrinsic good—place scripture into practical applications; modern

Catholic social teachings spring up from these understandings. The societal footprint of the Misericórdia, Cáritas Portugal, and other Catholic organizations (including orphanages and other child care facilities, nursing homes, medical clinics, family counseling centers, and hospitals) reflects this notion of intrinsic good and accounts for why these groups exist in the first place.

THE ECONOMIC CRISIS OF 2008 AND REFUNDAÇÃO

The global financial crisis of 2008 brought renewed focus on the societal need of non-governmental Catholic-based civic associations. As Miguel Glatzer points out in an earlier paper, Portugal was hit hard by the global financial crisis.[22] Although the government initially responded with stimulus (along with most of its European partners as well as the United States), interest rates on government debt rose significantly. Portugal passed austerity budgets in 2010 but was soon forced to seek an international bailout. The troika (the European Commission, the European Central Bank, and the International Monetary Fund) approved a bailout package of 78 billion Euros in May 2011, the third after Greece and Ireland. Tightened credit, reduced private sector demand, government austerity, and a slowdown in growth and slide into recession among most of its European trading partners caused the Portuguese economy to decline. The crisis led Portugal to experience a lost decade, with real GDP per capita returning to 2008 levels only in 2017.

In response to the economic crisis and the bailout conditions of the agreement with the troika, the Portuguese government committed itself to both austerity and structural reforms. It undertook a process referred to as rethinking, or *refundação*, of how the state provides services; that process eventually led the state to adopt several sharp policy changes, including reductions of public services, transfers, public investments, social pensions, and public employee salaries.[23]

The government tightened tax policies. Indirect taxes on goods and services (the Value Added Tax) were increased, pensions above 500 Euros were subject to a solidarity tax, and a number of personal income tax credits were eliminated.[24] Pensions were reduced on a progressive scale. Child benefits and the benefit of the social integration scheme (Rendimento Social de Inserção) were cut by close to a third, with eligibility for the latter also tightened.[25] Labor market regulations were liberalized, with protections reduced. The minimum wage was frozen, overtime pay was reduced by 50 percent, the thirteenth and fourteenth months of pay were eliminated, severance costs were cut, and criteria for dismissals were widened.[26]

Many people were badly hurt by the crisis and the measures implemented in response to it. Between 2010 and 2014, the poverty rate for working age adults (aged 18–64) increased from 12.9 to 19.3 percent.[27] Poverty increased by similar amounts among children. Reflecting limited access to unemployment benefits as well as cuts in both benefit levels and duration, poverty reached very high levels among the unemployed, 40.2 percent of whom were poor in 2012.[28] The number of unemployed soared, rising from 7.6 percent in 2008 to a peak of 16.2 percent in 2013 before falling to 12.4 percent in 2015. Broader definitions of unemployment, which include people discouraged from looking for work as well as part-time workers who wish to work full-time, reached 25.4 percent in 2013.[29] Cáritas Portugal—the official institution of the Portuguese Bishops' Conference—reports that demands for its services significantly increased, with almost a doubling in the numbers of families who were receiving support in 2011–2012. Similarly, Valentina Pop observes:

> Five years since the beginning of the crisis in 2008, there is little or no growth, there are ongoing massive increases in unemployment, and millions of people are living in poverty … The *Cáritas* report shows how these reforms translated into practice: people with disabilities and pensioners having to wait for months for their allowances and pensions because there is not enough personnel to process all the claims.[30]

To provide additional service, the government launched the Social Emergency Program in 2011 (Programa de Emergência Social—PES).[31] This program also attempted to increase the capacity of local non-profit organizations to deal with the crisis and to alleviate the suffering of the affected groups. Lino Maia reports that the government reached out to the CNIS as it developed this program, and that this association of third sector charitable organizations continues an excellent working relationship with the government:

> The CNIS gave many contributions to the definition of the Social Emergency Program for 2011. It was indeed consulted in advance and was the main "construction" of the program. Cooperation between the government and the CNIS is very good; we have monthly meetings with three social minis-

tries (Ministry of Solidarity, Employment and Social Security, Ministry of Education, and Ministry of Health). The CNIS is continually consulted to give advice on all legal documents of interest to the sector and a cooperative agreement just got approved by the Council of Ministers in a Decree Law. Not being a government organization and affiliated with no party (it cooperates and systematically dialogues with all parties), the CNIS feels very comfortable in the dialogue and cooperation with this government.[32]

Clearly, the government understood that the austerity program would have significant human consequences, and that its own state-run welfare services would not be able to keep up with the demand. The role of the CNIS, along with Union of Misericórdias (which has about 380 members) and the Union of Mutual Societies (with about 90 members), was essential to maintaining some degree of social harmony during the implementation of the austerity program.[33]

Anti-austerity Protests

At first, the Portuguese seemed resigned to these austerity measures. In time, however, anti-austerity protests were organized and reached a scale not seen in Portugal since the heady days of the April 25, 1974, revolution. Unlike the 1970s, however, some of these new groups were organized over social media.[34] One of the largest anti-austerity protests took place on March 12, 2011, when an estimated 300,000 people, calling themselves the Movimento 12 de Março (March 12, Movement) and the Geração à Rasca (Struggling Generation), protested in Oporto and in Lisbon. These protests did not reach the crisis level seen in Greece, but they nonetheless posed a potential challenge for the government: a civil society outraged against its elected officials does not bode well for the health of democracy. Indeed, a worrying effect of the 2008 crisis in the worst-affected countries was a steep drop in trust in national and European Union institutions. To the degree that Catholic civic organizations are responding to the needs of those hurt by the austerity measures—and thus toning down some of the anti-government and anti-system rhetoric of the protesters—one can say that the role and function they play in strengthening associational life indeed assists the larger deepening of Portuguese democracy.

QUESTION THREE: MEANS AND STRATEGIES

The question of means and strategies implies two interrelated concerns: first, the legal framework of how religious actors operate in the Portuguese public square; and second, their sources of income.

Legal Framework

The law of Religious Liberty of 2001 frames contemporary church–state relations in Portugal.[35] Among other provisions, it guarantees equal treatment for all confessions and the right of a religion to establish churches and run schools. Of note, Article 58 of the Law on Religious Liberty guarantees the Roman Catholic Church certain privileges not allowed to other confessions, because it left the Salazar-era 1940 Concordat between the Vatican and Portugal intact. That issue was remedied with the 2004 Concordat between the Vatican and Portugal, in which the Portuguese state affirmed the juridical position of the Catholic Church and its institutions, especially the church's jurisdiction in ecclesiastical matters, whereas the church recognized religious freedom in Portugal as a fundamental right for all people, and agreed to live within the democratic processes outlined in the constitution.

The four main legal documents governing how religious actors operate in the Portuguese public square are the 1983 IPSS statue, the 1992 *Despacho Normativo* (Legislative Order), the 1996 *Cooperation Agreement*, and the 2003 *Registo de Pessoas Colectivas Religiosas* (Register of Collective Religious Persons).[36] Combined, these measures aim at bringing some balance and structure to the relationship between the government and third sector organizations that had previously been very confused and unclear—due in part to the complicated historical path of the church–state relationship.

The IPSS statute of 1983 was the first step. Maria Barroco notes that this statute granted legal recognition to third sector organizations that advance societal justice and solidarity, and was a first attempt at harmonizing church–state relations in this area.[37] The 1992 *Despacho Normativo* allowed the state to provide technical support and subsidies to third sector organizations, as well as through the tax code (reimbursements, exemptions, abatements).[38] The ambitious 1996 *Cooperation Agreement for Social Solidarity* signed by the government, the Associação Nacional de Municípios (National Associations of Municipal and Civil Parish

Governments), the Associação Nacional de Freguesias (National Association of Local Parish Governments), representative bodies of IPSS members, the Misericórdias, and the Mutual Association members provides the legal basis for the coordination of social service work at both national and local levels of government, as well as the relevant civil society organizations.[39] Finally, the Registo de Pessoas Colectivas Religiosas, a register of faith-based organizations, was formally created by Decreto-Lei no. 134/2003 on June 28, 2003. Combined, these four steps have enabled the state to formally identify and regularize their relationship with religious third sector organizations and thereby to begin to bring some structure and logic to this relationship. With these developments, most works of third sector charity that were founded on a volunteer basis have now been framed within the IPSS structure, with access to public funding.[40]

Sources of Income

Given the terms of the 1996 Cooperation Agreement, many IPSS organizations now receive government subsidies. This arrangement is in harmony with Paul Hirst's argument that "the state should cede functions to such associations, and create the mechanisms of public finance whereby they can undertake them."[41] The policy implementation sector groups Santa Casa de Misericórdia de Lisboa, União das Misericórdias Portuguesa, CNIS, União das Mutualidades Portuguesas, and parochial social centers all receive substantial state support, working through contracts with the government which allocate funds for their services. Community sector groups such as Cáritas Portuguesa, SSVP, and Legião da Boa Vontade receive some government support, and philanthropic associations typically work outside of governmental grants. A 2005 study by the European Union found earned income (fees and sales) to be the dominant source of civil society organization revenue in Portugal (48 percent), followed closely by public sector support (40 percent), and finally, private philanthropy (12 percent).[42]

As these findings suggest, the church/state lines remain blurred. Catholic associations rely on state funding, and the state also relies on these institutions to deliver much needed social services at a lower cost than if the state performed all this work by itself. In this regard, Rui Branco notes that "one of the takeaways of the literature on social assistance in Portugal is that the state's direct effort is comparatively small, as it relies a great deal on the third sector … another is that the welfare civil society, and within it the religious welfare civil society, is one of the best, if not the best, organized sectors in the Portuguese civil society, and also one of the largest."[43]

QUESTION FOUR: EFFECTS

Numerous studies have documented the important contributions of third sector organizations in Portugal.[44] The October 2014 publication *Impactes Económico e Social das IPSS* (Economic and Social Impact of the IPSS), by the Confederação Nacional das Instituições de Solidariedade (National Confederation of the Solidarity Institutions), details the economic and social benefits of religious-based third sector activities.[45] Among the findings, the report reveals that the combined work of the main legal forms of IPSS, including the Santas Casas das Misericórdias; Centros Sociais e Paroquiais de Bem-Estar Social; Associações de Socorro Mútuo ou Mutualidades; and Associações de Solidariedade Social—the policy implementation sector—produced in the social economy in FY 2010, "36.8 % of production, 50.1 % of GVA (Gross Value Added), 63.4 % of employment, 42.6 % of earnings, 40.9 % of final consumption expenditure and 38.2 % of net borrowing of the social economy."[46] Similarly, Cáritas Portugal reports that in 2014 its Fundo Social Solidário (Social Solidarity Fund) supported 3957 persons facing difficulties with issues like housing costs, health, education, or jobs. Its Prioridade às Crianças (all priority to children) program assisted 115 children in 2014.[47]

In terms of gross numbers of Catholic-sponsored charitable organizations in Portugal, Miguel de Oliveira reports that as of 1994, there were 295 homes for the infirm, 26 hospitals, 42 outpatient departments and dispensaries, 201 child care centers, 795 social and parochial centers, and 3897 Catholic civic associations.[48] These numbers have increased over the last 20 years for both Catholic and non-religious third sector organizations. The Center for Civil Society reports that in 2010 there were 5022 IPSS. The European Union reports that as of September 2014, there were 5099 IPSS registered with the Portuguese social security system, including 3309 associations, 1004 social and parochial centers, 234 foundations, 208 institutes of religious organizations, and 344 Misericórdias.

As these numbers indicate, the effects of the work by these sector organizations in Portuguese civil society are quite important.[49] Significant pressures would be placed on the welfare state if these groups did not exist. Glatzer has noted that "the state has an important financial interest in delivering social services through the IPSS," given the significant cost savings of the delivery of these vital services. Agreeing, Manuel Morujão observes that "it's impossible to imagine the welfare state without the work of the Santas Casas da Misericórdia. If the *Misericórdias* were to close, the welfare state would collapse." Expanding on that notion, Morujão explains that in his view, "it would be extremely difficult to find alternatives. The Misericórdias have great structures, buildings, know-how, prepared personnel, strong tradition, and Christian inspiration to serve brothers and sisters, and this is significantly more than bureaucratic structures have to help people."[50]

QUESTION FIVE: PUBLIC PERCEPTION

How are these good works perceived by the population? Returning to the surveys completed in 2011 during the austerity crisis by the Centro de Estudos e Sondagens de Opinião at the Universidade Católica Portuguesa, and presented in Tables 5.4, 5.5, 5.6, 5.7, 5.8, and 5.9, we can find an overall appreciation of the role of Catholicism in contemporary Portuguese society.[51] Given the long and pronounced presence of the Roman Catholic Church in Portuguese society, these questions are particularly revealing: they help us gauge a general feeling of whether the people think that the Catholic Church is an antiquated vestige of the fascist past, or whether it continues to play a vital role in contemporary Portuguese society.

Table 5.4 Would there be more poverty if there were no Roman Catholic Church in Portugal?

	Percentage of respondents
Totally agree	29.1
Partially agree	20.3
Neither agree nor disagree	13.7
Partially disagree	8.1
Totally disagree	18.7
Don't know/no response	10.0
Total	100.0

Source: Centro de Estudos e Sondagens de Opinião and Centro de Estudos de Religiões e Culturas, "Identidades Religiosas em Portugal: Representações, Valores e Práticas," ed. Alfredo Teixeira, 2011 (summary of paper presented at the Plenary Assembly of the Conferência Episcopal Portuguesa, Fátima, April 16–19, 2012, Universidade Católica Portuguesa Com o patrocínio da Conferência Episcopal Portuguesa), http://www.esb.ucp.pt/sites/default/files/images/inquerito_2011_resumo.pdf

Table 5.5 Would many lack a purpose in life if there were no Roman Catholic Church in Portugal?

	Percentage of respondents
Totally agree	38.7
Partially agree	26.9
Neither agree nor disagree	11.4
Partially disagree	5.0
Totally disagree	10.3
Don't know/no response	7.7
Total	100.0

Source: Centro de Estudos e Sondagens de Opinião and Centro de Estudos de Religiões e Culturas, "Identidades Religiosas em Portugal: Representações, Valores e Práticas," ed. Alfredo Teixeira, 2011 (summary of paper presented at the Plenary Assembly of the Conferência Episcopal Portuguesa, Fátima, April 16–19, 2012, Universidade Católica Portuguesa Com o patrocínio da Conferência Episcopal Portuguesa), http://www.esb.ucp.pt/sites/default/files/images/inquerito_2011_resumo.pdf

Table 5.6 Would many die without hope if there were no Roman Catholic Church in Portugal?

	Percentage of respondents
Totally agree	44.2
Partially agree	24.7
Neither agree nor disagree	9.1
Partially disagree	4.9
Totally disagree	9.6
Don't know/no response	7.4
Total	100.0

Source: Centro de Estudos e Sondagens de Opinião and Centro de Estudos de Religiões e Culturas, "Identidades Religiosas em Portugal: Representações, Valores e Práticas," ed. Alfredo Teixeira, 2011 (summary of paper presented at the Plenary Assembly of the Conferência Episcopal Portuguesa, Fátima, April 16–19, 2012, Universidade Católica Portuguesa Com o patrocínio da Conferência Episcopal Portuguesa), http://www.esb.ucp.pt/sites/default/files/images/inquerito_2011_resumo.pdf

THE STATE, RELIGIOUS INSTITUTIONS, AND WELFARE DELIVERY... 123

Table 5.7 Would there be more progress if there were no Roman Catholic Church in Portugal?

	Percentage of respondents
Totally agree	6.5
Partially agree	10.0
Neither agree nor disagree	20.0
Partially disagree	13.7
Totally disagree	36.5
Don't know/no response	13.2
Total	100.0

Source: Centro de Estudos e Sondagens de Opinião and Centro de Estudos de Religiões e Culturas, "Identidades Religiosas em Portugal: Representações, Valores e Práticas," ed. Alfredo Teixeira, 2011 (summary of paper presented at the Plenary Assembly of the Conferência Episcopal Portuguesa, Fátima, April 16–19, 2012, Universidade Católica Portuguesa Com o patrocínio da Conferência Episcopal Portuguesa), http://www.esb.ucp.pt/sites/default/files/images/inquerito_2011_resumo.pdf

Table 5.8 Would there be more individual freedom if there were no Roman Catholic Church in Portugal?

	Percentage of respondents
Totally agree	8.7
Partially agree	12.4
Neither agree nor disagree	16.0
Partially disagree	13.6
Totally disagree	37.2
Don't know/no response	12.1
Total	100.0

Source: Centro de Estudos e Sondagens de Opinião and Centro de Estudos de Religiões e Culturas, "Identidades Religiosas em Portugal: Representações, Valores e Práticas," ed. Alfredo Teixeira, 2011 (summary of paper presented at the Plenary Assembly of the Conferência Episcopal Portuguesa, Fátima, April 16–19, 2012, Universidade Católica Portuguesa Com o patrocínio da Conferência Episcopal Portuguesa), http://www.esb.ucp.pt/sites/default/files/images/inquerito_2011_resumo.pdf

Table 5.9 Would there be more religious freedom if there were no Roman Catholic Church in Portugal?

	Percentage of respondents
Totally agree	13.4
Partially agree	12.2
Neither agree nor disagree	16.5
Partially disagree	10.7
Totally disagree	35.9
Don't know/no response	11.3
Total	100.0

Source: Centro de Estudos e Sondagens de Opinião and Centro de Estudos de Religiões e Culturas, "Identidades Religiosas em Portugal: Representações, Valores e Práticas," ed. Alfredo Teixeira, 2011 (summary of paper presented at the Plenary Assembly of the Conferência Episcopal Portuguesa, Fátima, April 16–19, 2012, Universidade Católica Portuguesa Com o patrocínio da Conferência Episcopal Portuguesa), http://www.esb.ucp.pt/sites/default/files/images/inquerito_2011_resumo.pdf

The Central Role of Combating Poverty

Table 5.4 asks about the social work of church and asks if there would be more poverty in Portugal without the Catholic Church. The survey finds that 49.4 percent of the Portuguese believe that there would be more poverty in Portugal without the Roman Catholic Church, with only 26.6 percent disagreeing. The 49 percent number approximates the number of practicing Roman Catholics in Portugal, but this result does seem to indicate a general appreciation for the charitable works of church-based organizations.

Tables 5.5 and 5.6 inquire about the ontological teachings of the church and ask if there would be less hope in Portugal without the Roman Catholic Church. The results indicate an appreciation for both the corporal works of mercy sponsored by church organizations and the hope contained in church teachings. Table 5.5 asks if people think there would be a lack of purpose in life without the Roman Catholic Church. A large percentage, 65.5 percent, agree that church teachings offer a purpose of life, with only 15.3 percent disagreeing. The strongest opinion was held by those who strongly agree with that statement, at 38.7 percent.

Similarly, Table 5.6 finds that 66.9 percent think that people would die without hope if there were no Catholic Church in Portugal. The strongest group, 44.2, totally agreed with the statement.

Tables 5.7, 5.8, and 5.9 all ask variations of questions concerning whether Portuguese society would be freer without the presence of the Roman Catholic Church. The results are somewhat surprising: the majority of Portuguese do not find the church to be an obstacle to individual freedom.

Table 5.7 asks whether Portugal would have more progress without the Roman Catholic Church. Only 16.5 percent agree with that statement, with 50.2 percent disagreeing. Of note, the strongest responses in this survey came from those who totally disagree with the statement.

Table 5.8 asks whether there would be more individual freedom in Portugal if there were no Roman Catholic Church. The results parallel the findings in Table 5.7: only 21 percent of the respondents agree with the statement, and 50.8 percent disagree. The strongest opinion was voiced by those who strongly disagree, at 37.2 percent.

Finally, Table 5.9 asks if people think that there would be more religious freedom if there were no Roman Catholic Church in Portugal; 46.6 percent disagree with that statement, and 25.6 percent agree. As is the case with the other tables, the largest percentage, 35.9 percent, totally disagrees with that statement.

These results clearly indicate a high appreciation of, and satisfaction with, the works of the Roman Catholic Church and its organizations in Portugal. Lino Maia explains:

> Maybe because of the great involvement of the Catholic Church and its IPSS (in combating poverty), there is a general appreciation for the Catholic Church, which has helped people to forget some "sins" of the Church. It is generally recognized that those who have done more to ensure that problems are not so onerous for the Portuguese, particularly in this (austerity) crisis, have been the Church and its institutions—not only the canonical structures in the IPSS, but also the Vincentians and *Cáritas*.[52]

Summing up the findings:

- A majority of Portuguese find that the Catholic Church provides needed services to combat poverty.
- A strong majority of Portuguese find that the Catholic Church provides ontological support (meaning and purpose of life).
- A plurality of Portuguese find that the Catholic Church does not impede personal or religious freedom.

Conclusion

How can a church in a newly consolidated democratic regime, in a time of economic crisis, with a past relationship to a fascist regime, and with declining numbers of adherents, contribute to the deepening of democracy? The concept of muted vibrancy is a particularly useful way to approach that question. It provides a nuanced understanding of the contemporary role of Catholicism in Portugal and takes us past a facile reading of their recent legislative defeats on moral issues.

Indeed, although the Portuguese Catholic Church has experienced a decrease in adherents over the past 30 years and has lost much influence in policy formation—as seen in the recent decisions by the government to decriminalize abortion and legalize same-sex marriage—the Portuguese Church remains vibrant. As the preceding discussion around our five key questions demonstrates, the social services provided by Catholic third sector organizations—whether they are part of the policy implementation sector, the community sector, or philanthropic associations—are greatly valued and have contributed to a strengthening of Portuguese associational life, especially so during the recent austerity crisis.[53] Father Lino Maia points out that "in Portugal there is a great sense of solidarity … almost all identify with the Judeo-Christian culture, and we are well aware that we are 'guards' of brothers and are called to 'feed the hungry.'"[54] Catholic social services—rooted in classic Christian understandings of the corporal works of mercy—have perhaps never been more in need. They are essential to combat poverty and to help to build a social consensus based on communitarian values. As such, they have clearly helped to strengthen Portuguese associational life, especially so after the austerity crisis of 2008.[55]

All of this brings us back to a fundamental contradiction in contemporary Portuguese society: although the numbers of baptized Catholics in Portugal participating in the life of their faith community have been decreasing over the past 30 years, perhaps due to the larger processes of secularization, the secular state in Lisbon still relies on the welfare services provided by those believing in corporal works of mercy. The twin processes of secularization and austerity have brought Portuguese Catholicism to this contradiction. Simply put, as the process of secularization tends to move people away from a daily spiritual reliance on organized religion, the politics of austerity requires more service to the poor by third sector organizations. Even though the good works of Catholic third sector organizations are clear signs of a vibrant, but perhaps muted, church, one must still wonder if the steady decline in the practice of Portuguese Catholicism may someday result in fewer numbers of Catholics able and willing to perform these services—thereby forcing the delivery of social services in Portugal onto a more secular path.

NOTES

1. Our thanks to Alfredo Teixeira for his permission to use the 2011 survey data in this chapter gathered by the Centro de Estudos e Sondagens de Opinião at the Universidade Católica Portuguesa.
2. Jeffrey Haynes and Anja Henning, *Religious Actors in the Public Square: Means, Objectives and Effects* (New York: Routledge, 2011), 3. Haynes and Hennig developed the questions on objectives, means and strategies, and effects.
3. W. Clyde Wilcox and Ted Jelen, *The One, the Few and the Many: Religion and Politics in Comparative Perspective* (Cambridge: Cambridge University Press, 2002).
4. Alfred Stepan, *Arguing Comparative Politics* (Oxford: Oxford University Press, 2001), 221. Stepan notes that Portugal is the only member of the European Union that expressly prohibits political parties from the use of religious symbols. This law dates from the 1974–1996 revolutionary period and is mitigated by the fact that there is a de facto Christian Democratic Party—the CDS, or Centro Democrático e Social-Partido Popular, CDS-PP—that is a member of international Christian Democratic organizations.
5. Centro de Estudos e Sondagens de Opinião and Centro de Estudos de Religiões e Culturas, "Identidades Religiosas em Portugal: Representações, Valores e Práticas," ed. Alfredo Teixeira, 2011 (summary of paper presented at the Plenary Assembly of the Conferência Episcopal Portuguesa, Fátima, April 16–19, 2012, Universidade Católica Portuguesa Com o patrocínio da Conferência Episcopal Portuguesa), http://www.esb.ucp.pt/sites/default/files/images/inquerito_2011_resumo.pdf.
6. "Portugal," Catholic Encyclopedia, http://www.newadvent.org/cathen/12297a.htm. See also Caroline Brettell, "The Priest and His People: The Contractual Basis for Religious Practice in Rural Portugal," in *Religious Orthodoxy and Popular Faith in European Society*, ed. Ellen Badone, 55–75 (Princeton: Princeton University Press, 1990); Thomas Bruneau, "Church and State in Portugal: Crisis of Cross and Sword," *Journal of Church and State* 18, no. 3 (1976): 463–90; Tom Buchanan and Martin Conway, *Political Catholicism in Europe, 1918–1954*

(Oxford: Clarendon Press, 1996); Gene Burns, *The Frontiers of Catholicism: The Politics of Ideology in a Liberal World* (Berkeley: University of California Press, 1992); Manuel Braga da Cruz, "A Igreja na Transição Democrática Portuguesa," *Lusitania Sacra* 8/9 (1996–1997): 519–36; Joyce Riegelhaupt, "Festas and Padres: The Organization of Religious Action in a Portuguese Parish," *American Anthropologist* (1973/75): 835–52; Paul Christopher Manuel, "Religion and Politics in Iberia: Clericalism, Anticlericalism and Democratization in Portugal and Spain," in *The One, the Few and the Many: Religion and Politics in Comparative Perspective*, ed. W. Clyde Wilcox and Ted Jelen, 71–96 (Cambridge: Cambridge University Press, 2002); Helena Vilaça, *Da Torre de Babel às Terras Prometidas—Pluralismo Religioso em Portugal* [From the Tower of Babel to the Promised Lands—Religious Pluralism in Portugal] (Porto, Edições Afrontamento, 2006); and Helena Vilaça, "Secularization and Religious Vitality of the Roman Catholic Church in a Southern European Country," in *The Social Significance of Religion in an Enlarged Europe: Secularization, Individualization and Pluralization*, ed. Gert Pickel, Olaf Müller, and Detlef Pollack, 77–94 (Aldershot, UK: Ashgate, 2012).
7. Hermínio Rico, email interview with Paul Manuel, May 6, 2015.
8. Lino Maia, email interview with Paul Manuel, June 8, 2015.
9. The corporal works of mercy are (1) to feed the hungry, (2) to give drink to the thirsty, (3) to clothe the naked, (4) to visit and ransom the captives, (5) to shelter the homeless, (6) to visit the sick, (7) to bury the dead. See United States Conference of Catholic Bishops, "The Corporal Works of Mercy," http://www.usccb.org/beliefs-and-teachings/how-we-teach/new-evangelization/jubilee-of-mercy/the-corporal-works-of-mercy.cfm. See also United States Conference of Catholic Bishops, "The Spiritual Works of Mercy," http://www.usccb.org/beliefs-and-teachings/how-we-teach/new-evangelization/jubilee-of-mercy/the-spiritual-works-of-mercy.cfm. The scriptural basis for the corporal works of mercy may be found in the Gospel of Matthew 25: 31–45, "*The Judgment of the Nations.* ˙31," http://www.usccb.org/bible/matthew/25.
10. See Santa Casa da Misericórdia de Lisboa (SCML), http://www.scml.pt/pt-PT/scml/5_seculos_de_historia/seculos_xv_e_xvi/.
11. *Registo de Pessoas Colectivas Religiosas* is governed under Decree Law 16/2001.
12. Lino Maia, email interview with Paul Manuel, June 8, 2015.
13. David Collier and Ruth Berins Collier, "Inducements verses Constraints: Disaggregating 'Corporatism,'" *The American Political Science Review* 73, no. 4 (1979): 967–86.

14. The Instituto Nacional de Estatística [National Statistical Institute] website contains the 2010 Satellite Account for Social Economy (SASE) and the 2012 survey on Volunteer Work, https://www.ine.pt/xportal/xmain?xpid=INE&xpgid=ine_publicacoes&PUBLICACOESpub_boui=157543613&PUBLICACOESmodo=2.
15. Santa Casa da Misericórdia de Lisboa, "Missão e Valores" [Mission and Values], http://www.scml.pt/pt-PT/scml/missao_e_valores/.
16. The Panthéon in the Latin Quarter in Paris was originally built as a Roman Catholic Church dedicated to St. Genevieve—the patroness of Paris. After many changes following the French revolution, it now functions as a secular mausoleum containing the remains of French heroes. However, a Christian cross remains atop the secular structure. See "Facts About the Pantheon in Paris," *The Pantheon Paris*, http://www.pantheonparis.com/history/facts.
17. Silvia Ferreira, email interview with Paul Manuel, May 5, 2015.
18. Hermínio Rico, email interview with Paul Manuel, May 6, 2015.
19. Lino Maia, email interview with Paul Manuel, June 8, 2015.
20. Sónia Sousa, email interview with Paul Manuel, May 11, 2015.
21. Von Essen, "Religious Perspective of Volunteering," 148.
22. Miguel Glatzer, "Fostering Civil Society: The Portuguese Welfare State and the Development of a Non-Profit Sector—from Growth to Euro Crisis," in *The European Union Beyond the Crisis: Evolving Governance, Contested Policies and Disenchanted Publics*, ed. Boyka Stefanova, 213–30 (London: Lexington Books, 2015).
23. See Ricardo Gonçalves, "A refundação do Estado em Portugal" [Refoundation of the State in Portugal], November 11, 2012, *EcosEconomia blog*, http://ecoseconomia.blogspot.com/2012/11/a-refundacao-do-estado-em-portugal.html. See also Sandra Henriques, "Passos Coelho defende que refundação evita segundo resgate" [Passos Coelho claims that refoundation avoids second bailout], *Antena 1, RTP Portugal*, October 30, 2012, http://www.rtp.pt/noticias/index.php?article=599307&tm=9&layout=123&visual=61.
24. See European Trade Union Confederation, Austerity Measures Adopted in Portugal, at http://www.etuc.org/portugal; International Monetary Fund, IMF Country Report No. 13/6, Portugal: Rethinking the State—Selected Expenditure Reform Options, January 2013, https://www.imf.org/external/pubs/ft/scr/2013/cr1306.pdf.
25. Maria Petmesidou and Miguel Glatzer, "The Crisis Imperative, Reform Dynamics and Rescaling in Greece and Portugal," *European Journal of Social Security* 17, no. 2 (2015): 151–81.

26. Amilcar Moreira, Ángel Alonso Domínguez, Cátia Antunes, Maria Karamessini, Michele Raitano, and Miguel Glatzer, "Austerity-Driven Labour Market Reforms in Southern Europe: Eroding the Security of Labour Market Insiders," *European Journal of Social Security* 17, no. 2 (2015): 202–25.
27. José António Pereirinha, "Pobreza e Novos Riscos Sociais em Portugal: Uma Análise da Despesa Social" [Poverty and New Social Risks in Portugal: An Analysis of Social Expenditure], in *Políticas Sociais em Tempo de Crise: Perspectivas, Tendências e Questões Críticas* [Social Policies in Times of Crisis: Perspectives, Trends and Critical Issues], ed. Cristina Albuquerque and Helena Amara da Luz, 125–44 (Lisbon: PACTOR, 2016), 128.
28. Organisation for Economic Co-operation and Development (OECD), *Economic Surveys: Portugal 2014*, 94, https://doi.org/10.1787/eco_surveys-prt-2014-en.
29. Ministério do Trabalho, Solidariedade e Segurança Social, *Livro Verde Sobre as Relações Laborais 2016* (Lisbon: Gabinete de Estratégia e Planeamento do Ministério do Trabalho, Solidariedade e Segurança Social, 2016), 83.
30. Valentina Pop, "Charity documents 'human cost' of EU austerity," *EU Observer*, March 27, 2014, https://euobserver.com/social/123643; Ann Leahy, Seán Healy, and Michelle Murphy, *A Caritas Monitoring Report: The European Crisis and Its Human Cost: A Call for Fair Alternatives and Solutions. A Study of the Impact of the Crisis and Austerity on People, with a special focus on Cyprus, Greece, Ireland, Italy, Portugal, Romania and Spain*, http://www.caritas.eu/sites/default/files/caritascrisisreport_2014_en.pdf.
31. Government of Portugal, 2012 Social Emergency Program, http://www.mercadosocialarrendamento.msss.pt/docs/programa-de-emergencia-social.pdf. Also available at http://www.mercadosocialarrendamento.msss.pt/programa_emergencia_social.jsp; Paul Krugman, "Can Europe be Saved?," *New York Times Magazine*, January 16, 2011, http://www.nytimes.com/2011/01/16/magazine/16Europe-t.html?_r=0.
32. Lino Maia, email interview with Paul Manuel, June 8, 2015.
33. Lino Maia, email interview with Paul Manuel, June 8, 2015. It is unclear to what extent the social emergency plan of the PDS-CDS government during the recent crisis was just purely a matter of *policy choice* as opposed to a *policy legacy* inherited from previous governments. It is certainly true that contrary to Spain and Greece, Portugal has a rich history of third sector involvement in policy making via articulation agreements with the state.

34. The social media anti-austerity movement was led by Alexandre de Sousa Carvalho, João Labrincha, and Paula Gil.
35. José de Sousa de Brito, "Covenantal and Non-Covenantal Cooperation of State and Religion in Portugal," in *Religion and Law in Dialogue: Covenantal and Non-Covenantal Cooperation between State and Religion in Europe...*, ed. Richard Puza and Norman Doe (Leuven: Peeters Publishers, 2006).
36. Ascoli, Glatzer, and Sotiropulos, "Southern European Welfare," 19. Glatzer has usefully observed that prior to the 1983 statue "the relationship of the state to civil society organizations in this field was ad hoc, unsystematic and based on a high level of discretion."
37. Maria de Fátima Barroco, "As Instituições Particulares de Solidariedade Social: Seu Enquadramento e Regime Jurídico," in *As Instituições Não-Lucrativas e a Acção Social em Portugal*, ed. Carlos Pestana Barros and José C. Gomes Santos, 59–74 (Lisbon: Editora Vulgata, 1997), 66.
38. Barroco, "As Instituições Particulares de Solidariedade Social." Barroco notes that the exact details of the subsidies, etc., are revisited and codified annually in agreements between the relevant ministry and the IPSS union. See also Maria de Fátima Barroco, *Pessoas Colectivas e Solidariedade Social: Legislação e Diplomas Complementares* (Lisbon: Arco-Íris: Cosmos, 1996).
39. Barroco, "As Instituições Particulares de Solidariedade Social."
40. Rui Branco, email interview with Paul Manuel, May 5, 2015. More recently, the government has sought to extend the role of these organizations. Rui Branco notes that "one of the recent developments during the (austerity) crisis has been the expanding role of the third sector following a number of extended protocols and agreements since the present government took office in 2011; namely, the extension of third sector activities to school canteens or to funeral services. Actually, one bone of contention with the current socialist opposition is the will to roll back some of the added influence the welfare civil society has gained."
41. Paul Hirst, *Associative Democracy: New Forms of Economic and Social Governance* (Oxford: John Wiley & Sons, 2013), 21.
42. European Union, *Study on volunteering in the European Union: Country Report on Portugal*, 2005, http://ec.europa.eu/citizenship/pdf/national_report_pt_en.pdf.
43. Rui Branco, email interview with Paul Manuel, May 5, 2015. See also Branco, "A Sociedade Civil de Welfare em Portugal—Uma Perspetiva Histórica e Comparada" [The Civil Society of Welfare in Portugal—A Historical and Comparative Perspective], in *Politica Comparada. O Sistema Político Português numa Perspectiva Comparada* [Comparative Politics. The Portuguese Political System in a Comparative Perspective], ed. Conceição Pequito Teixeira, 403–31 (Cascais, Portugal: Principia, 2016).

44. See the 2010 Satellite account for social economy Report, *Instituto Nacional de Estatística* [National Institute of Statistics], https://www.ine.pt/xportal/xmain?xpid=INE&xpgid=ine_publicacoes&PUBLICACOESpub_bou i=157543613&PUBLICACOESmodo=2; the social networking website *Rede de Serviços e Equipamentos, Carta Social* also has useful information, http://www.cartasocial.pt/index2.php.
45. Confederação Nacional das Instituições de Solidariedade [National Confederation of the Solidarity Institutions], *Impactes Económico e Social das IPSS* [Economic and Social Impact of the IPSS], October 2014, http://novo.cnis.pt/Cnis_Impactes_RFinal_revisto.pdf.
46. *Impactes Económico e Social das IPSS* [Economic and Social Impact of the IPSS], 200.
47. Ana Carvalho, "Quantifying the Third Sector in Portugal: An Overview and Evolution from 1997 to 2007," *Voluntas* 21 (2010): 588–610. See also Ann Leahy, Seán Healy, and Michelle Murphy "Poverty and Inequalities and Inequalities on the Rise: Just Social Models Needed as the Solution! A Study of the Impact of the Crisis and Austerity on People, with a Special Focus on Cyprus, Greece, Ireland, Italy, Portugal, Romania, and Spain," *Caritas Monitoring Report*, 2015, http://www.caritas.eu/sites/default/files/caritascrisisreport_2015_en_final.pdf; Government of Portugal, *Programa de Emergência Social* [Program for the Social Emergency], http://www.portugal.gov.pt/media/747090/programa%20emergencia%20social.pdf.
48. P. Miguel de. Oliveira, *História Eclesiástica de Portugal* [Church History of Portugal] (Lisbon: Publicações Europa-America, 1994): 280. See also Helena Vilaça and Maria João Oliveira, "Portrait du Catholicisme au Portugal" [Portrait of Catholicism in Portugal], in *Portraits du Catholicisme. Une Comparaison Européenne* [Portraits of Catholicism: An European Comparison], ed. Alfonso Perez-Agote, 209–54 (Rennes, France: Presses Universitaires de Rennes).
49. Manuel Morujão, email interview with Paul Manuel, May 13, 2015. See also Américo Mendes, "Volunteering in Portugal," *European Social Innovation Research Blog*, June 14, 2013, http://siresearch.eu/blog/volunteering-portugal.
50. Manuel Morujão, email interview with Paul Manuel, May 13, 2015.
51. Also see *Religion and Culture in the Process of Global Change: Portuguese Perspectives*, José Tolentino Mendonça, Alfredo Teixeira, and Alexandre Palma, editors, Washington, DC: The Council for Research in Values and Philosophy, 2016, at http://www.crvp.org/publications/Series-VIII/19-Portugal.pdf.
52. Lino Maia, email interview with Paul Manuel, June 8, 2015.

53. Ipek Göçmen, "Role of Faith-Based Organizations," *Nonprofit and Voluntary Sector Quarterly* 42, no. 3 (2013): 495–516; Jacques Barou, "Faith-based Organizations and Social Exclusion in France," in *Faith-Based Organisations and Social Exclusion in Greece, in France and in Portugal*, ed. Leonidas Oikonomakis, Jacques Barou, and Andres Walliser, 47–75 (Leuven: Acco, 2011).
54. Lino Maia, email interview with Paul Manuel, June 8, 2015.
55. Rui Branco, email interview with Paul Manuel, May 5, 2015. Branco asks this very important question: "Will the crisis merely follow a path-dependent course, or will it have path-shifting consequences, upsetting the previous policy balance?"

CHAPTER 6

Church–State Relations in Today's Crisis-Beset Greece: A Delicate Balance Within a Frantic Society

Periklis Polyzoidis

Introduction: The Path of Church–State Relations in Greece

Understanding the complex relationship between the church in Greece and the Greek state is a difficult task; understanding it from a Western point of view is a tour de force—unless you start from the beginning. External analyses of Greek Orthodoxy might well be a partial misinterpretation for Western spectators who have not been able to recognize the same forms of social engagement in the Greek Orthodox Church that have been dominant in the West.[1] For the purpose of our study, we divide the history of the development of the church–state relations in the Orthodox world into four large consecutive periods.

P. Polyzoidis (✉)
Democritus University of Thrace, Xanthi, Greece

© The Author(s) 2019
P. C. Manuel, M. Glatzer (Eds.), *Faith-Based Organizations and Social Welfare*, Palgrave Studies in Religion, Politics, and Policy,
https://Doi.org/10.1007/978-3-319-77297-4_6

The Apostolic Era: "Give Back to Caesar What Is Caesar's and to God What Is God's"

The first interpretation of the intended relationship between Christianity and political authority belongs to Jesus Himself.[2] The building of the strong relationship between orthodoxy and the Greek language had begun very early, as religion first spread in the predominantly Greek-speaking eastern half of the Roman Empire. The empire itself had no reason to oppose Christianity, because it didn't represent a threat to its authority. However, the secrecy of the rituals of the Christians and their refusal to participate in public religion aroused growing suspicion among the pagan population accustomed to religion as a public event; this contributed to a general hostility against Christians. The first systematic persecution of the early Christian church by the Roman government took place under the emperor Nero in 64 A.D. and thereby forced it to become an underground movement, until the year 313 when the Roman emperors Constantine the Great and Licinius jointly promulgated the Edict of Milan, which legalized the Christian religion.

The Byzantine Period: The Supremacy of the Two-Headed Eagle

Constantine the Great reorganized the empire, made Constantinople the new capital, and legalized Christianity, which later was established as the state religion in the eastern part of the Roman Empire when Theodosius I convened the First Council of Constantinople[3] in 381. Heraclius adopted the Greek language for official use instead of Latin, while the general Hellenization of the empire was growing in the seventh century. Thus, although the Roman state continued, Byzantium was something new, insofar as it was centered around Constantinople, oriented toward the Greek rather than the Latin culture, and characterized by the orthodox Christianity.

The Orthodox Church had a prominent role in civilizing, humanizing, and uniting the many nations that had to live peacefully within the empire, and very soon Byzantine culture and orthodoxy were synonymous concepts. The official state symbol of the late Byzantine Empire was the double-headed eagle. Semantically, it symbolizes the unity between the Byzantine Orthodox Church and the state, a harmonic relationship between the civil and the ecclesiastical functions of the emperor; that is also why the claws of the eagle hold a cross and an orb.[4] Literature and art became chiefly religious. The power of the church, under the patriarch of Constantinople, became increasingly important and shaped public affairs. Theology thrived, cultivated by emperors and monks alike.

Most major intellectual, cultural, and social aspects of development in the Christian Church took place within Byzantium where the Greek language was widely spoken and used for most theological writings. Over time, most parts of the liturgy, traditions, and practices of the church of the empire, which still provide the basic patterns of contemporary orthodoxy, spread into the wider sphere of its influence and were adopted within the territory that later formed the Eastern Church. It came to be called "Greek" Orthodox just as the Western Church is called "Roman" Catholic. Christian preaching encouraged charity, and numerous charity foundations connected with the church were established.

The Ottoman Period: Angels and Demons vis-à-vis the Untutored and Deprived Population

Under the Ottoman Empire (1453–1821), the Orthodox Church was an accepted institution, and the Church of Greece maintained an important degree of independence. Christian churches were endowed with civil as well as ecclesiastical power over all Christians in Ottoman territories. There are two completely different approaches concerning the role of the church under the Ottoman Empire. On the one hand, it is stressed that the church was only a mechanism that the Ottomans used to keep the Greeks under absolute control and financially exploit them, sometimes with a virulence hardly imaginable. In keeping with this viewpoint,[5] it is obvious that the attitude of the church toward independence was dissuasive or even hostile, while the Christian population saw the church not as an agent of deliberation, but rather as the long hand of the sultan over Christianity. Mainstream approaches though adopt a completely different point of view, arguing that the Orthodox religion and its priests were an important element for the conservation and the definition of the Greek nationality, language, culture, traditions, and history; Orthodoxy has been seen as embedded in Greek national identity ever since.[6] The existence of many clergymen among the New Martyrs, who had been tortured and executed during Ottoman rule as a result of their constant struggle to avoid forced Islamization, is considered strong evidence of the real role which the church played during this period.[7]

Modern Times: Building a Fragile Equilibrium upon the Devastated Land

In the first years after the Revolution of 1821 and the formation of the Greek state, the Church of Greece was nationalized and came under the direct control of the state, which mobilized the capacity of Orthodoxy and used its authority and popularity among the citizens in order to legitimize its policies. On the other hand, the church has gradually become dependent upon the state in order to establish a centralized and hierarchical organizational structure. The first Greek Constitution[8] was dedicated "In the name of the Holy, Consubstantial and Indivisible Trinity," and it institutionalized the Eastern Orthodox Church of Christ as the prevailing religion of Greece. Adherence to the church has been established as a definitive hallmark of Greek ethnic identity in every Constitution ever since. The victorious War of Independence left behind a ruined land and thousands of handicapped fighters, widows, and orphans. Social protection was typically in the hands of the local governments, but in fact it was run exclusively by the church and some benefactors from abroad.

At the beginning of the twentieth century, the church continued its action through both its local facilities and the institutions of the Archdiocese. Its priorities were the maintenance of institutions and the protection of children and of the poor elderly. In 1922 and afterwards, the social policy was compulsorily focused on the encounter of the huge problems created by the influx of 1.5 million refugees of Smyrna and the other cities of the lost Greek territory of the Near East. During the German occupation, the Metropolises of the church all over Greece were active in distributing food, medicine, and clothes. Many priests were manhandled, tortured, and killed because of their acts of resistance against the Nazis.[9]

THE CHANGING RELIGION PATTERNS IN CONTEMPORARY GREECE

The Prominent Status of the Church of Greece

The Greek Constitution establishes the Eastern Orthodox Church of Christ as the prevailing religion in the country. The change from the previous constitutional term "state religion" manifests a significant recognition of religious plurality. The church constitutes a public law entity supervised by the Ministry of Education and Religious Affairs and thus enjoys tax exemption. The state is committed to cultivating the "national and religious conscience" of the Greek people through its educational function, to subsidizing the church budget, and to administrating its property.[10] Priests have the status of public servants paid by the state at rates comparable to those of teachers, an obligation arising from the confiscation of church property.

Religious rituals accompany every official state ceremony and also take place at the beginning of every school year; major church holidays are also state holidays. Greek flags are permanently displayed in all Orthodox churches, while the flag itself depicts a blue canton in the upper hoist-side corner bearing a white cross that symbolizes Eastern Orthodox Christianity. Parliament members as well as the president must take a religious oath,[11] and school starts every day with a religious prayer.[12] Religious marriages and baptisms are legally equivalent to their civil counterparts, and the relevant certificates are issued by officiating clergy. All Greek students in primary and secondary schools in Greece attend Christian Orthodox classes, although there is an exemption system for students who do not wish to attend, as long as the exemption is requested by both parents. Recently, a vital controversy between the church and the Ministry of Education about the content of this instruction has begun. When the Greek prime minister proceeded to a government reshuffle in 2016, Education and Religion Minister Nikos Philis lost his post. It was just three days after the Archbishop of Athens attacked him during a television interview regarding religious education.

An important element of the orthodox tradition is that the Head of the Church is Jesus Himself, and there is no Bishopric head, such as a Pope. The Church of Greece has a relatively loose federal structure with no efficient centralized bureaucracy.[13] Its primate is the Archbishop of Athens and All Greece. Four different Orthodox ecclesiastical statuses exist within the territorial limits of the Greek state.[14] The church is divided into 81 dioceses, called "Metropolises." Dioceses are divided into parishes. The Holy Synod is the supreme authority; it consists of all the diocesan bishops who have metropolitan status and deals with general church questions under the presidency of the Archbishop. The Standing Synod consists of the primate and 12 bishops, each serving for one term on a rotating basis and deals with details of administration. By virtue of its status as the prevailing religion, the canon law of the church is recognized by the Greek government in matters pertaining to church administration. This is governed by the "Constitution of the Church of Greece," which has been ratified into law by the parliament.

Orthodoxy and Religious Pluralism: The Master of a Game Whose Rules Are Changing

The vast majority of Greeks, a proportion between 88.1 percent[15] and 97.9 percent[16] of the population, are Orthodox, but there is evidence of a negative trend[17] (Fig. 6.1). There are no official statistics on religious groups; the census after 1991 did not ask for religious affiliation. The Greek Constitution provides for the right of all citizens to practice the religion of their choice but strictly prohibits proselytizing actions by all denominations, though previous regulations applied this term only against the Church of Greece. Religions with smaller numbers of followers include Judaism, Islam, Roman Catholic, and Jehovah's Witnesses.

Besides the Orthodox Church, only Judaism and Islam are also considered to be "legal persons of public law," having the right to own property including houses of prayer. All other religions are considered "legal persons of private law," so they cannot own property as religious entities; the property must belong to a specifically created legal entity rather than to the religious body itself (Fig. 6.2).

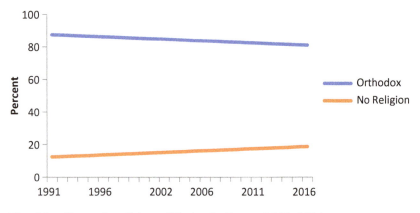

Fig. 6.1 Change in religious affiliation in Greece, 1991–2016

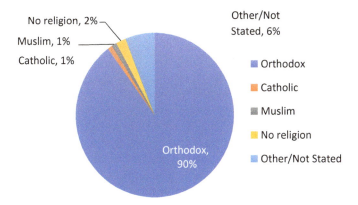

Fig. 6.2 Religious affiliation in Greece, 2016

The Muslim population in Greece is not homogeneous, since it consists of different ethnic, linguistic, and social backgrounds that often overlap. In Thrace, Northern Greece, there is an indigenous Muslim minority who have lived in Greece since the times of the Ottoman Empire; it consists of Turkish-speaking, Pomac-speaking,[18] and Romani-speaking populations. Their total number is estimated to be 97,604 people (0.95 percent of the total population), according to the 1991 census.[19] A total of 375 mosques exist in the region; the Greek state pays the salaries and some expenses of the two official Muslim religious leaders (muftis) and provides a small monthly allowance to imams, while Sharia, the Muslim religious law, is officially recognized by the state as the law regulating family and civic issues of the Muslim minority in Thrace. There is also a growing Muslim community in Athens, consisting mainly of immigrants from South Asia and the Middle East (mainly of Pakistani, Afghani, and Bangladeshi origin) who began arriving in Greece in the last quarter of the twentieth century. According to estimations, as there are no official records, their number is about 380,000.[20] The Muslim population is increasing rapidly with the arrival of refugees from Syria and other Muslim immigrants.

Even today there is no official mosque nor any official cleric to officiate at religious functions, including funerals, outside Thrace. Press reports state that the number of unofficial prayer rooms in Athens ranges from 25 to 70.[21] Members of the Muslim community use the official Muslim clerics in Thrace for official religious rites. The Greek government approved the building of a mosque in Athens in 2006 with public money; the leadership of the Orthodox Church publicly supported the decision, and the church donated 300,000 square feet, worth an estimated $20 million, for the purpose of establishing a Muslim cemetery. The project has been blighted by legal complications, and only after one decade of long debates and tumultuous objections from religious and citizen groups has the Greek Parliament definitively re-approved the building of the mosque; the government has also promised that a Muslim cemetery will be built.

The Muslim share of Greece's total population will increase between 2010 and 2050, from about 5.9 percent to 10.2 percent. A variety of factors, including higher birth rates, a bulging youth population among Muslims, and immigration, underlie this expected increase. The estimated Muslim share in Greece in 2050 is nearly 2 percentage points higher than in an alternative scenario with no new immigration. Indeed, more than half of the prospective growth of Europe's Muslim population can be attributed to the new immigration.[22]

The Jewish community in Greece currently amounts to roughly 5500 people.[23] There also exist 200,000 Roman Catholics,[24] 20,000–35,000 Greco-Armenians,[25] 41,376 Protestants, belonging to both the Greek Evangelical Church and Free Evangelical Churches,[26] about 28,000 Jehovah's Witnesses,[27] and about 2000 supporters of the controversial Hellenic ethnic religion.[28] Members of minority denominations report only minor incidents of societal discrimination.[29]

The World of Religion from the Secularist Point of View

In 2014, the church, seen positively by 57% of the population, was the fourth most trusted institution in Greece (the first three being the military with 80 percent, the police with 70 percent, and "the people" with 67 percent). One year later, it came down to the seventh place (62 percent).[30] Archbishop Ieronymos gathers an overwhelming 67 percent of positive views; 47 percent of citizens consider public statements of clerics on issues of public and foreign policy as "uniting," whereas 38 percent consider them as "divisive."[31] Between 2001 and 2015, there were significant changes in the relationship between the Greek population and the church. The percentage of true believers dropped from 86 percent to 52 percent; the percentage of those who pray daily from 54 percent to 25 percent; and the percentage of the every-Sunday-churchgoers from 23 percent to 7 percent. The influence of the church in society has significantly decreased during the same period. About 50 percent of the Greeks are now against the use of religious symbols in schools, courts, and state offices; 82 percent favor civil marriage, 73 percent cremation of the dead, and 50 percent same-sex marriages. Of respondents, 64 percent of the Greeks state that they are "little" or "not at all" satisfied with the current activity of the church, while only 5 percent are "very" and another 27 percent "quite" satisfied. About half the people (47 percent) believe that the role of the church is now weaker than ever.[32]

At the same time, more and more people believe that too many problems have found their way into the body of the church, including the lack of the ecclesiastical ethos of self-reproach and self-criticism. Some clergy and officers of the church enjoy luxurious living and cozy relationships with state power, and this has resulted in their bureaucratization and professionalization. This proximity to power does not allow church personnel at all levels to distance itself from the patron/client mindset, from populism, and from the widespread corruption of the Greek political system. Many priests are isolated form the real world, and they do not really care about the problems of the people. According to the findings of a special committee formed to investigate the demands of the people on the church, more transparency is needed regarding financial management and stronger participation of the secular when it comes to church matters.[33] People also demand more ethical and better educated priests; changes to the existing system of electing bishops; and stronger support of the participation of young people in the church.

Church, Welfare, and Financial Crisis: Spiritual Infusions in a Material World

Welfare State and Welfare Church

The church is an official partner of the state in matters of social protection. There are institutional provisions for a Synodical Committee, which has consultative status regarding social welfare.[34] Furthermore, there are provisions for official representation with consultative status of the church in the Advisory Committee for the reconstruction of social welfare and the establishment of new social protection institutions (Law 2082/1992); the church is de jure member of the Council of Social Welfare, which is the supreme consultative institution of the Ministry of Health and Welfare (Law 2646/1998).

Within the church, the provision of welfare services is organized at four levels: locally, through the large churches; regionally, through the Dioceses and through the Monasteries; and centrally, through the Holy Session. The Holy Session also controls the Synodical Committee for Social Welfare and Charity, which has only consultative status on analyzing actual social problems and proposing measures: despite its central position, it is not active in coordinating and monitoring the rest. In fact, there is no central authority, and every level has its own administrative and financial independence.[35] In general, local dioceses ("Metropolises") provide for regional charity funds and welfare institutions, while local parishes, based in large churches, provide for local charity funds and distribution of free meals. The church's charity mission has always been very significant both at national[36] and local levels.[37]

In contrast to the social protection provided by the state, which is largely compensatory—that is, not complimentary—all church welfare provisions are non-contributory and are offered for free. In many cases, beneficiaries are not only Orthodox Greeks, but also people of different ethnic origins or religions. The social welfare contribution of the church is far from trivial. The church spent more than 120 million Euros on charities in 2015, directly serving about 1.2 million people, which amounts to an impressive 10 percent of the total population. The lion's share of this amount (about 30 million Euros) was directed to the 327 soup kitchens throughout Greece, which were visited by more than half-a-million people affected by the crisis. Another 25 million Euros were allocated to the 73 ecclesiastical homes for the elderly, and about the same amount was distributed as social assistance benefits through the 80 central and 1946 parochial charity funds to quarter of a million people.[38] The church also provides for a large variety of other initiatives and institutions.[39] More than 40 percent of the Greeks see the role of the church in the financial crisis as positive, with another 25 percent having no clear opinion.[40]

Nevertheless, the church by no means wishes to suggest that it can shape economic and social policies better than the Greek state or the European Union. On the contrary, it keeps a very low profile, respecting the basic teachings of Orthodox faith that charity should remain secret.[41] There is harmonious and well-coordinated cooperation with the government and its respective ministries at all levels. The church doesn't seek to replace the state, but rather to complement it. Church parishes constitute the oldest, largest, and most active social welfare volunteer network, which extends all over Greece, even to the most isolated villages or islands.

Financial Crisis: Contemporary and Future Challenges

The situation in Greece has gone from bad to worse ever since 2009, when the financial crisis hit the Western world. Greece is the country with the lowest life satisfaction rating out of all OECD nations. Since 2007, life satisfaction in Greece has plunged 27.3 percentage points. The proportion of Greek people reporting that they trust the government in Greece fell from 38 percent to 13 percent between 2007 and 2012, while the proportion of people who were optimistic about the future was just 20 percent in 2011. Other countries impacted by the financial crisis, such as Ireland and Spain, have also experienced a decline in life satisfaction, though nowhere near as severe as that experienced in Greece.[42] The crisis has also exerted dangerous downward pressure on labor and social rights.[43]

More than one out of two Greeks (55.1 percent) reported in 2015 that they believe that things are only going to get worse. Furthermore, 71.5 percent think that the situation in Greece took a turn for the worse, while in terms of their personal finances and family structure, 65.6 percent of Greeks stressed that their situation has worsened. Another 57.7 percent of Greeks appear pessimistic about the country's economic future.[44] An impressive 80 percent believe that "things are going to the wrong direction"; the same proportion is disappointed with the government; and 90 percent believe that their financial situation will worsen in the future.[45] In 2006, the most common feelings to be reported were anger (34 percent) and disappointment (37.7 percent).[46]

You don't have to be a social policy expert to explain these findings. Greece experienced one of the largest falls in real wages across OECD countries, more than 5 percent per year on average since the first quarter of 2009.[47] Unemployment reached 25.2 percent in June 2016. Greece's unemployment rate continues to remain the highest within the European Union. The youth unemployment rate averaged 34.57 percent from 1998 until 2016, reaching an all-time high of 60 percent in March of 2013. In June 2016, it was 47.70 percent. Household income dropped by a third between 2007 and 2014, and private consumption has dropped around 30 percent since 2010.[48]

In 2014, more than a third of the population was at risk of poverty or social exclusion in Greece (36.0 percent). From 2008 to 2014, the highest increase of the at-risk-of-poverty or social exclusion rate among all EU members was recorded in Greece (from 28.1 percent in 2008 to 36.0 percent in 2014). The percentage of people at risk of income poverty is

22.1 percent, the number of those materially severely deprived in 2014 was 21.5 percent, and the share of those materially severely deprived was another 21.5 percent.[49] The explosive financial situation of Greece is matched with an increasingly unstable geopolitical environment in the wider region because of the internal conflict in Syria (displaced populations in neighboring Turkey and Lebanon exceed one million in each country), the newly founded Islamic State, and the political situation in Turkey.[50] Greece has been faced with a significant increase in arrivals of illegal immigrants and asylum seekers from Syria and the wider region (as well as African and Asian countries) in 2014 (about 23,000 apprehensions at the Greek Turkish borders during the first six months of 2014). In July 2015, 50,242 people arrived in Greece, as compared to 43,500 for the whole previous year. The total number of refugees and immigrants arriving in Greece exceeds than 160,000.[51]

The welfare state, which has contributed to the fiscal crisis of the state with its huge deficits in key programs such as pensions and health itself, is rapidly collapsing. Pensioners are hit hardest by the crisis. Pensions have been slashed by as much as 60 percent to an average of 830 Euros a month, while at the same time, prices have been rising. Greece's creditors are demanding the government cut pensions further, by an equivalent of 1 percent of the gross domestic output.[52] The deficit in the pension system is 9 percent of GDP, while pension funds have lost at least 25 billion Euros since 2012. Enhancing the capacity of social protection requires considerable reconfiguration and the proper funding of social safety nets, but now the crisis and the measures to counter it deprive the welfare state of resources.[53]

Out of a population of nearly 11 million, Greece has 3.6 million workers—but 2.66 million pensioners and 1.2 million are unemployed. One in three Greeks is over 60, with the rate growing proportionately through 2050.[54] Greece has one of the world's most rapidly aging populations, and by 2050, it is estimated that the number of adults over 60 will have risen to 40.8 percent of the population.[55] Under the current circumstances, the effects on pension and social security systems may be irreversible. The health system is also on the verge of collapse, and all health indices show that the health of the population is getting worse.[56]

The financial crisis has affected the church in three ways. First, it has multiplied the number of people seeking social assistance, exactly at a time when the state is incapable of facing its obligations. Second, since the clergy are civil servants, the drastic reduction of new recruitments in the public sector due to the fiscal consolidation of the Greek economy deprives the church from necessary human resources. Finally, the growing impoverishment of large swaths of the population has resulted in a dramatic reduction in the faithful's contributions, on which the church primarily relies for its social and philanthropic work. Driven by the cruelty of the crisis, the church has gone far beyond the rigid notions that it should focus on its spiritual mission and not deal with worldly problems or get involved in political and economic issues; now it plays an important role in stemming the effects of this crisis, using every means at its disposal to provide an enormous amount of charitable and social work.

On the other hand, though, the church's very spiritual mission has not been forsaken. The church tries hard to further highlight, within the public sphere, the primacy of freedom and human dignity as a universal and fundamental fact of human existence. Orthodox teaching places at its center the human being made in the image of God rather than the *homo economicus* who is ruled by finances and consumerism. In every activity organized by the church, such as Sunday services, spiritual speeches, and other cultural events, great efforts for a spiritual restoration of the human person are made; people are called to denounce the domination of the markets, to examine their own mistakes and omissions, to become united for the sake of social cohesion, and to become creative, proposing and taking realistic steps for exiting the crisis.[57]

The future role of the church as a significant provider of social assistance in broader welfare reform isn't clear, as it depends on the direction of the evolution of the state–church and church–society relationships, based on the prospects for the invigoration of the civil society; on the future form of competition among multiple new and old social and religious factors; and on the extent to which forthcoming substantial organizational and contextual changes could facilitate autonomous activity.[58] At the same time, to the extent that reception and acceptance of others, especially the poor and foreigners, is a fundamental element of the Orthodox tradition and identity, the rise across Europe of neo-Nazism and Fascism will also constitute a great challenge for the church in the near future.

THE HOLY BLOWS: FIGHTING FOR THE STATUS QUO IN A *NOVUS ORDO MUNDI*

The institutionalization of Greek Orthodoxy as the official state religion as well as its historical role as described above gives the church a powerful voice in policy making and the organization of society. More often than not, this voice leads to tensions with the government, as the church has a vested interest in preventing social reforms that would weaken the established social order. Controversial points include fundamental issues, such as the church–state separation, the management of the large church property, and the erasing of one's religious orientation on identity cards, as well as other issues such as civil marriage ceremonies, religious teaching at school, praying before school class, the incineration of the dead, abortions, and same-sex marriages.

The socialist government that came into power in 1981 promised to promote the separation of church and state. In subsequent years, the church, supported by the conservative opposition, objected strongly to the separation and forced capitulation or compromise on most issues. Recently history repeated itself, as the new left-wing government announced when it took power in 2015 its intention to separate church and state, though not hastily or confrontationally. Apart from minor issues like putting a stop to the prayers and confessional instruction that are part of program for almost all pupils at state schools,[59] it seems that neither the government itself nor other advocators who strongly support the separation have an agenda on the actual format of the alleged separation. The varying degrees of separation are dependent upon the applicable legal structures and prevalent views toward the desired relationship between religion and politics,[60] and there are many different points of view.[61]

A full separation would probably imply depriving the church of its constitutionally guaranteed role as the "prevailing religion," stripping priests and other church personnel from their status as public servants, and putting them out of the state payroll (78 percent of the Greeks would prefer the church to pay the salaries of the priests[62]), redefining the status of the vast church property, and ending all tax exemptions for church institutions. Taxation of the church and its assets can yield significant amounts that are necessary for the public budget. Nonetheless, current tax exemption of the church is not so high as many believe: yearly tax payments of the church exceed 12 million Euros.[63] A head-on confrontation with the church is not possible, as it would take an enormous amount of political energy and time. Changing even one word of the Constitution is a burdensome procedure and can't be done in the lifetime of a single parliament. The church has no special relation with any political party,[64] but it can block talks before they even start. At least half the Greeks (75 percent in one survey[65] and 53 percent in another[66]) are in favor of separation, while 82 percent believe that after separation, the church could not financially survive.[67]

The ownership of church property[68] has always been a controversial issue. Although the church handed over a considerable part of its property, including land, to the state, which in turn took on the responsibility of paying salaries to priests from the budget, the Orthodox Church is still the largest single landowner in Greece, and the church has the institutional duty to manage its property in the most efficient way.[69] When the socialist government proposed transferring arid farmland owned by the church to petty farmers for cultivation, the church, supported by large numbers of citizens, saw it as an attack on church prerogatives, and so a bill that was passed was never enforced.

In 1992 the European Parliament issued a strong recommendation urging the Greek government to modify its entire legal framework regarding potential religious discrimination. A year later, the socialist government attempted to abolish religion from identity cards, causing huge frustration in the church. The Archbishop of Athens and Greece, Christodoulos, was furious about this proposal, and tensions exploded in society, resulting in massive protests. A rally in Athens gathered together more than 500,000 demonstrators organized in favor of the church's position. Driven by this success, the church started a petition demanding a national referendum to assess public opinion on the new ID cards, and very soon more than 3 million people had signed it. The government rejected the demand, arguing that a referendum is not a legal way to decide when basic human rights are at stake. By this time, 46 percent of Greeks favored the inclusion of information about religion on the IDs (14 percent were undecided).[70] The church gave up the battle over the identity cards, when it was ensured of the probable constitutional status quo and the European Union's benevolent collaboration; a rapid integration of the church in the Europeanization process began right afterward, combined with an important financial subvention of European funds.

Regarding social policy, church's dependence on the state implies significant institutional limitations with respect to its capacity to express an active stance and organize collective action in social welfare matters, a condition that hardly encourages activism around issues of social justice and social welfare on behalf of the church.[71] Thus, the church sooner or later had to acquiesce to state liberalized laws. Until 1983 the church had recognized only religious marriages; when the government issued a new family law promoting the legalization of civil marriage ceremonies, it did not succeed in rendering religious marriage merely an optional ceremony, and so both forms remain yet legal.

Until 2016 cremation of the dead was not allowed in Greece because of church opposition. Today it is forbidden only for church members. Abortion is another case in point. The church did protest the legalization of abortion in 1986, but its reaction was distinctly subdued in comparison to other major confrontations.[72] Regarding emerging social policy issues, delays and restrictions caused by the church were neither systematic nor extensive. In general, despite its adherence to tradition, the church has proven relative flexible in adapting its services to the rapidly changing social environment.

THE FUTURE OF CHURCH–STATE RELATIONS IN GREECE: STRATEGIC MANEUVERS ON QUICKSAND

Historically a central pole of national identity, religion has always played an important role in Greek political, cultural, and social life. Today the status of the Orthodox Church is largely based on the role the church played in the preservation of the Greek nation throughout the years of the Ottoman Empire but also on the role it played in the Greek War of Independence. The Constitution adopted after the restoration of democracy states that "the Eastern Orthodox Church of Christ" is the "prevailing religion in the country," a status that guarantees the church the monopoly on cooperation with the state and provides it with a standard clientele. Officially, the Orthodox Church and the state are separate, but this separation is not written or regulated in the Constitution; the state has a commitment to cultivate the "national and religious conscience" of the Greek people through its educational task. The government financially supports the church; for example, it pays the salaries and for religious training of clergy, and it finances the maintenance of church buildings.

Along with the fact that church members comprise the vast majority of Greeks, the institutionalization of Greek Orthodoxy as the official state religion gives the church a powerful voice in policy making and the organization of society, and it exerts significant political and economic influence. On the other hand, there are tiny but clear signs that since the last decade the influence of the church on the society has started to deteriorate: a proportion of ex-members is turning its back on the church, while the church itself is mutating to a rather bureaucratic than spiritual institution.

The charity mission of the church is, and has always been, very significant; the church cooperates at many levels with the state on fighting poverty, supporting seniors and disabled citizens, and boosting the social integration of immigrants. This mission is today more important than ever, as the financial crisis affecting Greece is also a humanitarian one, with serious consequences for people's lives and for the social cohesion. The pressure that would be brought onto the welfare state if these services were stopped would be vast; apparently, no other mechanism could totally replace it for many years to come.

Historically, there have always been tensions in the church–state relationships. When it comes to minor issues, such as civil marriage, abortions, and cremation of the dead, the reaction of the church has been moderate, and adaptations to the new standards of society have occurred in time and without serious conflict; the dependence of the church on the state may have played a significant role in its compromise. Nevertheless, when it comes to major issues, such as the separation by the state or the management of its property, that threaten the very hardcore of its prominent position in society, the church mobilizes all its powers to defend its positions. The pressure for the ultimate arrangement of these issues grows stronger, and sooner or later the windbag of Aeolos will open. The church bides its time and keeps a low profile; it meticulously assesses its friends and enemies within the political system and society and carefully prepares its future movements.

NOTES

1. Yannis Stavrakakis, "Politics and Religion: On the 'Politicization' of Greek Church Discourse," *Journal of Modern Greek Studies* 21 (2003): 18–45.
2. Mark 12:13–17: "[some of the Pharisees and Herodians] came to him [Jesus] and said, 'Teacher, we know that you are a man of integrity. You aren't swayed by others, because you pay no attention to who they are; [...] Is it right to pay the imperial tax to Caesar or not? [...].' 'Why are you trying to trap me?' asked [Jesus]. 'Bring me a denarius and let me look at

it.' They brought the coin, and he asked them, 'Whose image is this? And whose inscription?' 'Caesar's,' they replied. Then Jesus said to them, 'Give back to Caesar what is Caesar's and to God what is God's.' And they were amazed at him."
3. Or second ecumenical council. The council was very important from both a theological and geopolitical point of view, as it was an effort to attain consensus in various vital issues through representing the whole of Christendom.
4. The heads also symbolize the dual sovereignty of the Byzantine Emperor, with the left head representing Rome (the West), and the right head representing Constantinople (the East).
5. This school of thought is mainly based on the widely read pamphlet "Hellenic Nomarchy," published in Italy short before the outbreak of the Greek War of Independence (1821). It was written by "Anonymous the Greek" and advocated the ideals of freedom, social justice, and equality as the main principles of a well-governed society.
6. Elizabeth Prodromou, "Towards an Understanding of Eastern Orthodoxy and Democracy Building in the Post-Cold War Balkans," *Mediterranean Quarterly* 5, no. 2 (1994): 115–38; Mathew Blinkhorn and Thanos Veremis, *Modern Greece, Nationalism and Nationality* (Athens: ELIAMEP, 1990); Georgios Georgiades, "The Greek Church of Constantinople and the Ottoman Empire," *The Journal of Modern History* 24, no. 3 (1952): 235–50.
7. George Metallinos, *Ottoman Occupation Period* (Athens: Akritas, 1998).
8. "Epidaurus Law" of 1822.
9. Agathanggelos Charmantidis, *Memories and Testimonies from the '40 and the Occupation Period. The Contribution of the Church of Greece* (Athens: EMYEE Publication Branch, 2001).
10. Archbishop Hieronymous, *Church Property and the Payroll of the Clergy* (Athens: Friends of the Centre of Church Charity of Oinophyta Viotoias, 2012).
11. Yet there are also provisions for those who are non-religious.
12. A former obligation that is made optional by the current government.
13. Its canonical territory is confined to the borders of the land prior to World War I, while the rest of Greece is subject to the jurisdiction of the Ecumenical Patriarchate of Constantinople. For practical reasons though most of the dioceses are de facto administered as part of the Church of Greece.
14. The Orthodox Church of Greece (divided into 78 dioceses, named "Metropolises"), the semi-autonomous Orthodox Church of Crete (8 dioceses), the dioceses of the Dodecanese Islands (4 dioceses), which directly depend upon the Patriarchate of Constantinople and the autonomous,

self-governing monastic community of "Agion Oros" (Mt. Athos, the Holly Mountain), which has constitutionally guaranteed autonomy.
15. Pew Research Center, "Religious Belief and National Belonging in Central and Eastern Europe," May 10, 2017, http://www.pewforum.org/2017/05/10/religious-affiliation/, Table 1.
16. According to the 1951 census, 7,472,559 people or 97.9 percent are Orthodox.
17. In a recent survey (Kappa research, "Poll on Religious Matters," published in the newspaper *To Vima*, April 12, 2015), only 81.4 percent of the Greeks state that they are Orthodox (95 percent in an identical survey 15 years ago), and 14.7 percent state that they are non-religious (2 percent 15 years ago). On the other hand, Pew Research Center ("Religious Belief and National Belonging in Central and Eastern Europe," May 10, 2017, http://www.pewforum.org/2017/05/10/religious-belief-and-national-belonging-in-central-and-eastern-europe/) still identifies only 2 percent non-religious Greeks.
18. Pomacs; their estimated population is 50,000. The majority are Muslims, but some of them are Greek Orthodox. Carl Skutsch, *Encyclopedia of the World's Minorities* (London: Routledge, 2005).
19. Foreign Ministry, *Muslim Minority of Thrace, Greek Commission for the Management of Water Resources: Data from the Current Census* (Athens: Foreign Ministry Information Department, 1991); U.S. Department of State, *International Religious Freedom Report 2006: Greece* (Bureau of Democracy, Human Rights, and Labor, 2006).
20. Pew Research Center, "The Future of World Religions: Population Growth Projections, 2010–2050. Why Muslims Are Rising Fastest and the Unaffiliated Are Shrinking as a Share of the World's Population," April 2, 2015, http://www.pewforum.org/2015/04/02/religious-projections-2010-2050/.
21. Kostas Onisenko, "O fákelos "Tzamí stin Athína,"" *Kathimerini*, published November 16, 2014, http://www.kathimerini.gr/792201/article/epikairothta/ellada/o-fakelos-tzami-sthn-a8hna.
22. Pew Research Center, The Future of World Religions.
23. Central Board of Jewish Communities in Greece, "Pre-War Communities," July 1, 2009, https://kis.gr/en/index.php?option=com_content&view=section&layout=blog&id=16&Itemid=.
24. Greek Helsinki Monitor Minority Rights Group—Greece, *Human Rights in Greece and Beyond*, 2002, http://www.greekhelsinki.gr/bhr/english/organizations/ghm_mrgg_religious_freedom_2002.rtf.
25. Evi Saltou, "Páno apó 40.000 Arménioi zoun stin Elláda," *Ta Nea*, April 9, 2015, http://www.tanea.gr/news/greece/article/5229605/genoktonia-armeniwn/.

26. Operation World, Country Lists, "—Greece," 2018, http://www.operationworld.org/gree.
27. Jehovah's Witnesses Organization, *2015 Yearbook of Jehovah's Witnesses*, 2015, https://www.jw.org/en/publications/books/2015-yearbook/.
28. Matthew Brunwasser, Letter from Greece: The Gods Return to Olympus. *Archeology* 58, no. 1 (January/February 2005), http://www.archaeology.org/0501/abstracts/letter.html.
29. U.S. Department of State, "Greece: International Religious Freedom Report 2006, Bureau of Democracy, Human Rights, and Labor, 2006, https://www.state.gov/j/drl/rls/irf/2006/71383.htm; Ioannis Ktistakis and Nikolaos Sitaropoulos, "*Discrimination on the Grounds of Religion and Belief: Greece*," June 22, 2004, http://edz.bib.uni-mannheim.de/daten/edz-ath/gdem/04/religion_el.pdf.
30. *Public Issue*, "Annual Research on Institutional Confidence," November 30, 2015, http://www.publicissue.gr/tag/greek-index-of-confidence-in-institutions/.
31. Dimitris Raptis and Matthew Schmidt, *Nationwide Poll on the Separation of State and Church in Greece*, 2015, posted at https://www.facebook.com/bridgingeurope.
32. Kappa Research, "Poll on Religious Matters," published in the *To Vima*, April 12, 2015.
33. George Papathanasopoulos, "Analysis of the Kappa Research Poll on Religious Matters," *To Vima*, April 12, 2015.
34. Law 590/1977 Constitutional Charter of the Church of Greece.
35. George Diellas, *The Contribution of the Church of Greece in the Formation of the "Welfare State" and Its Participation in the Social Care System* (Athens: Synodical Committee for Social Welfare and Well-Being, 2011–2015).
36. Demitrios Constantelos, *Poverty, Society and Philanthropy in the Later Mediaeval Greek World* (New Rochelle, NY: Aristide D. Caratzas, 1992); Leonidas Patras, *Social Policy* (Athens: Sakkoulas Bros, 1974); Sophia Mourouka, *The Social Work of the Church and the Role of Saint Filothei* (Athens: Church of Pure Christians of Greece, 1997); John Petrou, *Church and Politics in Greece* (Athens: Sakkoulas Bros, 1992); John Petrou, *Christianity and Society* (Thessaloniki: Vanias, 2004).
37. Joseph Tagarakis, *The Charity Work of the Greek Orthodox Community of Thessaloniki 1840–1928* (Thessaloniki: History Centre of the Municipality of Thessaloniki, 1994).
38. The Holy Synod of the Church of Greece, "Philanthropic Work of the Church of Greece Today," *Towards the People* 48, no. 6 (2016), 67–78.
39. Including 14 orphanages, 21 boarding schools (providing shelter and meals to poor students of the public universities), 16 nursery homes for the

chronically ill or people with disabilities, 9 centers for mental health, 6 projects for the "help at home" for needy people, 21 clinics, 23 protection shelters, 20 kindergartens, 11 preschools, 23 schools, 207 vocational schools, 78 supporting schools, 4 student dormitories, 266 scholarships, 203 cultural centers, 142 "social groceries" (where people can source food and other items for free), 69 places for free of charge distribution of clothes, 3 doctor's offices and 3 drugstores, 10 blood banks, and 266 scholarships.
40. Raptis and Schmidt, *Nationwide Poll.*
41. Maria Petmesidou and Periklis Polyzoidis, "Religion, Values and the Welfare State in Greece," in *Religion, Values and the Welfare State*, ed. H.-R. Reuter and K. Gabriel, 177–314 (Stuttgart: Mohr Siebeck, 2013).
42. Organisation for Economic Co-operation and Development (OECD), "Measuring National Well-Being: International Comparisons; Office for National Statistics," July 1, 2015, https://www.ons.gov.uk/peoplepopulationandcommunity/wellbeing/articles/measuringnationalwellbeing/2015-07-01.
43. Maria Petmesidou and Ana Guillén, "Economic Crisis and Austerity in Southern Europe: Threat or Opportunity for a Sustainable Welfare State?" (European Social Observatory, Research Paper No. 18, 2015), http://www.ose.be/files/publication/OSEPaperSeries/Petmesidou_Guillen_2015_OseResearchPaper18.pdf.
44. Kappa Research, "Poll on Religious Matters."
45. University of Macedonia, *Survey 1–2 September 2016* (Thessaloniki: Unit for the Research of Public Opinion, 2016).
46. Thegreekzcom.com, *Poll: Disappointment and anger against the government*, 2006, www.thegreekz.com/forum/showthread.php?736854.
47. OECD, "Measuring National Well-Being."
48. European Union, *In-Depth Analysis. Greece's Financial Assistance Program* (Brussels: Directorate General for Internal Policies, Economic Governance Support Unit, 2016), http://www.europarl.europa.eu/cms-data/120262/Study%20-%20Greece-Regional%20policy%20and%20economic%20and%20social%20situation.pdf.
49. Eurostat, "17 October: International Day for the Eradication of Poverty" (Brussels: Eurostat News Release 181, 2015).
50. Anna Triandafyllidou, *Migration in Greece: Recent Developments* (Athens: Hellenic Foundation for European and Foreign Policy, 2015).
51. United Nations High Commissioner for Refugees (UNCHR), "Number of Refugee Arrivals in Greece," 2015, http://www.unhcr.org/news/latest/2015/8/55d32dcf6/numbers-refugee-arrivals-greece-increase-dramatically.html.
52. EU, *In-Depth Analysis.*

53. Manos Matsaganis, "The Welfare State and the Crisis: The Case of Greece," *Journal of European Social Policy* 21, no. 5 (2011): 501–12.
54. Byron Kotzamanis, *Greek population projected in 2050* (Volos: Laboratory of Demographic and Social Analysis, 2016).
55. HelpAge International, *Ageing in the Twenty-First Century: A Celebration and a Challenge* (New York, 2015), http://www.helpage.org/silo/files/ageing-in-the-21st-century-contents-and-intro.pdf.
56. Maria Petmesidou, Stephanos Papanastasiou, Maria Pempetzoglou, Christos Papatheodorou, and Periklis Polyzoidis, *Health and Long-Term Care in Greece* (Athens: Observation for Economic and Social Evolution INE GSEE, 2015); Charalambos Economou, Daphni Kaitelidou, Alexander Kentikelenis, Aris Sissouras, and Anna Maresso, *The Impact of the financial crisis on the Health System and Health in Greece* (Brussels: WHO, European Observatory on Health Systems and Policies).
57. Ignatius of Demetrias, "The Orthodox Church of Greece and the Economic Crisis," Public lecture organized by the Hellenic Observatory of the London School of Economics, November 12, 2014.
58. Petmesidou and Polyzoidis, "Religion, Values and the Welfare State."
59. Under the changes implemented, the lessons on religion in Greek elementary, junior high, and high schools will not be Orthodoxy-centered, as they will present all religions in the world; the church called changes "unacceptable and dangerous," and Archbishop Ieronymos said that they "will not bear fruits, they will damage our culture and society and will cause a rift between Church and State." Philip Chrysopoulos, "New Clash Between Church and Education Minister in Greece, *Greek Reporter.com*, September 21, 2016, http://greece.greekreporter.com/2016/09/21/new-clash-between-church-and-education-minister-in-greece/. At the same time, 49 percent of the Greeks believe the religion class should be optional. See Raptis and Schmidt, *Nationwide Poll*.
60. Evagelos Venizelos, *Towards a Meta-Representative Democracy* (Athens: Polis, 2008).
61. Nikiforos Diamanturos, *Politics and Culture in Greece, 1974–1991: An Interpretation* (Basingstoke, UK: Macmillan, 1993); Anastassios Anastassiadis, "Religion and Politics in Greece: "Conservative Modernization" in the 1990s" *Questions de Recherché*, 11 (2004): 2–35.
62. Kappa Research, "Poll on Religious Matters."
63. The Holy Synod of the Church of Greece, Special statement on February 22, 2012.
64. Venizelos, *Towards a Meta-Representative Democracy*.
65. Raptis and Schmidt, *Nationwide Poll*.
66. Kappa Research, "Poll on Religious Matters."
67. Kappa Research, "Poll on Religious Matters."

68. "Church property" consists of the property of all ecclesiastical legal entities of public law.
69. John Konidaris, *Law 1700/1987 and the Recent Crisis in Church–State Relations* (Athens: Ant. Sakkoula, 1991); John Konidaris, *Fundamental Regulations of the State–Church Relationship* (Athens: Ant. Sakkoula, 1999).
70. B.A. Robinson, "Greek Orthodox Church and Identity Cards," *Religious Tolerance.org*, August 30, 2001, http://www.religioustolerance.org/chr_orthi.htm.
71. Petmesidou and Polyzoidis, "Religion, Values and the Welfare State in Greece."
72. George Mavrogordatos, "Church–state Relations in the Greek Orthodox Case" (paper presented to the Workshop "Church and State in Europe," ECPR Joint Sessions, Copenhagen, April 14–19, 2000).

PART II

Countries with Competing Religious Societies and with a Formerly Dominant Church

CHAPTER 7

Combining Secular Public Space and Growing Diversity? Interactions Between Religious Organizations as Welfare Providers and the Public in Sweden

Annette Leis-Peters

The Nordic countries, Sweden in particular, have for a long time been perceived as clear-cut examples for the social–democratic welfare regime.[1] During the last decade, the strong Lutheran tradition has gained more attention in research as one of the roots for this welfare system. The universal and comprehensive welfare state model presupposes both strong and stable bonds between church and state and a state-friendly theology like the Lutheran doctrine of the Two Kingdoms.[2] At the same time, international value studies like the World Value Survey point to the Nordic countries as the region that is in the forefront of individualization, secularization, and post-materialism.[3] How do these two different pictures fit together? What do they mean for the religious organizations acting in this welfare context?

A. Leis-Peters (✉)
VID Specialized University, Oslo, Norway

This chapter examines the role, effects, perceptions, and strategies of religious actors in Swedish society by analyzing the results of several quantitative and qualitative studies in the field of religion and welfare. It consists of four parts and a conclusion: the first part sketches the current religious landscape and highlights important changes in the relationship between religion/church and state; the second tries to evaluate the effect of the work of religious actors based on quantitative studies in the field; the third explores expectations in the population with regard to religious actors in welfare provision; and the fourth part analyzes two qualitative studies about the role of religion in welfare to learn more about objectives and strategies of religious actors. The conclusion discusses how this research in the field of welfare can contribute to a better understanding of the role of religious actors in the public sphere.

Sweden: A Complex Nordic Case?

Sweden has developed from a religiously almost homogeneous country to a society with a great variety of faiths and beliefs within the last few decades. One of the obvious reasons for this is the growing immigration to Sweden since the 1960s that includes both waves of migrant laborers from Europe and waves of refugees from all over the world. While only 4 percent of all people registered in Sweden were foreign born in 1960, this number has increased to 17.9 percent in 2016.[4] Most foreign-born citizens are not Lutheran, but belong to other Christian denominations or religions outside Christianity and thereby contribute to growing religious diversity. Therefore, it is not surprising that the proportion of Church of Sweden members has decreased while Swedish society has become more diverse. As late as 1972, 95 percent of all people living in Sweden were members of the Church of Sweden. By 2016, this proportion had dropped to 61.2 percent. The loss of members has accelerated since the year 2000 due to both immigration and defections from the Church of Sweden.[5] (See Figs. 7.1 and 7.2.)

Swedish statistics do not register religious affiliation. The numbers for Figs. 7.1 and 7.2 are calculated by the author based on population development statistics provided by Statistics Sweden,[6] the membership development statistics of the Church of Sweden,[7] and the yearly statistics of the Swedish Agency for Support to Faith Communities (SST) about

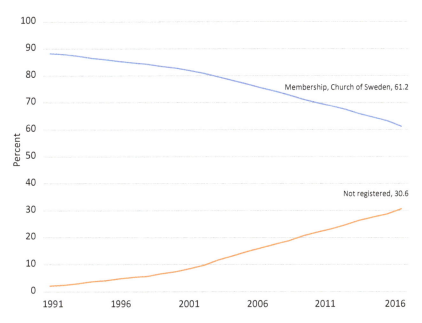

Fig. 7.1 Membership, Church of Sweden, 1991–2016

how many persons the different faith communities serve. With the exception of the membership numbers for the Church of Sweden, all numbers included in the calculation are estimates. The faith communities themselves estimate how many persons they serve. In the years 1991–1992, the SST complemented estimates of the faith communities with its own estimates. Until the year 2000, it was also possible to be both a member of the Church of Sweden and other faith communities. Therefore, the numbers up until 2000 (and also some years after the disestablishment of the Church of Sweden) are misleading. They most likely include several double memberships. Nevertheless, there is no way to calculate the number of people who are not registered in any faith community other than adding the numbers of the Church of Sweden membership to membership numbers of the other faith communities and subtracting them from the number of the total population of Sweden.

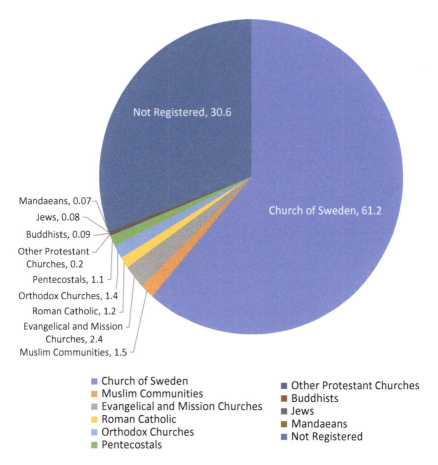

Fig. 7.2 Membership, Church of Sweden, 2016

From State Church to Semi-official Church

While the statistics register rapid change, a historical perspective points to lengthier processes that underlie these changes. From the Protestant Reformation in the sixteenth century until the middle of the nineteenth century, the church was closely intertwined with the state, both on the national and local levels. The Reformation resulted in the establishment of an Evangelical-Lutheran state church in 1593, which tied king, people, and church to one another. Every Swedish citizen automatically became a member of the Church of Sweden. It took until the mid-eighteenth century to officially approve a small number of faith communities outside the Church of Sweden. These included the Reformed Church and the Anglican Church and later the Roman Catholic Church and the Jewish community. The dominance of the state church is illustrated by the conditions under which the awakening movement took place in the late eighteenth century and during the nineteenth century. In this period, any religious meeting that the Church of Sweden did not control was still forbidden.[8]

A first step toward the separation of church and state was taken in 1862 when municipal laws for the first time distinguished between civil and church municipalities. These two units had been interwoven almost indistinctly before.[9] At the same time, it also became easier for churches outside the Church of Sweden to become officially approved. Still, it was not until 1951 that full religious freedom was guaranteed in Sweden. It then became possible to leave the Church of Sweden without joining one of the officially approved religious communities. However, only in the year 2000, when the Church of Sweden became a free folk, did its status as a state church end.

This historical background is important for understanding why on the one hand it was not easy to draw a line between church and state and why on the other it became important to strive for more equality for the other faith communities in the country. "Ambiguity between disestablishment and religious control" is the subtitle of an article by Swedish sociologist of religion Per Pettersson about the relationship between state and religion.[10] His research is part of the Nordic research project "The Role of Religion in the Public Sphere. A Comparative Study of The Five Nordic Countries (NOREL)" that was conducted between 2009 and 2014. NOREL investigated how the interplay between religion and society changed from the 1980s to 2014 in the fields of religion and politics, religion and media, religion and state, and religion and civil society during this period.[11] Furseth and colleagues concluded that they needed the concept of complexity to understand the religious changes in the five Nordic countries: Denmark, Finland, Iceland, Norway, and Sweden. While many developments in the Nordic countries can easily be explained by institutional differentiation, one of the key elements of secularization theory, the links of the Nordic states with the majority churches and more recently also with the other faith communities, weakens this argument.[12]

Pettersson's article illustrates this Nordic complexity in religion. He shows that the change of status of the Church of Sweden from state church to free folk church was an important divide in church–state relationships in Sweden, but at the same time not as complete as it seems. For Pettersson, the term "semi-official" church is the appropriate description of the actual status since the state still delegates official tasks to the Church of Sweden. Most important among these is the administration and maintenance of almost all burial grounds in Sweden (including special sections for people of other religions) and the preservation of the cultural heritage of the country that consists not least of many church buildings. The law also demands that the king be a member of the Church of Sweden. The preparatory government bills for the Church of Sweden Act of the year 2000 aiming to regulate the transition of the Church of Sweden from state church to folk church also indicate the Swedish state's desire to maintain a certain control over the church. It prescribes that the Church of Sweden should be Evangelical-Lutheran, democratic, and an important part of welfare society. Last but not least, this law enables Swedish tax authorities to collect church taxes for the Church of Sweden from its members without charging it for this service.[13] The semi-official status is mirrored in the public theology of the Church of Sweden. The church considers itself not an interest group, but a folk church responsible for all people in Sweden.[14]

Promoting and Controlling Religious Diversity

But what does this mean for the political goal of disestablishing the Church of Sweden and the reforms that have been discussed and conducted as a part of this aim since the 1960s, namely equal treatment of all faith communities and a "religiously neutral and secular state"?[15] It is an interesting illustration of the Swedish history of state–religion relationships that the state established a new authority to equate the other faith communities with the Church of Sweden. The Swedish Agency for Support to Faith Communities (SST) was founded in 1971 as a consequence of the proposal for state financing for independent faith communities (i.e., outside the Church of Sweden). This proposal was based on the state–church report of 1968 that was commissioned by the minister of church affairs. It formulated that it was necessary that the state gives financial support to all faith communities, and not only to those few that were already officially established. The proposition clearly aimed to give equal opportunities to all faith community and suggested an active policy to achieve this. It is noteworthy that the proposal drew a very positive picture of the role of faith communities in society. They were considered to be important because they answer to religious and cultural needs of the Swedish population and represent different values, beliefs, and worldviews that are crucial for a lively democracy.[16] However, funding them also means controlling them, since the faith communities must comply with certain conditions, such as having a minimum size or having democratic structures.[17]

In 2016, SST paid altogether almost 89 million Swedish Crowns to the faith communities, funding general organizational costs, projects, activities for refugees, theological education, and pastoral care in the health care system.[18] In the context of state–religion relationships, it is also interesting that the SST has recently redefined its own role as public authority for faith communities. It has redesigned its website, developing it from an administrative site for those who want to apply for public support for their faith community to an information portal about religion in Sweden. It has published several books about different religions in Sweden, and the director says clearly on his blog that he wants religion to become more visible in Swedish society.[19] Like the new relationship between church and state that makes the Church of Sweden a semi-official church, the active policy of the public authority SST can be interpreted as promotion of religious diversity and support for faith communities and at the same time as public control of the religious sector.

Religious Diversity in Semi-secular Sweden

The short survey about state–religion relationships may give the impression that religious actors in Sweden experience some control but mainly positive support from the public. In other words, Swedish society could be expected to give them the preconditions to engage and flourish in all parts of society, including the field of welfare. However, the situation is more complicated. As mentioned in the introduction, Sweden is one of the most secularized, individualized, and post-materialist countries in the world.[20] Moreover, the political aim to re-organize the relationships between state and faith communities focused not only on achieving equal treatment of all communities, but also on creating a religiously neutral and secular state. Value studies find that a majority of Swedes already have secular beliefs and practices. According to the European Values Survey 2008–2010, for example, fewer than 37 percent of all Swedes believe in God and 66 percent go to religious services (except baptisms, weddings, and funerals) less than once a year.[21] Qualitative studies that try to understand the beliefs of the majority of Swedes who seem to be rather indifferent to both religious doctrines and practices indicate that many Swedes expect the public sphere to be secular. But they highlight also that it would be wrong to define as non-religious all those who cannot be characterized as religious. Swedish religious studies' scholar Ann af Burén uses the term "semi-secular" to describe this group, which demonstrates little interest in religion or in combining different religious doctrines and practices, yet is not hostile toward religions either. Af Burén's research is important for understanding the expectations toward the public sphere because her research indicates that it is common among the semi-secular Swedes to think that their way of perceiving and handling religion is "normal."[22]

For religious actors, this means that they must act in a public sphere where the majority is not very interested in religious expressions and practices. The majority of the Swedish population, like other Nordic citizens, instead understands religion as part of the private sphere, a distinction that often automatically and unconsciously implies that the public sphere should be secular and free from religious expressions.[23] How do religious actors that depend on public funding act in a public sphere that is expected to be secular?

Welfare as a Public Arena for Religious Actors?

In Nordic countries, welfare is an interesting field to explore in these contexts. While the universal, social–democratic welfare state can be traced back to Lutheran roots, the establishment of this welfare system is also a process of institutional differentiation: namely the Church of Sweden and other religious actors are losing responsibility for the field of welfare, which has increasingly shifted to the public sphere. The grand aim of the social–democratic welfare regime is to provide general, professional, and equal welfare services for all citizens in the whole country.[24] Against this background, it is natural that the state and the municipalities become the dominant actors in welfare when the welfare state was established in the second half of the 20th century, as funders, governors, and providers. Only they can ensure that even citizens in remote places are covered by the promises and services of the universal welfare state.

A speech by the well-known Swedish social–democrat Alva Myrdal on the conference for church social work in 1971, at the peak of the Swedish welfare state, illustrates the location of religious actors in the welfare system, as assigned by welfare politicians. Myrdal emphasizes the importance of faith communities to accompany and support individuals in situations of existential crisis. About professionalized welfare services she says that the public welfare system will take over all institution-based health care and social work. Hence, she recognizes the need for religious actors in the private sphere of welfare, but claims that the state should take on public, institutionally based, and professionalized welfare tasks.[25]

During the last three decades, the perception of civil society actors, including religious actors, as welfare providers has changed fundamentally. Austerity in the welfare sector and the growing diversity that is accompanied by a greater variety of welfare needs both made Nordic welfare politicians reconsider the role of the civil society organizations.[26] In a public investigation about the future of care, one of the main questions was how civil society actors could be encouraged to participate more in the provision of professional care services.[27] Religious actors have been and can be counted among them. Against this background, it is natural to ask: How has the role of religious actors in Swedish welfare society changed, and how could it be described today? Can religious actors today be found both in the professionalized and institutionalized public sphere of welfare work and in the individualized, existential welfare in the private sphere?

VISIBLE OR INVISIBLE IN WELFARE WORK?

Traces of Professional Religious Welfare Work?

If religious actors have entered the public sphere through welfare, their activities must be detectable in some kind of documentation. The question then is this: How can the effects of the welfare activities of religious actors be measured? A quantitative approach would be to look for these activities in statistics. Sweden is known as a country with comprehensive public data collection documenting almost all aspects of Swedish society. However, there is no explicit statistical overview that gives an impression of the share of religious actors in welfare provision. To get an impression of their participation, neighboring fields must be consulted. Researchers have, for example, been interested in finding out if the growing political interest in civil society organizations as providers of welfare services has resulted in a higher share of them among the welfare providers. Their studies show that the participation of civil society, non-profit providers in welfare has not increased remarkably during the last decades, while the share of private, for-profit welfare providers has grown. This development is most striking in Sweden, where the private, for-profit sector in welfare has increased considerably.[28] Some researchers point to the European Union (EU) as a major reason for growing numbers of for-profit actors in Swedish welfare provision. Following up on the EU regulation that all public orders and services must be offered to tender, within just a few years Sweden has together with the Netherlands become one of the EU countries with the highest proportion of public procurements.[29]

Religious actors are counted as a part of the civil society organizations in general studies, but their contribution is rarely singled out. However, based on general studies, it could be concluded that religious actors have not enlarged the engagement in welfare provision like the rest of the civil society organizations. Obtaining exact numbers about the activities and effects of religious actors in welfare is also difficult because there is no Swedish umbrella organization for religious welfare providers that could provide data for this part of the civil society sector. Some religious actors are members in overarching umbrella organizations for non-profit providers such as FAMNA (http://www.famna.org/), but these organizations do not document the religious organizations specifically either. Against this background, it is not possible to obtain a quantitative picture of activities, nor, consequently, of the effects of religious actors in welfare.

Knowledge and research about religious actors in welfare is limited not simply because there is no umbrella organization that can provide data. Due to the lack of such an organization, congregation-based welfare work and independent professional religious welfare providers, like diaconal institutions or religious foundations that run hospitals, are rarely seen together. The research in this field is characterized by a lack of clarity in the use of concepts. In religious studies and sociology of religion, the term "religious organizations" is common, while researchers with a civil society interest often use the term faith-based organization (FBO) or religious non-governmental organization (RNGO). Nordic studies in the field of welfare and religion often focus on locally based organizations that can be characterized as a kind of congregation. An exception is the Norwegian sociologist Harald Askeland, who has studied professional religious welfare providers in Norway. According to him, it is important to distinguish between religious actors with the purpose to provide professional welfare and religious actors in general, for which welfare work is one among a whole variety of expressions of faith in practice. Askeland defines religious organizations with an identity and a specific aim that is self-imposed and derived from a religious tradition as "FBOs," while it is the task of "religious organizations" to gather believers in different religious practices.[30] The basic conditions in welfare work differ between these two types of religious organizations. Professional faith-based welfare providers must relate to both professional and economic logics. They act therefore in a hybrid setting, while the welfare activities of religious organizations with a general focus often concern individual, existential needs and have a supplementary character to the professional welfare services.

Askeland is one of the few Nordic researchers who points to the need to be aware of and explicit about what type of religious actor the research focuses on. Most researchers choose one type of religious actor and treat it as representative of all religious actors. Since faith-based welfare organizations offering professional services are most likely to become visible in general statistics, this section starts by examining research about them. The only recent example of quantitative research about professional FBOs in welfare in the Nordic countries is a long-term comparison of the proportion of diaconal institutions in different welfare and health services in Norway. The results show that there has been a constant decrease of involvement of diaconal institutions in almost all areas of welfare and health care since the 1980s.[31] This contradicts the political pleas for more civil society involvement that have characterized Norwegian welfare policy in the last decade. Altogether, the few available quantitative studies do not indicate a growing effect of religious actors in welfare. On the contrary, they point instead to a stagnating or even decreasing trend. However, the difficulty in capturing all types of religious actors in one study could suggest that the existing results reveal only a part of the picture.

Welfare Work as a Part of the Practice of Religious Actors

Welfare activities of religious actors are obviously hard to find in public documentation. It might be easier to trace them by starting with the religious actors themselves and looking at their activities and practices. An example of a research project that explores welfare work as part of all activities of religious organizations is the nationally representative survey of Muslim congregations in Sweden by sociologist Klas Borell and social work researcher Arne Gerdner.[32] The survey shows that Muslim congregations focus not only on religious teachings and encounters between believers but also on a variety of social activities. Most of them have various groups and programs for children and young people. Many offer services for refugees and newly arrived immigrants and run visiting services that look after the elderly and the ill. Some of them even visit prisons or offer help to substance abusers. Even though their work concentrates mainly on their own members, the congregations report that the welfare work helps them to establish a social network in society. Borell and Gerdner's representative survey draws attention to welfare activities that earlier have often been overlooked in research and public discourse. However, one could ask whether this welfare work takes place in the public sphere, or whether it belongs instead to the private sphere, since it focuses on individual, existential needs.

The last quantitative study that must be mentioned regarding the possible effect of religious actors in the public sphere is a report about the social contribution of faith communities that was commissioned by the Swedish Ministry of Health and Social Affairs in 2015. Before this report, in 2014, the Ministry published a booklet about faith communities together with the SST that had the title "a good force in society."[33] The title itself indicates a new recognition of the social role of faith communities in the Ministry. The foreword of the report[34] confirms that the Ministry acknowledges the growing role of religion in society and wants to explore the potential of faith communities to solve the social challenges that Swedish society faces currently and will face in the future.

The report presents the importance of faith communities in welfare by classifying their contribution in four categories: The first dimension includes the contexts of meaning-making and social community that faith communities create. This category comprises what the report calls core activities of the faith communities—that is, religious services, pastoral care, activities for children and youth, baptisms, weddings, funerals, and activities for elderly people in the congregation. The second dimension has the heading "the unique contribution of faith communities in public tasks" and embraces all the chaplaincies in various public institutions, such as health care institutions, prisons, the army, and the police. In addition, the role of faith communities in emergency teams is highlighted. This field is dominated by chaplains from the Church of Sweden and the traditional Free Churches. Chaplains from other Christian denominations and Islam serve only in larger numbers in prisons.[35]

The third dimension gives an overview of denominational alternatives to public services offered by faith communities. More concretely, this section focuses mainly on elementary schools, adult education centers, and higher education institutions run by faith communities. Since the free school reform in 1992, about 65 elementary schools with a religious profile have been established in Sweden. Among them, 30 have a background in Protestant churches outside the Church of Sweden, 10 in Muslim organizations, 2 in the Church of Sweden, 1 in an Orthodox Church, 4 in the Roman Catholic Church, and 2 in Jewish communities. Eighteen are run by organization with Christian values, but without any denominational bonds.[36] The second area that is mentioned is nursing homes for elderly people. In addition to three bigger diaconal institutions that run a greater variety of care services, the report mentions nine care institutions that are run by different churches, including Free Churches. Altogether, the report illustrates that there are very few denominational alternatives to public services. The last dimension is the shortest section in the report and tries to give an overview of faith communities as advocates in public debate. The researchers find that the public discourses about refugee policy and climate policy engage faith communities the most and that they contribute actively. In these areas, they are part of national campaigns that attract a lot of attention. Otherwise, it is difficult to get an overview of the contribution of faith communities to the public debates because many of the initiatives are based in local contexts.

The report draws attention to the large variety of social activities that the Church of Sweden, Free Churches, and other Christian denominations and religions work with continuously. However, many of the listed activities are part of the core work of faith communities and/or belong to the field of personal spiritual support, that is, to the private sphere. In other words, the report does not indicate a growing role for religious actors in (professional) welfare provision and in the public sphere.

In all the studies and reports presented in the section above, there is no evidence that religious actors have had a larger presence in professional welfare provision during recent decades. They are still barely visible in this type of services. This does not mean that religious actors are not important for welfare in Sweden. The studies illustrate that welfare work forms part of the core activities of most religious organizations and that many of them also develop additional initiatives in this field. Even though not many new welfare activities of religious organizations could be detected in the studies presented above, the existence of such reports indicates a change. Researchers and public officials have both become more aware of and interested in the social activities of faith communities.

Expectations from a Secular Public Sphere

The sections above show that while religious actors have not necessarily become more numerous in welfare, they have become more visible. Welfare politicians express clearly that they want more civil society organizations in welfare provision. These political calls extend to religious actors, which sometimes are even mentioned or addressed explicitly.[37] But what about the secular Swedish population? Do they really want religious actors among the welfare providers? Or do they prefer real secularism when it comes to welfare?

Again, there is not much research that specifically examines the attitudes of the Swedish population toward religious actors as welfare providers. An exception is a representative survey that was conducted on behalf of the Church of Sweden in 2012. The aim was to discover if there really is an interest in a greater role of the Church of Sweden in welfare. This main question was approached from different angles and even included a comparison with other faith communities and civil society organizations.

The survey illustrates how established the system of public provision of welfare services is in Sweden. Only 48.1 percent of the respondents felt positively about alternative welfare providers. The analysis relates this partly to a critical debate about shortcomings in private, for-profit care services at the time the survey was conducted. Nevertheless, the scores of the Church of Sweden are even lower than alternative welfare providers in general. Only 45.1 percent want the Church of Sweden as a provider of welfare services, while 43.7 percent are positive about religious providers in welfare in general.[38]

The picture becomes murkier when the survey asks about different types of welfare services and whether the Church of Sweden should be able to run them. The evaluation differs considerably between those respondents who are generally negative, those who are generally positive, and those who sympathize with the church. Still, there are some services that a majority of all respondents think that the Church of Sweden can provide: 69.1 percent of those who are negative and 86.7 percent of the sympathizers think that the Church of Sweden can run shelters for homeless people, while 57 percent of those who are critical and 80.9 of those who are supportive can imagine the church taking responsibility for day care services for homeless people.[39] The services that both the critics and the supporters are most skeptical about are elementary and upper secondary schools. Only 2.3 percent of those who are negative and only 28.3 percent of the sympathizers want the Church of

Sweden to run their own elementary schools. This is interesting because this is an area in which faith communities have had the ability to run their own institutions for more than two decades. At the same time, the opening of the school sector to private non-profit and for-profit providers is one of the reforms that has recently been discussed quite critically in Swedish public debate. This policy is blamed for the fact that Swedish pupils score worse in international comparisons than they did 20 years ago.

It is interesting that most of the respondents, no matter how they feel about the Church of Sweden, believe that the church would be suited for services for the most marginalized, like homeless people. Services for refugees might have scored higher after the start of the European refugee crisis in 2015 than they did in 2012. In that year, only 31 percent of the critics and 53.4 percent of the sympathizers could imagine the Church of Sweden as responsible for reception centers for refugees.[40]

The researchers conclude that the survey reveals a "Swedish dilemma."[41] There is a positive attitude to an active social role of the Church of Sweden. But at the same time, many of the respondents do not want the religious values of the church expressed in the welfare work that it does. It is religion as faith—that is, as a system of doctrines and religiously motivated beliefs and practices—that is experienced as problematic in the public sphere, whereas religion as a social system is welcomed.[42] This applies even more to faith communities outside the Church of Sweden. The studies presented in earlier sections show that religious actors have become more visible in the public sphere. The survey on expectations toward the Church of Sweden in the field of welfare clouds the picture. Greater visibility of religious actors does not necessarily mean that a majority of the Swedish population wants to have religious actors as part of professional welfare provision and the public sphere.

LOCAL COMMUNITIES AS AN ARENA FOR PARTICIPATION OF RELIGIOUS ACTORS

Questions about the objectives, strategies, and methods of religious actors in the public sphere can only be touched on briefly in this chapter. There are no Swedish studies that explicitly study this topic, but there are several projects, large and small, that can contribute pieces of the puzzle. Most of these projects are local case-studies that provide important insights, but only a bit of general information.

While the role of religious organizations in welfare has not attracted very much attention in quantitative research, it has become a popular theme in qualitative research in Sweden. Many projects analyze the contribution of religious organizations to different areas of welfare in selected local communities. Examples include three European projects in the field of welfare and religion in which Swedish researchers were involved or were coordinators: the project Welfare and Religion in a European Perspective (WREP), which was funded by The Swedish Foundation for Humanities and Social Sciences[43]; the project Welfare and Values in Europe—Transitions related to Religion, Minorities or Gender (WaVE)[44]; and the project Faith-Based Organisations and Social Exclusion in European Cities (FACIT)[45]—all financed by the European Commission. The following section focuses on research from the WREP and the FACIT projects to highlight two case-studies, one focusing on the Church of Sweden and the other on Muslim congregations.

Prepared to Cooperate

The WREP project included eight Western European countries (Sweden, Norway, Finland, Germany, France, the United Kingdom, Italy, and Greece). The project consisted of eight local case-studies, one in each country, in which the researchers explored in one selected municipality how majority church representatives, representatives of the municipality, and the local population thought about the role of the majority church in welfare.

The Swedish case-study in a middle-sized town shows that the local population, church representatives, and representatives of public authorities agree on the fundamental and overarching role of the state and the public sector in welfare.[46] All of them underline that the state should be responsible for all welfare services. Other civil society organizations, including the Church of Sweden, were welcome to complement and to assist under the governance of the public sector. The church perceived itself mainly as a "religious specialist"[47] that contributed with worship services and with social gatherings. Most of the church's social activities took place on church premises. Examples of activities included choirs, groups for children and young people, cafés, counseling groups and individual counseling, financial assistance in situations of special need, family guidance, and home visits. All these activities could be categorized as core work of the church. Most of them can be understood as answering personal and existential needs and therefore be placed in the private sphere.[48]

At the same time, church representatives in the municipality were open to cooperation with other local actors and the public authorities. This resulted in a number of publicly funded welfare services that are run by the church. Among them are preschools, a youth center, and a hostel for homeless people. Moreover, the church also participated in joint ventures with the public sector and other local actors in emergency counseling, emergency groups, and a family center.[49] Compared to the results of the quantitative overviews of welfare activities run by religious actors that only detected a few professionalized welfare services delegated by the public sector to religious actors, the Church of Sweden congregations in the town in the case-study seemed to be rather successful in contributing to local welfare provision. Their strategy was to function as religious specialists in the local community and at the same time to be open to cooperation. The mapping of church activities shows that Church of Sweden congregations were actually invited into cooperative projects and that the public authorities even delegated public tasks to them. This presupposes public authorities with a positive attitude toward the church and church representatives who take part in the local community and are prepared to take on new tasks when needed.

Preconditions for Identity Building

The second Swedish case-study discussed in this chapter is part of the European research project FACIT, which examined how FBOs deal with social tensions and social exclusion in big city regions. Other European countries involved in the project were Belgium, Germany, the Netherlands, Spain, Turkey, and the United Kingdom. The Swedish case-study was the only Nordic case-study in the project and examined the three biggest cities in Sweden: Stockholm, Gothenburg, and Malmö. The case-study included the Church of Sweden, Christian minority churches, faith communities outside Christianity, and even some professionalized faith-based welfare providers like the city missions. The collected data was based both on interviews and on ethnographic work. The study examined whether the austerity of the welfare state has resulted in more participation of religious actors in the field of welfare in Stockholm, Gothenburg, and Malmö.

The overall result is very much in line with other Swedish research in the field. The religious actors considered the public sector to be responsible for welfare. Sometimes they took on complementary welfare initiatives. However, their main welfare contributions were social community, meaningful leisure time activities, and spiritual gatherings.[50]

This section focuses in particular on the results from the analysis of the data from the Muslim congregations. Summarizing their findings, political scientists Charlotte Fridolfsson and Ingemar Elander point out that minority faith communities, such as Muslim congregations, not only focused on religious services, but also arranged for social encounters and promoted networking with the majority society.[51] This is in line with what Borell and Gerdner see in their representative study,[52] although there are differences among Muslim congregations. How well the congregations networked with other actors in the local community depended on the communication skills of individual representatives in responsible positions within the congregation.

The interviews with the representatives of the Muslim congregations drew the attention of the researchers to two further factors that affect how religious actors relate to the public sphere. First, the researchers point to the challenge faced by representatives of Muslim organizations who continuously had to relate and react to Islamophobic discourse in society. Being in the public sphere meant that they were confronted with negative stereotypes of Islam. The Muslim respondents underlined repeatedly how difficult this cultural climate made it for them to develop an identity as Swedish Muslims. In other words, public discourses about religion matter and have an impact on the social engagement of religious actors. The second factor that Fridolfsson and Elander detect is also related to the issue of identity in society. Muslims in Sweden found themselves in a society and landscape formed and dominated by Christianity and limited by a consensus to keep the public sphere secular. In this landscape (or public sphere), Muslim congregations requested proper sacral buildings that helped them form their identity. The Muslim respondents in the case-study emphasized that a mosque is much more than a place for religious practice; they also perceived mosques as "intellectual and social hubs for Muslims: places for creating both bonding and bridging social capital."[53] Consequently, mosques were presented not only as arenas for identity building but also as platforms for social activities that can contribute to welfare. The examples from the FACIT case-study invert the problem.

The question is not only how and if religious actors contribute to welfare and thereby act in the public sphere; it is just as important to ask what society must provide to enable religious actors to contribute to welfare and to the public sphere.

Conclusion

Based on studies in the field of welfare and religion, this chapter tries to discuss the question of how religious actors in Sweden relate to the public sphere and how the social changes of the recent decades have affected their role. Given the changes both in state–religion relationships and in welfare society, one would expect religious actors to play a much more active role in the public sphere than they did 20 years ago. However, none of the reviewed studies gives any indication that the engagement of religious actors in professional welfare provision, that is, in the public sphere of welfare, has significantly increased. Moreover, less than half of the Swedish population is interested in welfare providers with a strong religious profile. Does this mean that religious actors and their welfare engagement should remain in the private sphere, where the majority of the Swedish population wants them to be?

Yet, the studies presented in this chapter also show that something has changed. Religious actors have recently received much more attention and acknowledgment for their activities in welfare than they did before. Today, both public authorities and the population know more about how religious actors attend to the existential and spiritual needs of their members and how they create identity, community, and social networks. This is particularly important with regard to immigrants and refugees who come to Sweden. Does this mean that it has become of public interest what religious actors do in the private sphere?

The two qualitative case-studies about the welfare contributions of religious actors in local communities lead to additional questions. Is it appropriate to ask about the objectives, methods, and strategies of religious actors in order to understand their role in the public sphere? Is it not just as important to examine the opportunities and hindrances that the religious actors meet in welfare work and the public sphere? Who defines the public sphere? In what ways is the public sphere defined? And how have these definitions changed over recent decades? Is it the privilege of the public actors and the majority of the population to define what the public sphere should look like? What would researchers find when exploring the public sphere from the perspective of religious actors? All these are important questions for researchers to address to understand the changed role of religious actors in a changed public sphere in Sweden.

NOTES

1. Gøsta Esping-Andersen, *The Three Worlds of Welfare Capitalism* (Cambridge: Polity Press, 1990).
2. Philip Manow and Kees van Kersbergen, "Religion and the Western Welfare State: The Theoretical Context," in *Religion, Class Coalitions and Welfare States*, eds. Kees van Kersbergen and Philip Manow, 1–38 (Cambridge: Cambridge University Press, 2009); Susanne Wallman Lundåsen and Lars Trägårdh, "Social Trust and Religion in Sweden: Theological Belief versus Social Organization," in *Religion and Civil Society in Europe*, ed. Joep de Hart, Paul Dekker, and Loek Halman, 109–24 (Heidelberg: Springer, 2013).
3. Christian Welzel, *Freedom Rising: Human Empowerment and the Quest for Emancipation* (New York: Cambridge University Press, 2013).
4. Statistics Sweden, 2017, http://www.scb.se.
5. Svenska kyrkan [Church of Sweden], 2017, http://www.svenskakyrkan.se.
6. Statistics Sweden, *Befolkningsutveckling: födda, döda, in- och utvandring, gifta, skilda 1749–2016* [Population development: born, died, immigration and emigration, married, divorced 1747–2016], 2018, https://www.scb.se/hitta-statistik/statistik-efter-amne/befolkning/befolkningens-sammansattning/befolkningsstatistik/pong/tabell-och-diagram/helarsstatistik--riket/befolkningsutveckling-fodda-doda-in--och-utvandring-gifta-skilda/.
7. Svenska kyrkan, *Svenska kyrkans medlemsutveckling år 1972–2016* [The Membership Development in the Church of Sweden in the Years 1972–2016] (Uppsala: Svenska kyrkan, 2017).
8. Oloph Bexell, ed., *Sveriges kyrkohistoria, part 7. Folkväckelsens och kyrkoförnyelsens tid* [The Church History of Sweden, Volume 7. The Time of the Popular Revival Movements and of Church Re-Newal] (Stockholm: Verbum, 2003).
9. Anders Bäckström, Ninna Edgardh Beckman, and Per Pettersson, *Religious Change in Northern Europe. The Case of Sweden* (Stockholm: Verbum, 2004).
10. Per Pettersson, "State and Religion in Sweden. Ambiguity between Disestablishment and Religious Control," *Nordic Journal of Religion and Society* 24, no. 2 (2011): 119–36.
11. Inger Furseth, ed., *Religious Complexity in the Public Sphere: Comparing Nordic Countries* (London: Palgrave Macmillan, 2018).

12. Inger Furseth, "Secularization, Deprivatization or Religious Complexity," in *Religious Complexity in the Public Sphere: Comparing Nordic Countries*, 291–312 (London: Palgrave Macmillan, 2018), 294.
13. Pettersson, "State and Religion in Sweden," 123–25.
14. Thomas Ekstrand, "Thinking Theologically about Welfare and Religion," in *Welfare and Religion in 21st Century Europe II: Gendered, Religious and Social Change*, eds. Anders Bäckström, Grace Davie, Ninna Edgardh, and Per Pettersson, 107–50 (Farnham, UK: Ashgate, 2011).
15. Pettersson, "State and Religion in Sweden," 120.
16. Myndigheten för stöd till trossamfund, Nämnden för statligt stöd till trossamfund [The Board for State Support to Faith Communities], 2017a, http://www.sst.a.se/download/18.3e8d58c211f8378233080009349/ Uppfoljningrapport2.pdf.
17. Annette Leis-Peters, Martha Middlemiss Lé Mon, and Magdalena Nordin, "Religiösa organisationer och civilsamhället" [Religious organisations and civil society], in *Sociologiska perspektiv på religion i Sverige* [Sociological Perspectives on Religion in Sweden], eds. Mia Lövheim, and Magdalena Nordin, 107–22 (Malmö, Sweden: Gleerups, 2015).
18. Myndigheten får stöd till trossamfund, Utbetalda statsbidrag år 2016 [Paid Benefits Year 2016], 2018, http://www.sst.a.se/download/18.23a06a21 15bf5bc807eb03ab/1495536449631/17a+Utbetalda+statsbidrag+%C3 %A5r+2016%2C+ny+sortering.pdf.
19. Myndigheten för stöd till trossamfund, Direktören Åke Göranssons blogg [The Blog of the Director Åke Göransson], 2017b, http://www.sst.a.se/ kontakt/akesblogg.4.11165b2c13cf48416deda9.html; Annette Leis-Peters, "Religious Literacy in Welfare and Civil Society: A Nordic Perspective, in *Re-imagining Religion and Belief for 21st Century Policy and Practice*, ed. Christopher Baker, Beth R. Crisp, and Adam Dinham (Bristol, UK: Polity Press, forthcoming 2018).
20. Welzel, *Freedom Rising*.
21. Inger Furseth, Lars Ahlin, Kimmo Ketola, Annette Leis-Peters, and Bjarni Randver Sigurvinsson "Changing Religious Landscape in the Nordic countries," in *Religious Complexity in the Public Sphere: Comparing Nordic Countries*, ed. Inger Furseth, 31–80 (London: Palgrave Macmillan, 2017).
22. Ann af Burén, *Living Simultaneity: On Religion among Semi-Secular Swedes*, Södertörns University, 2015, https://www.diva-portal.org/ smash/get/diva2:800530/FULLTEXT01.pdf.
23. Inger Furseth, "Secularization, deprivatization or religious complexity," in *Religious complexity in the public sphere: Comparing Nordic countries*, ed. Inger Furseth, 291–312 (London: Palgrave Macmillan, 2018b).
24. Esping-Andersen, *Three Worlds of Welfare Capitalism*.

25. Alva Myrdal, "Samhälle—Samfund—Individ" [Society—Community—Individual], in *Diakoni i 70-talet* [Diaconia in the 70s], ed. Svenska kyrkans Diakoninämnd, 99–115 (Stockholm: Verbum, 1971); Annette Leis-Peters,. "Hidden by Civil Society and Religion? Diaconal Institutions as Welfare Providers in the Growing Swedish Welfare State," in *Religion and the Welfare State*, ed. Pirjo Markkola and Ingela Nauman, 105–27, Special Issue of the *Journal of Church and State* 56, no. 1 (2014).
26. Karin Busch Zetterberg, *Det civila samhället i socialstaten. Inkomstkällor, private transfereringar, omsorgsvård*, Socialstatsprojektet (Stockholm: City University Press, 1996), 2.
27. SOU, *Vårda vården—samverkan, mångfald och rättvisa. Slutbetänkande från Utredningen Vårdens ägarformar—vinst och demokrati* [To Care for Care—Cooperation, Diversity and Justice. Final Report from the Public Investigation the Ownership of Care—Profit and Democracy] (Stockholm: Fritzes, 2003), 23.
28. Karl Henrik Sivesind, "The Changing Roles of For-Profit and Nonprofit Welfare Provision in Norway, Sweden, and Denmark," in *Promoting Active Citizenship. Markets and Choice in Scandinavian Welfare*, ed. Karl Henrik Sivesind and Jo Saglie, 33–74 (London/New York: Palgrave Macmillan, 2017); Karl Henrik Sivesind, "Endring av fordelingen mellom ideelle, kommersielle og offentlige velferdstjenester i Skandinavia" [Changes in the Distribution Between Value-Based, Commercial, and Public Welfare Services in Scandinavia], in *Mot en ny skandinavisk velferdsmodell? Konsekvenser av ideell, kommersiell og offentlig tjenesteyting for aktivt medborgerskap* [Towards a New Scandinavian Welfare Model? Consequences of Value-Based, Commercial and Public Service Provision for Active Citizenship], ed. Karl Henrik Sivesind, 17–39 (Oslo: Institutt for samfunnsforskning, 2016); Ola Johansson, *Tjäna eller tjäna? Om vård och vinst. Privatisering av vård, omsorg, skola—vilka tar över?* [To Serve or to Gain? About Care and Profi. Privatization of Nursing, Care, School—Who Takes Overs?] (Stockholm: Famna, 2011).
29. Clas Rehnberg, "Jämförelse av förutsättningar for idéburne vårdgivare inom EU/EES området" [Comparison of Preconditions for Idea-Based Care Providers in the EU/EES Area]. In SOU, *Vård med omsorg. Möjligheter och hinder* [Care with Care. Possibilities and Obstacles], 263–90 (Stockholm: Fritzes, 2007), 37.
30. Harald Askeland, *Hverdagsledelse: Diakoni, verdier og ledelse i praksis* [Everyday leadership. Diaconia, values and leadership in practice] (Oslo: VID vitenskapelige høgskole/Det teologiske menighetsfakultetet, 2016), 44f.
31. Olav Helge Angell, "Institusjonsdiakoni i den norske velferdsstaten [Institutional diaconia in the Norwegian welfare state]," in *Kan institusjoner elske? Samtidsessayer om diakonale virksomheter* [Can institutions love. Contemporary essays about diaconal services], ed. Einar Aadland, 31–49 (Oslo: Akribe, 2009).

32. Klas Borell and Arne Gerdner, "Hidden Voluntary Social Work. A Nationally Representative Survey of Muslim Congregations in Sweden," *British Journal of Social Work* 41, no. 5 (2011): 968–79.
33. Myndigheten för stöd till trossamfund, "Trossamfunden—en god kraft i samhälle" [Faith Communities—a Good Force in Society], 2014, http://www.sst.a.se/nyheter/nyhetsarkivaktuellt/trossamfundenengodkraftisamhallet.5.38228ad4143b35110977082.html.
34. Socialdepartementet, *Trossamfundens sociale insatser. En preliminär undersökning* [The Social Activities of Faith Communities. A Preliminary Study] (Stockholm: Fritzes, 2015).
35. Socialdepartementet, *Trossamfundens sociale insatser*, 44.
36. Socialdepartementet, *Trossamfundens sociale insatser*, 55.
37. Socialdepartementet, *Trossamfundens sociale insatser*.
38. Socialdepartementet, *Trossamfundens sociale insatser*, 62.
39. Anders Bäckström, "Välfärdsinsatser på religiös grund. Förväntningar och problem. En teoretisk inledning" [Welfare Activities on Religious Ground. Expectations and Problems. A Theoretical Introduction], in *Välfärdsinsatser på religiös grund. Förväntningar och problem. En teoretisk inledning* [Welfare Activities on Religious Ground. Expectations and Problems], ed. Anders Bäckström, 11–30 (Skellefteå, Sweden: Artos & Norma), 95.
40. Bäckström, "Välfärdsinsatser på religiös grund," 95.
41. Socialdepartementet, *Trossamfundens sociale insatser*, 65.
42. Socialdepartementet, *Trossamfundens sociale insatser*.
43. Anders Bäckström, Ninna Edgardh Beckman, and Per Pettersson, *Welfare and Religion in 21st Century Europe I. Configuring the Connections*, ed. Anders Bäckström and Grace Davie with Ninna Edgard and Per Pettersson (Farnham, UK: Ashgate, 2010).
44. Lina Molokotos-Liederman, Anders Bäckström, and Grace Davie, eds., *Religion and Welfare in Europe: Gendered and Minority Perspectives* (Bristol: Policy Press, 2017).
45. Charlotte Fridolfsson and Ingemar Elander, "Faith and Place. Constructing Muslim Identity in a Secular Lutheran Society," *Cultural Geographies* 20, no. 3 (2013): 319–37.
46. Ninna Edgardh and Per Pettersson, "The Church of Sweden. A Church for All, Especially the Most Vulnerable," in *Welfare and Religion in 21st Century Europe I. Configuring the Connections*, ed. Anders Bäckström and Grace Davie with Ninna Edgard and Per Pettersson, 39–56 (Farnham, UK: Ashgate, 2010).
47. Edgardh, Ninna, and Pettersson, "The Church of Sweden," 44.
48. Edgardh, Ninna, and Pettersson, "The Church of Sweden," 45.
49. Edgardh, Ninna, and Pettersson, "The Church of Sweden."

50. Ingemar Elander and Charlotte Fridolfsson, *Faith-based Organisations and Social Exclusion in Sweden* (Leuven/Den Haag: Acco, 2011).
51. Fridolfsson and Elander, "Faith and Place."
52. Borell and Gerdner, "Hidden Voluntary Social Work."
53. Charlotte Fridolfsson and Ingemar Elander, "Faith and Place. Constructing Muslim Identity in a Secular Lutheran Society," *Cultural Geographies* 20, no. 3 (2013): 319–337, 330.

CHAPTER 8

Social Capital and Religion in the United Kingdom

Steven Kettell

INTRODUCTION

In the past few decades, social capital has become one of the most influential concepts in the social sciences, offering an explanatory framework for analyzing issues such as social cohesion, multiculturalism, trust, and political engagement. A central claim in the literature on this topic is that a key source of social capital is provided by religion. Notions of divine morality, a commitment to ethical codes of conduct, and an emphasis on community are said to promote pro-social behavior and to do so more effectively than non-religious motivations.

These assumptions underpin an increasingly close relationship between government and faith-based organizations in the United Kingdom (UK). Starting with the New Labour administrations led by Tony Blair, successive governments have seen faith-based organizations as a valuable source of social capital via their role in providing voluntary and charitable services,

S. Kettell (✉)
University of Warwick, Coventry, UK

© The Author(s) 2019
P. C. Manuel, M. Glatzer (eds.), *Faith-Based Organizations and Social Welfare*, Palgrave Studies in Religion, Politics, and Policy,
https://doi.org/10.1007/978-3-319-77297-4_8

as a mechanism for promoting social cohesion and engaging "hard-to-reach" groups, and as a means of plugging the gap in welfare provision left by the politics of austerity and the withdrawal of the state.

Scholarly research into the issue of social capital, however, has centered primarily on North America (principally, the United States) and, to a lesser degree, Europe.[1] Research into the UK context has been far less extensive and has tended to focus on causes and consequences that overlook the religious dimension.[2] As a result, the evidence base for the relationship between religion and social capital in the United Kingdom remains comparatively thin. As Annette observes, "There is no hard data on the nature and extent of faith-based community action in the UK."[3] And as Wharton and de Las Casas put it, "Faith-based charities as a group are not well understood."[4]

The purpose of this chapter is to examine the evidence on the link between social capital and religion in the United Kingdom. It begins by exploring some of the conceptual dimensions of social capital, considers the way in which the idea of a link has underpinned relations between government and faith-based organizations, and analyzes the extent to which the empirical evidence supports or challenges this assumption.

Conceptualizing Social Capital

The idea of social capital derives from the work of several key thinkers (the most influential of these, perhaps, are Pierre Bourdieu, James Coleman, and Robert Putnam). While scholars have approached the concept from a number of different perspectives, the core of the idea refers to the way in which the shared values and interconnections within and between social groups contribute to pro-social behavior.[5] As Putnam writes, "Whereas physical capital refers to physical objects and human capital refers to the properties of individuals, social capital refers to connections among individuals—social networks and the norms of reciprocity and trust-worthiness that arise from them."[6] Or, as Field pithily observes, the concept can be summarized in just two words: "relationships matter." As he explains: "People connect through a series of networks and they tend to share common values with other members of these networks; to the extent that these networks constitute a resource, they can be seen as forming a kind of capital."[7]

Theorists typically distinguish between different forms of social capital, principally focusing on their *bonding*, *bridging*, and *linking* effects. Bonding social capital centers on the way in which groups generate interpersonal solidarity, connecting members together and enhancing the cohesiveness of the relationships between them. This type of social capital is often found in groups that are relatively small and homogeneous (either ethnically or in terms of shared values or beliefs), and in groups based on enduring, mutually supportive commitments, such as friends or family. In contrast, bridging social capital refers to the interconnections that exist horizontally between members of different groups that have shared or overlapping interests, such as neighbors or groups within a community. Whereas bonding social capital focuses on inward-looking relations, bridging social capital centers on broader intergroup dynamics and is said to foster an improved sense of wider civic responsibility, social trust, and cooperation. In contrast to both bonding and bridging social capital, linking social capital refers to vertical interconnectivity, as people make connections that go beyond their normal social boundaries. Linking social capital can enable individuals to forge relationships across markers of social similarity (such as class or status), allowing them to access resources from outside their usual circles.[8]

Social capital is beneficial in a variety of ways. For individuals, it can facilitate access to resources and influence as well as provide a shared sense of identity and belonging. Studies have also shown positive links to improved levels of personal well-being, life satisfaction, and increased outcomes across a variety of health indices.[9] The broader community effects are also significant. Social capital is often described as a form of "social glue," providing the mutual endeavor that is essential for the flourishing of civic and democratic life. Higher levels of social capital have been positively associated with (inter alia) lower mortality rates, reduced levels of crime, economic growth, higher educational attainment, and political engagement.[10]

A key claim in the scholarly literature on this subject is that religion provides a unique source of social capital. For this, there are two alternative explanations. One approach, centering on the role of values, contends that religion provides adherents with a set of divinely ordained moral codes, a sense of meaning and a core identity that together promote ethical and pro-social behavior. A second approach centers on the role of social networks and claims that membership of a religion embeds adherents within a moral community, creating practical opportunities for developing civic skills and engaging in communal activities.[11] For these reasons, faith-based organizations are often said to be more effective at promoting social capital than their non-religious counterparts. As Weller notes, a central theme on this topic is that "religion and religious organizations form a substantial part of civic society and that they contribute significantly to the preservation and development of both bonding and bridging social capital."[12]

This claim is supported by a substantial body of evidence. Research has found that people who attend religious services more frequently make higher financial donations to charity[13]; that members of a congregation are more likely to connect to individuals from outside their everyday social circle[14]; that members of a church are more likely to join voluntary organizations[15]; and that religious volunteering has a "spillover effect" to civic engagement in general (one study, for instance, found that people involved in religious volunteering were almost 3.6 times more likely to volunteer for non-religious causes).[16]

A more detailed inspection of the evidence, however, reveals that this link is far from straightforward. One issue is that different dimensions of religiosity produce varying degrees of social capital. The regularity of attendance at a place of worship, for example, is more strongly linked to civic engagement than religious affiliation or belief.[17] The specific form of religion involved plays a critical role as well. Hierarchical religions (such as Roman Catholicism, Orthodox Christianity, and Islam) are commonly said to be negatively associated with social capital compared to non-hierarchical religions (most notably Protestantism). While hierarchical religions are believed to produce close church and family ties, emphasize vertical social structures, and rely on government to address social problems, non-hierarchical religions are said to encourage civic engagement and participation in social networks outside of the church and family.[18]

Another problem concerns the benefits that religion is thought to produce. Research into the link between religion and personal well-being has found a range of negative as well as positive results,[19] and higher than average levels of religiosity have also been linked to unfavorable effects at the country level, including shorter life expectancy and higher levels of infant mortality, violent crime, corruption, abortion rates, and income inequality.[20] In contrast, the least religious and most secular countries in the world are often ranked higher across a range of quality of life and equality indicators.[21]

Studies have also found that higher levels of religiosity (especially in smaller and more conservative groups) can promote greater levels of bonding social capital, creating and reinforcing sharp in/out-group dynamics that can generate intolerance and prejudicial attitudes toward non-group members.[22] Research from the United States has found that involvement with a religious organization can have a negative impact on involvement with non-religious groups (contrary to the idea of a "spill-over effect")[23] and that a significant proportion of religiously inspired volunteering and giving is directed to activities within and around religious groups themselves as opposed to the wider community.[24]

Government and Faith-Based Organizations in the United Kingdom

The assumption of a link between religion and social capital underpins recent government efforts to engage more closely with faith-based organizations in the United Kingdom. Government interest in faith-based organizations began to develop during the 1980s and became particularly intense under the New Labour administrations from 1997 to 2010.[25] This trend continued under the Conservative–Liberal Democrat coalition from 2010 to 2015 and shows little sign of abating.

The closer engagement between government and faith-based organizations has been promoted through a range of policies and institutional mechanisms. These include the creation of a Faith Communities Unit in the Home Office in 2003, the establishment of a Faith Communities Consultative Council in 2005, the forming of a Faith and Social Cohesion Unit in 2007, and the provision of financial support to faith-based organizations via a Faith Communities Capacity Building Fund designed to enable faith-based organizations to play a greater role in civil society and link more effectively with public authorities.[26]

The official rationale for this policy shift has centered on three principal themes. The first of these was based on the view that faith-based organizations could be harnessed as useful partners in projects of urban regeneration as well as the promotion of voluntary and charitable activities.[27] The New Labour Prime Minister, Tony Blair, described faith groups as being "some of the most effective voluntary and community organisations in the country"[28] and maintained they had "a critical role to play in meeting community and individual needs."[29] The view of the then Home Secretary,

David Blunkett, was that the government wanted to "mobilise the strength and commitment of faith communities as part of the renewal of civil society and engagement in active citizenship."[30]

The view of religion as a wholly benevolent force was challenged by the second thematic influence, which saw faith as a remedy for social problems relating to issues of social cohesion. This became increasingly influential in the wake of the Cantle report into ethnically fuelled disturbances in several northern cities in 2001, as well as the terrorist attacks of 9/11 and July 7, 2005, which highlighted the dangers posed by radical forms of Islam.[31] From this perspective, engagement with faith-based organizations was seen by government officials as a useful means of connecting with "hard-to-reach" social groups and for helping them to integrate into mainstream life in the United Kingdom.[32] As the Commission on Integration and Cohesion (2007) put it, faith-based organizations helped "to build integration and cohesion through their community buildings and leaders on the ground, their support for projects and networks, and the promotion of shared values."[33]

The third theme underpinning government–faith-based organization relations emerged with the introduction of austerity policies by the Conservative–Liberal Democrat coalition and has seen engagement with faith groups as a means of filling the gap in welfare provision prompted by the withdrawal of the state.[34] One of the central themes of this period was the "Big Society" agenda, a key objective of which was to create an expanded voluntary sector with a greater role for faith-based organizations in proving welfare and social services. As Eric Pickles, the then Secretary of State for Communities and Local Government, put it: "For years, faith communities have been quietly making a huge difference day-in and day-out, to every single neighbourhood in the country."[35] Baroness Warsi, then co-chair of the Conservative Party, declared that the goal of the Big Society was to "unleash the positive power of faith."[36]

THE CASE FOR FAITH

One of the main arguments in support of the view that religion provides a valuable source of social capital is that faith-based organizations are engaged in a wide range of voluntary endeavors. These include the provision of food banks, street pastors, youth clubs, advice and information services, education and training courses, family support and mental health services, the cooking and delivering of community meals, and participation in local governance. Many charities, such as Tearfund, World Jewish Relief, Christian Aid, Barnardo's, CAFOD, and Oxfam, are also religious (or religiously inspired), and as Wharton and de Las Casas point out, 26.6 percent of charities in Great Britain are faith-based (a total of 49,881 from 187,495 registered in 2015). Evidence suggests that they are well equipped to provide bridging social capital. More than 85 percent of faith-based charities responding to a recent survey said that they were engaged in collaborative activities with other groups and institutions, and 80 percent rated themselves as "good" or "excellent" in their ability to work with others.[37]

A number of qualitative studies (typically drawing on focus groups, surveys, and interviews) make similar claims. Research conducted by Morris and colleagues concluded that "faith groups provide an impressive range of valuable services and benefits to their local communities."[38] Cairns and colleagues found that local churches were "playing an important role in the development of social capital and more cohesive communities."[39] Baker and Skinner found that churches were "engaged in highly creative and innovative regeneration and social capital enterprises ... with a wide variety of both faith-based and secular partners."[40] The Commission on Urban Life and Faith concluded that "faith-based organisations make a decisive and positive difference to their neighbourhoods through the values they promote, the service they inspire and the resources they command."[41]

These claims are also supported by quantitative data. A poll conducted for the BBC by ComRes in 2014 found that religiosity was positively linked to the production of pro-social behavior. More than three quarters (77 percent) of respondents actively practicing a religion reported giving money to charity during the previous month, compared to 67 percent of people who did not practice a religion.[42] These findings mirrored those of a 2007 report by the National Centre for Social Research, which found that 67 percent of people actively practicing a religion engaged in some form of formal volunteering compared to 55 percent of those who were not actively religious, and 55 percent of those with no religion.[43] The same pattern was evident for charitable donations, with 87 percent of respondents practicing a religion claiming to have donated during the last four weeks, compared to 80 percent of people not actively practicing a religion and 74 percent of the non-religious.[44] Recent figures from the

National Council for Voluntary Organisations found that 35 percent of those actively practicing a religion engaged in formal voluntary activities at least once a month, compared to 24 percent of those not practicing.[45] A study commissioned by ResPublica in 2013 showed that 79 percent of Church of England congregations engaged in formal voluntary action during the past 12 months compared to 40 percent of the general population, and found that 90 percent of congregations were involved in informal voluntary activity compared to 54 percent of the general population.[46] This report also supported the link between attendance and social capital, with 84 percent of churchgoers who attended at least once a week claiming to have taken part in formal social action compared to 66 percent of those attending less than weekly.[47]

These findings are further supported by research into the distribution of voluntary activities in the United Kingdom. This has found that a significant amount of voluntary activity is conducted by a small group of people, described as a "civic core" (in this case: 8.9 percent of the population are responsible for 50.9 percent of all volunteering hours and 42.5 percent of charitable giving), and that members of this group are significantly more likely to say that they are "actively practicing their religion" (at 42.4 percent) than members of "non-core" (26.5 percent) and "disengaged" (24.7 percent) groups.[48]

Questioning the Link

The view that religion provides a unique source of social capital is problematic in a number of important respects. One issue is that the large majority of the voluntary and community sector is "secular" rather than "religious." Inverting the figures provided by Wharton and de Las Casas, for example, highlights the fact that almost three quarters (73.4 percent) of registered charities in Great Britain are driven by motivations that are not grounded in faith.[49] A second point is that defining voluntary activity itself remains a difficult task,[50] and statistics on religious volunteering often lack detail about the role of "faith" as a motivating factor. This methodological issue poses a serious dilemma for researchers, since the lines of causality can run in different directions. It is not always clear whether volunteering is being driven by religiosity or whether individuals that are more predisposed to volunteering are themselves more likely to join and attend religious organizations.[51]

This makes it difficult to know whether religious individuals are volunteering directly because of their faith or whether other factors such as peer-group influence are just as, or more, important.[52] Research by Jochum and colleagues found that the impact of faith on volunteering was subordinate to social factors such as levels of age and education, leading them to conclude that: "Religious affiliation makes little difference in terms of volunteering."[53] A study conducted by the National Centre for Voluntary Organisations found that religious reasons were ranked considerably lower than other motivations in a list of those that drove voluntary behavior. Religious belief ("It is part of my religious belief to help people") was placed 11th out of 15 in a series of reasons why people took part in voluntary activities, being cited by just 17 percent of respondents, some way behind: "I wanted to improve things, help people" (61 percent), "The cause was really important to me" (41 percent), "Had spare time to do it" (34 percent), "Thought it would give me a chance to use my existing skills" (30 percent), and "Wanted to meet people/make friends" (30 percent).[54] A similar study conducted by the National Centre for Social Research placed religious belief at 13th place out of 17 in a list of reasons why people had made a recent charitable donation, being cited by just 12 percent of respondents, far behind motivations such as: "Work of charity important" (52 percent), "Right thing to do" (41 percent), "Just feel like giving" (31 percent), and "Can afford to" (20 percent).[55]

Citizenship Survey figures produced by the Department for Communities and Local Government further challenge the idea of a clear link between religion and social capital. Statistics collected in 2010/2011 (the last time the survey was taken) showed there to be no meaningful difference between religious and non-religious individuals in terms of their propensity to take part in voluntary and civic activities. Levels of "civic participation" for people self-identifying as "Christian" and those identifying as having "no religion" stood at 34 percent each, and the figures for formal volunteering were 40 percent and 37 percent, respectively. The figures for "all activities" (including civic activism and consultation) were 58 percent for Christians and 56 percent for no religion.[56] A similar point can be discerned from research into the characteristics of the "civic core." While figures show that members of the core were more likely to be actively practicing a religion than those outside it, more than half of those within the civic core (57.6 percent) did not actively practice a religion. By the same token, the large majority (73.5 percent) of people engaged in voluntary and charitable activities outside the core were not religiously active.[57]

Another problem with the assumption of a link between religion and social capital is that the beliefs and practices that bind faith groups together can often impede their ability to engage in community activities, producing bonding rather than bridging or linking social capital. In the UK case, this point has been observed by a number of studies. Cairns and colleagues note that while Faith-based organizations can create social cohesion, their role in developing bonding rather than bridging social capital "may currently be more substantial."[58] Jochum et al. similarly maintain that "most faith-based organisations are more likely to create bonding social capital," and that "too much bonding social capital can be exclusive and at times even destructive."[59] These claims are supported by figures from the Charities Aid Foundation showing that religious organizations and causes are the largest recipients of charitable donations. The single largest "cause area" to which donors gave money in 2016 was "Religious organisations," which attracted 20 percent of all donations made in that year. The next largest area, by comparison, was "Overseas aid and disaster relief" (with 10 percent of donations) followed by "Medical research," "Hospitals and hospices," and "Children or young people" (with 8 percent each). Religious causes also attracted the highest donations from the oldest and the most religious age cohort (the over sixty-fives), receiving 22 percent of their donations.[60] An earlier study by the Charities Aid Foundation (2013) found that members of the civic core were also more inclined toward voluntary activities based around faith, with 37 percent having an interest in religious causes compared to 20 percent of the "Middle Ground" group and 10 percent of "Zero Givers."[61] On the same theme, figures produced by ResPublica show that the highest rated type of voluntary activities cited by people who volunteered in the last 12 months were closely linked to issues of faith, namely: "promoting church" (with 66 percent), "Christian charities" (with 60 percent), "Choral/musical" and "cultural activities, hobbies" (33 percent), and "pastoral care" (31 percent).[62]

The view that religion tends to produce bonding social capital is supported by a range of other studies. Research based on data from the Ethnic Minority British Election Study found that religious affiliation was negatively associated with civic engagement in groups where the respondent's religious or ethnic group was in a minority, suggesting that "ethnic and religious minority organizations may be especially unlikely to promote other types of organizational involvement."[63] A study conducted by Lukka and colleagues found that the ability of many faith communities to engage with bridging activities was hampered by internal issues (such as an insistence on specific roles for men and women) and concluded that "there may be pressure to challenge the traditions of some minority cultures in order to create "bridging" as well as "bonding" social capital."[64] A review conducted under the auspices of the Office of the Deputy Prime Minister came to a similar conclusion, noting that sex roles in some faith groups were so sharply divided that it was difficult to imagine how they could contribute toward bridging social capital, and finding that "the faith-based sector existed in a parallel universe to the mainstream voluntary and community sector."[65]

This tendency toward bonding social capital underpins concerns that faith-based organizations will use their voluntary activities to proselytize and discriminate against individuals who do not share their religious beliefs and values. While such claims have been strenuously rejected by faith-based organizations—a joint report by Christians in Parliament and the Evangelical Alliance dismissed such fears as "false"—research suggests that the matter might not be so clear cut.[66] Figures from ResPublica show that almost half (48 percent) of church members who engaged in volunteering activity said that they considered this to be a means of promoting their faith and converting others (a statement to which just 21 percent disagreed).[67] A study conducted by Wharton and de Las Casas (despite claiming that there was "little evidence to justify fears of proselytism") found that a significant proportion of religious volunteers used these activities "to try and increase the number of people who share our faith." Almost a fifth (19 percent) of religious volunteers strongly agreed with a statement to this effect (23 percent strongly disagreed), while almost half (48 percent) of Christian respondents "agreed" or "strongly agreed" with this view. Given that almost two-thirds (64.5 percent) of faith-based charities in Great Britain are Christians, this figure is far from insubstantial.[68] The issue is all the more problematic given the stance taken by many religious organizations on equality issues such as gender, sexual, and reproductive rights, much of which diverges from the norms of mainstream public opinion. The latest findings from British Social Attitudes revealing how much more conservative the views of religious individuals are on issues such as premarital sex, same-sex relationships, transgenderism, abortion, and euthanasia highlight just how potentially problematic this divergence can be.[69]

A final point to be highlighted in this respect is that, while the number of people becoming involved in voluntary activities has increased throughout the post-war period—the average number of associational memberships increased by 44 percent between 1959 and 1990 according to Hall—religion itself has experienced a sustained process of decline.[70] Figures produced by British Social Attitudes show that the proportion of the adult population describing themselves as "Christian" fell from 61 percent to 41 percent between 1991 and 2016. A growth in the proportion of adults adhering to non-Christian faiths (from 3 percent to 6 percent during the same period) remains insufficient to offset the overall trend, while the proportion of UK adults self-identifying as having "no religion" has substantially increased from 35 percent to 53 percent.[71] Figures 8.1 and 8.2 are set out below.

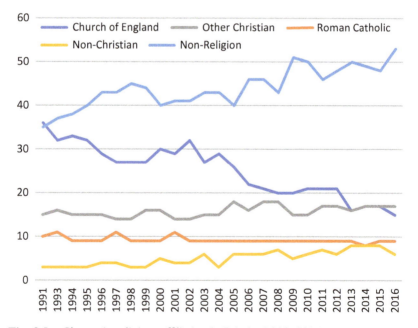

Fig. 8.1 Change in religious affiliation in Britain, 1992–2016

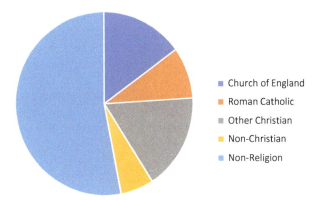

Fig. 8.2 Religious affiliation in Britain, 2016

CONCLUSION

It is estimated that more than 14 million people in the United Kingdom take part in some kind of formal voluntary activity at least once a month, creating an annual benefit to the national economy of more than £22 billion[72] (other estimates put this figure even higher).[73] Volunteering also has a significant role to play in sustaining the welfare state, particularly in an era of politically imposed austerity. In the absence of official figures, it is hard to arrive at a precise picture of the extent to which voluntary activity underpins the welfare state—indeed, there are ongoing debates over whether, and to what degree, government spending on welfare can "crowd out" voluntary behavior,[74] but a report by the King's Trust has estimated that the health and social care sector in England alone is supported by around three million volunteers.[75] As Bussell and Forbes note, key elements of the welfare state "are now dependent on the voluntary sector and volunteer involvement."[76]

Clearly, faith-based organizations have a substantial impact in this area. Yet, estimating their value to the welfare state is an even more difficult task given the lack of officially recorded figures on the work that faith-based organizations have undertaken with government institutions and the methodological conundrums involved in disentangling the motivating role of "faith" in voluntary activity. Nevertheless, the assumption that there exists a well-established and valuable link between religion and social capital remains pervasive. Religious organizations are said to provide their adherents with a divinely inspired ethical framework and a sense of communal obligation, making them uniquely attuned to the production of pro-social behavior. These assumptions have helped to drive and to justify moves toward a closer relationship between government agencies and faith-based organizations in the United Kingdom. Government officials have seen faith-based organizations as a useful source of voluntary and charitable activities, as a channel through which to promote social cohesion, and as a means of filling in gaps in welfare provision left by a withdrawal of the state.

The empirical evidence to support the assumption that such a link exists remains problematic. The claim that religiously active individuals are more likely to engage in voluntary and charitable behaviors is significantly flawed, and while faith-based organizations can and do produce social capital, it is often likely to assume a more negative form (bonding, rather than bridging or linking social capital). Much religious involvement in voluntary activity is directed toward religious causes themselves, and issues of proselytization remain a cause for concern. Given these difficulties, the idea that faith-based organizations are uniquely well placed to provide an effective solution to problems such as social integration and a retrenchment of welfare services must remain open to question.

Notes

1. Justin Beaumont, "Faith Action on Urban Social Issues," *Urban Studies* 45, no. 10 (2008): 2019–34.
2. For example, see, Peter Hall, "Social Capital in Britain," *British Journal of Politics* 29, no. 3 (1999): 417–61; Performance and Innovation Unit [PIU], "Social Capital: A Discussion Paper," Cabinet Office, London; Paul Weller, "Religions and Social Capital. Theses on Religion(S), State(S), and Society(ies): With Particular Reference to the United Kingdom and the European Union," *Journal of International Migration and Integration* 6, no. 2 (2005): 271–89.
3. John Annette, "Faith Communities, Communitarianism, Social Capital and Youth Civic Engagement," *Ethnicities* 11, no. 3 (2011): 383–97.
4. Rachel Wharton and Lucy de Las Casas, "What a Difference a Faith Makes: Insights on Faith Based Charities," New Philanthropy Capital, London, 2016.
5. For overviews, see John Field, *Social Capital* (London, Routledge, 2003); and James Farr, "Social Capital: A Conceptual History," *Political Theory* 32, no. 1 (2004): 6–33.

6. Robert Putnam, *Bowling Alone: The Collapse and Revival of American Community* (New York, Simon and Schuster, 2000), 19.
7. Field, *Social Capital*.
8. See Field, *Social Capital*; Robert Furbey, Adam Dinham, Richard Farnell, Doreen Finneron, and Guy Wilkinson, with Catherine Howarth, Dilwar Hussain, and Sharon Palmer, *Faith as Social Capital: Connecting or Dividing?* Joseph Rowntree Foundation (Bristol, UK: Policy Press, 2006); Chris Baker and Jonathan Miles-Watson, "Faith and Traditional Capitals: Defining the Public Scope of Spiritual and Religious Capital—A Literature Review," *Implicit Religion* 13, no. 1 (2010): 17–69.
9. Greg Smith, "Does faith make you healthy and happy? The Case of Evangelical Christians in the UK," *Journal of Religion and Society* 19 (2017): 1–15.
10. For example, Hall, "Social Capital"; Office for National Statistics, "Social Capital: A Review of the Literature," ONS Social Analysis and Reporting Division, 2001; PIU, "Social Capital"; Baker and Miles-Watson, "Faith."
11. See Baker and Miles-Watson, "Faith"; Wharton and de Las Casas, "What a Difference."
12. Weller, "Religions and Social Capital."
13. For example, Peer Scheepers, Manfred te Grotenhuis, and Jan Reitsma, "Dimensions of individual religiosity and charity: cross national effect differences in European countries?" *Review of Religious Research* 47, no. 4 (2006): 347–62.
14. For example, Robert Wuthnow, "Religious involvement and status-bridging social capital," *Journal for the Scientific Study of Religion* 41, no. 4 (2002): 669–84.
15. Pui-Yan Lam, "As the Flocks Gather: How Religion Affects Voluntary Association Participation," *Journal for the Scientific Study of Religion* 41, no. 3 (2002): 405–22.
16. See Stijn Ruiter and Nan Dirk de Graf, "National Context, Religiosity and Volunteering: Results from 53 Countries," *American Sociological Review* 71 (2006): 191–210.
17. Penny Edgell Becker and Pawan Dhingra, "Religious Involvement and Volunteering: Implications for Civil Society," *Sociology of Religion* 62, no. 3 (2001): 315–35; Ruiter and De Graf, *National context*; Patty Van Cappellen, Vassilis Saroglou, and Maria Toth-Gauthier, "Religiosity and Prosocial Behavior Among Churchgoers: Exploring Underlying Mechanisms," *International Journal for the Psychology of Religion* 26, no. 1 (2016): 19–30.
18. See Anneli Kaasa, "Religion and Social Capital: Evidence from European Countries," *International Review of Sociology* 23, no. 3 (2013): 578–96; Lam, *As the flocks*; Pui-Yan Lam, "Religion and Civic Culture: A Cross-

National Study of Voluntary Association," *Journal for the Scientific Study of Religion* 45, no. 2 (2006): 177–93; Ellen Dingemans and Erik Van Ingen, "Does Religion Breed Trust? A Cross-National Study of the Effects of Religious Involvement, Religious Faith, and Religious Context on Social Trust," *Journal for the Scientific Study of Religion* 54, no. 2 (2015): 1–17.
19. Baker and Miles-Watson, "Faith and Traditional Capitals."
20. For example, Tomas James Rees, "Is Personal Insecurity a Cause of Cross-National Differences in the Intensity of Religious Belief?" *Journal of Religion and Society* 11 (2009): 1–24.
21. For example, Phil Zuckerman, *Society Without God: What the Least Religious Nations Can Tell Us About Contentment* (New York: New York University Press, 2010).
22. See Cairns, Jared Kenworthy, Andrea Campbell, and Miles Hewstone, ed., "The Role of In-Group Identification, Religious Group Membership and Intergroup Conflict in Moderating In-Group and Out-Group Affect," *British Journal of Social Psychology* 45, no. 4 (2006): 701–16; Ruud Koopmans, "Religious Fundamentalism and Hostility against Out-Groups: A Comparison of Muslims and Christians in Western Europe," *Journal of Ethnic and Migration Studies* 41, no. 1 (2015): 33–57.
23. Lam, "As the Flocks Gather."
24. Luke Galen, "Does Religious Belief Promote Prosociality? A Critical Examination," *Psychological Bulletin* 138, no. 5 (2012): 876–906; Jesse Lee Preston and Ryan Ritter, "Different Effects of Religion and God on Prosociality with the Ingroup and Outgroup," *Personality and Social Psychology Bulletin* 39, no. 11 (2013): 1471–83; Van Cappellen et al., *Religiosity*.
25. İpek Göçmen, "The Role of Faith-Based Organizations in Social Welfare Systems: A Comparison of France, Germany, Sweden, and the United Kingdom," *Nonprofit and Voluntary Sector Quarterly* 42 (2013), no. 3: 495–516.
26. Veronique Jochum, Belinda Pratten, and Karl Wilding, eds., "Faith and Voluntary Action: An Overview of Current Evidence and Debates" (London: National Council for Voluntary Organisations, 2007); Department for Communities and Local Government, *Face to Face and Side by Side: A Framework for Partnership in Our Multi Faith Society*" (London, 2008); Annette, "Faith."
27. Baker and Miles-Watson, "Faith and Traditional Capitals."
28. Cited in Greg Smith, "Faith in Community and Communities of Faith? Government Rhetoric and Religious Identity in Urban Britain," *Journal of Contemporary Religion* 19, no. 2 (2004): 185–204.
29. Tony Blair, Speech at Faithworks, March 22, 2005, http://webarchive.nationalarchives.gov.uk/20080909054223/http://www.number10.gov.uk/Page7375.

30. Cited in Smith, "Faith in Community."
31. Home Office, "Working Together: Co-Operation Between Government and Faith Communities," Faith Communities Unit, London, 2004; Chris Baker and Hannah Skinner, "Telling the Stories: How Churches Are Contributing to Social Capital," (Manchester, UK: William Temple Foundation, 2005).
32. Smith, *Faith*.
33. Commission on Integration and Cohesion, "Our Shared Future," Wetherby, 2007.
34. Angus McCabe, Heather Buckingham, and Steve Miller, with Marcianne Musabyimana, "Belief in Social Action: Exploring Faith Groups; Responses to Local Needs," Third Sector Research Centre, Working Paper 137, 2016.
35. Eric Pickles, "Ministers Talk Big Society with Faith Leaders," *Communities and Local Government News*, July 19, 2010.
36. Sayeeda Warsi, "Christianity and Public Life: A New Beginning for Relations Between Society, Faith, and the State," Speech to the Bishops of the Church of England, September 15, 2010; on these points also see Steven Kettell, "Religion and the Big Society: a match made in heaven?," *Policy and Politics* 40, no. 2 (2012): 281–96.
37. Wharton and de Las Casas, "What a Difference."
38. Zoe Morris, Kath Maguire, and Jenny Kartupelis, "Faith in Action: A Report on Faith Communities and Social Capital in the East of England" (paper presented at the East of England Faith Leadership Conference, 2003).
39. Ben Cairns, Margaret Harris, and Romayne Hutchison, "Faithful Regeneration: The Role and Contribution of Local Parishes in Local Communities in the Diocese of Birmingham," Centre for Voluntary Action Research, Aston Business School, 2004.
40. Baker and Skinner, "Telling the Stories."
41. Commission on Urban Life and Faith, "Faithful Cities: A Call for Celebration, Vision and Justice" (London: Church House Publishing, 2006); on these points also see Furbey et al., *Faith as Social Capital*.
42. BBC, "Religion—Charitable Giving Survey," 2004, http://www.secularism.org.uk/uploads/bbc-eligion-charitable-giving-march-2014-england-only.pdf.
43. Natalie Low, Sarah Butt, Angela Ellis Paine, and Justin Davis Smith, "Helping Out: A National Survey of Volunteering and Charitable Giving," Office of the Third Sector, Cabinet Office, London, 2007, Table 3.4.
44. Low et al., "Helping out," Table 11.6.
45. National Council for Voluntary Organisations [NCVO], *UK Civil Society Almanac*, 2017, https://data.ncvo.org.uk/.

46. James Noyes and Phillip Blond, "Holistic Mission: Social Action and the Church of England" (Lincoln, UK: ResPublica, 2013).
47. Noyes and Blond, "Holistic Mission," Table 1.
48. John Mohan and Sarah L. Bulloch, "The Idea of a "Civic Core": What Are the Overlaps Between Charitable Giving, Volunteering, and Civic Participation in England And Wales?" Third Sector Research Centre, Working Paper 73, 2012.
49. Wharton and de Las Casas, "What a Difference," Table 1.
50. Andrew Haldane, "In Giving, How Much Do We Receive? The Social Value of Volunteering," Speech to the Society of Business Economists, London, 2014, http://www.bankofengland.co.uk/publications/Documents/speeches/2014/speech756.pdf.
51. For example, Christopher J. Einolf, "The Link Between Religion and Helping Others: The Role of Values, Ideas and Language," *Sociology of Religion* 72, no. 4 (2011): 435–55.
52. Humanists UK, "Religion, Belief and Volunteering," 2010, https://humanism.org.uk/wp-content/uploads/1bha-briefing-volunteering-12-10-final.pdf.
53. Jochum et al., "Faith."
54. NCVO, *UK Civil Society*.
55. Low et al., "Helping out," Figure 13.1.
56. Department for Communities and Local Government (2011), Citizenship Survey, April 2010–March 2011, tables available from: http://webarchive.nationalarchives.gov.uk/20120919165040/http://www.communities.gov.uk/publications/corporate/statistics/citizenshipsurveyq4201011.
57. Mohan and Bulloch, "The Idea," Table 1.
58. Cairns et al., "Faithful Regeneration."
59. Jochum et al., "Faith."
60. Charities Aid Foundation, "UK Giving 2017: An Overview of Charitable Giving in the UK" (Kent, UK: Charities Aid Foundation, 2017).
61. Charities Aid Foundation, "Britain's Civic Core: Who Are the People Powering Britain's Charities?" (Kent, UK: Charities Aid Foundation, 2013).
62. Noyes and Blond, "Holistic Mission," Figure 5.
63. Ingrid Storm, "Civic Engagement in Britain: The Role of Religion and Inclusive Values," *European Sociological Review* 31, no. 1 (2015): 14–29.
64. Priyya Lukka and Mike Locke, with Andri Soteri-Proctor, "Faith and Voluntary Action: Community, Values and Resources" (London: Institute for Volunteering Research, 2003).
65. Office of the Deputy Prime Minister, "Review of the Evidence Base on Faith Communities," London, 2006.

66. Christians in Parliament and the Evangelical Alliance, "Faith in the Community: Strengthening Ties Between Faith Groups and Local Authorities," 2013, http://www.eauk.org/current-affairs/publications/loader.cfm?csModule=security/getfile&pageid=38452.
67. Noyes and Blond, "Holistic Mission," Figure 3.
68. Wharton and de Las Casas, "What a Difference."
69. British Social Attitudes, 34th Report, National Centre for Social Research, 2017.
70. Hall, "Social Capital"; for an overview, see Steve Bruce, "Post Secularity and Religion in Britain: An Empirical Assessment," *Journal of Contemporary Religion* 28, no. 3 (2013): 369–84.
71. British Social Attitudes, 34th Report.
72. NCVO, *UK Civil Society*.
73. For example, Haldane, *"In Giving."*
74. For example, Isabelle Stadelmann-Steffen, "Social Volunteering in Welfare States: Where Crowding Out Should Occur," *Political Studies* 59, no. 1 (2013): 135–55.
75. Chris Naylor, Claire Mundle, Lisa Weaks, and David Buck, "Volunteering in Health and Care: Securing a Sustainable Future" (London: The King's Fund, 2013).
76. Helen Bussell and Deborah Forbes, "Understanding the Volunteer Market: The What, Where, Who and Why of Volunteering," *International Journal of Nonprofit and Voluntary Sector Marketing* 7, no. 3 (2002): 244–57; 244.

CHAPTER 9

Faith-Based Organizations Under Double-Pressure: The Impact of Market Liberalization and Secularization on Caritas and Diakonie in Germany

Josef Hien

Germany is like no other country when it comes to faith-based welfare provision. The two largest organizations, Catholic Caritas and the Protestant Diakonie, are an essential part of the German welfare state. Caritas's annual report indicates that it had 617,193 employees in 2015, making it the largest private employer in Germany.[1] Through the expansion of their welfare services, Caritas and Diakonie together have become Germany's second largest employer (after the state) in all categories and employ together 1,142,900 people in part- and full-time contracts equaling an 826,580 full-time equivalents in 2015.[2] Internationally operating German companies like BMW (124,729 employees) or Bayer (115,200 employees) only employ one-tenth of what Caritas and Diakonie employ in Germany. Both faith-based welfare providers have steadily expanded their services and employees since the end of World War II.

J. Hien (✉)
University of Milan, Milan, Italy

© The Author(s) 2019
P. C. Manuel, M. Glatzer (eds.), *Faith-Based Organizations and Social Welfare*, Palgrave Studies in Religion, Politics, and Policy, https://doi.org/10.1007/978-3-319-77297-4_9

Most of the staff of both faith-based welfare providers work in the care sector. Within the care sector, Caritas and Diakonie employ most personnel in the medical sector (260,679 full-time equivalents), in hospitals or ambulant care. The second largest sector is child and youth care. Here Caritas and Diakonie have together 211,679 full-time equivalent employees, mostly in kindergartens and day care facilities. Elder care is the third largest sector, in which 183,320 staff are employed. Disabled care with 119,441 employees comes fourth. Poor relief, such as food banks or shelters, and family care play only a residual role, with 31,270 and 7372 employees (see Tables 9.1 and 9.2). While employment in the health care sector, family care, and poor relief has slightly decreased since the 1990s, child care (+48 percent), elder care (+63 percent), and disabled care (+46 percent) are the growth engines of the two largest German faith-based providers between 2012 and 2015.

Together, Caritas and Diakonie are responsible for 80 percent of the welfare work of all secular and religious charitable institutions of the German system of care service provision [Wohlfahrtspflege]. Caritas and Diakonie have together a share between one-fifth and one-fourth of the care market.

Both non-profit faith-based organizations have a considerable annual budget. Caritas's annual budget report indicates a budget of 167,833,000 Euros, of which 74,759,000 come from the federal government and 1,0890,000 from the German Catholic Church (which is funded to a large part by a church tax collected by the state on behalf of the churches from every member). That means 67.2 percent of Caritas's annual budget is funded directly or indirectly through the federal government. The rest comes from donations, membership fees, and profits from assets such as real estate.

Table 9.1 Employees of faith-based welfare organizations in Germany, 1990–2012

	Elderly	*Disabled*	*Child/Youth*	*Poor relief*	*Medical*	*Family*
FBO 2000/1990	112,424	81,823	143,256	33,314	263,545	23,616
FBO 2012	164,607	108,183	188,542	37,549	256,748	7589
	+46.4%	+32.2%	+31.6%	+12.7%	−2.6%	−67.8%

Figures are calculated by the author as full-time employment equivalent, following the template of the German federal statistics authority, one part-time employee equals half a full-time employee. Sources: Data for 2000/1990 based on comparing Diakonie data for 2000 with Caritas data for 1991 due to a lack of data on Caritas for 2000; figures for 2012 are from 2012 for Diakonie and Caritas

Table 9.2 Employees of faith-based welfare organizations in Germany, 2012–2015

	Elderly	Disabled	Child/Youth	Poor relief	Medical	Family
FBO 2012	164,607	108,183	188,542	37,549	256,748	7589
FBO 2015	183,320	119,441	211,679	31,270	260,679	7372
	+63%	+46%	+48%	−20%	+2%	−3%

Source: Numbers for 2015 come from the last available statistic of the Caritas (survey conducted December 31, 2014) and Diakonie (survey conducted January 1, 2016)

The number of employees and the budget of Diakonie and Caritas make Germany the country in Europe with the greatest share by far of faith-based welfare activity. Comparable figures are hard to come by and do not always seem to capture accurately the situation in different countries, but taken as a percentage of the total population, Belgium, the country with the second largest share of faith-based welfare activity in continental Europe, has little more than half of the volume of faith-based welfare service employees. Of the German population (82.5 million), 1.3 percent works for Caritas or Diakonie. This chapter will address six major aspects of faith-based welfare service development in Germany: the evolution of the religious composition of the country and its demographic development; the path of church–state relationship development in the country and the interconnectedness of German faith-based organizations with the evolution of the German welfare state; the aims of faith-based welfare service providers and their relation to the public and the state; the relationship between faith-based welfare providers and the state; the conflicts between faith-based welfare providers and the German public; and the question of what would happen if faith-based welfare providers stopped their services.

THE RELIGIOUS DEMOGRAPHICS OF GERMANY

Germany has, with its fractured political history, experienced significant shifts in and changes to its denominational composition. The German Empire was founded by Bismarck in 1871 as a Protestant nation, but one-third of its population was Catholic.[3] Defeat in World War I brought a revolution leading to the establishment of the Weimar Republic in 1918. According to the census of 1925, 64.1 percent were Protestant and 32.4 were Roman Catholic, with a 0.9 percent share of Jewish and 2.6 percent others.[4] This changed after the end of the Nazi dictatorship with the defeat in World War II and the ensuing loss of large parts of the Eastern territory. It was exacerbated through German partition. West Germany became 45.8 percent Catholic and 50.6 percent Protestant. In East Germany (GDR), the 1950 census showed 85 percent Protestants and 10 percent Catholics. Through a strong policy of de-Christianization, the GDR brought these figures down to 25 percent Protestants, 5 percent Catholics and 70 percent unaffiliated in 1989 on the eve of reunification.[5] Before reunification, West Germany experienced only a slight drop in church affiliation (though church attendance dropped remarkably) (see Fig. 9.1). In 1987, 42.9 percent were Catholic, while Protestants became with a drop to 41.6 percent for the first time a minority. The percentage of unaffiliated people had risen from 3.6 in 1950 to 11.4 in 1987.[6] Through the strong decrease in church affiliation in the East, reunification boosted the "non-members of a statuary religious corporation," as the census of 2011 put it, to 33 percent in the same year. Catholic Church membership sunk to 31 percent of the population, and Protestant church membership to 30.8 percent.

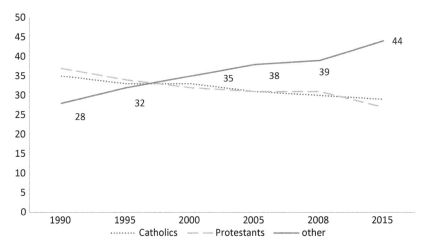

Fig. 9.1 Change in religious affiliation in Germany, 1990–2015. Sources: Data from Catholic and Protestant Church Germany; and Joachim Eicken and Ansgar Schmitz-Veltin, *Die Entwicklung der Kirchenmitglieder in Deutschland* (Destatis, 2010), https://www.destatis.de/DE/Publikationen/WirtschaftStatistik/ Gastbeitraege/EntwicklungKirchenmitglieder.pdf?__blob=publicationFile

The past 25 years also brought a pluralization of religious affiliation in Germany (see Fig. 9.2). The 2011 census, the last available at the time of writing, sees evangelical Free Church members at 0.9 percent of the population, Eastern Orthodox Church at 1.3 percent, and Muslims between 4 and 4.2 percent.[7] In 2015, the federal statistical agency calculated the percentage of Muslims in the German population between 5.4 and 5.7, the increase stemming from immigration of Muslims between 2011 and 2015 (about 1.2 million). Through the influx of approximately 1 million predominantly Muslim asylum seekers between 2015 and 2016, the figures should have risen in 2017 to 6.4 or 6.7 percent; however, no one knows how many will be granted asylums status and no precise census existed at the time of writing.[8] The decline in church membership and the religious pluralization stands in sharp contrast to the increase of traditional Protestant or Catholic welfare service provision faith-based activity in Germany, leading some commentators to speak of a "confession paradox."[9]

Germany, like most Western European countries, has a rapidly aging society. When Bismarck introduced old age insurance in the late 1880s, only every 22nd member of the Kaiser Reich was older than 65 years.

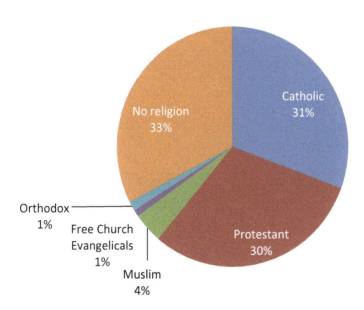

Fig. 9.2 Religious affiliation in Germany, 2011

In the 1970s, a bit less than 100 years later, already every sixth German was over 65 years old.[10] In 2014, every fifth German was older than 65, and this put the country with 20.8 percent second (just after Italy) in the classification of all Europe 27 countries regarding its 65-plus population.[11] With a fertility rate way beyond reproduction, this development poses a great deal of stress on the refinancing of pension in the future. It also creates a care gap for elderly care and disability care. Since the 1970s, ever more women in (West) Germany have entered the labor market. The percentage of women in work rose form 45.9 percent in 1970 to 74.5 percent in 2016. Today Germany is the European country with the second highest percentage of active women in the labor market.[12]

In a Christian Democratic or Conservative welfare state structured around the male breadwinners, the unpaid domestic work within the household such as child and elderly care has been ascribed to women. The churches and their political allies the Christian Democrats were strongly involved in institutionalizing and guarding this system from the 1950s to the 1990s.[13] The increase in female labor market participation since the 1970s triggered a shortage of care in German families for children, elderly, and disabled. Paradoxically, faith-based welfare providers like Caritas and Diakonie profit from this care gap due to their possibilities to expand in the child, elderly, and disability care markets.[14] However, the increasing employment of Christian faith-based care service providers in sensible segments like child and elderly care also creates frictions in a pluralizing society. Now the first-generation Muslim working migrants (mostly from Turkey) from the 1960s are becoming frail. In cities like Berlin, one can sometimes spot caretaking agencies that explicitly target Muslim clients, but frictions may arise between Christian faith-based care service and Muslim clients.

The Path of the Church–State Relationship in Germany

Research on continental European faith-based welfare providers by political scientists and sociologists is dominated by macro-sociological approaches focusing primarily on institutions.[15] In particular, it has been found that the church–state conflicts of the nineteenth century determined the degree to which faith-based welfare organizations became incorporated into European welfare states. This is certainly true for Germany, but no detailed empirical study on how the interaction effect unfolded exists.[16] Bismarck aimed at assimilating the Catholic subculture into the Protestant *Leitkultur* [lead culture] of the empire, but after a failed *Kulturkampf* in the 1870s [Culture War], he had to give in and grant the Catholics a series of concessions to make them political allies for his crusade against socialism. Part of these concessions was to revoke the suppression of Catholic auxiliary organizations, leading to a flourishing of Catholic social and civil society organizations which made Catholic Germany the "pride of Europe."[17] In 1897, the existing Catholic charities were partly brought together under the roof of the newly found Caritas, which from then on existed in parallel to the Protestant Diakonie (Innere Mission), which had been formed in 1848. Moreover, a forerunner of the subsidiarity principle was introduced into the German welfare state, which was further elaborated and institutionalized during Weimar times.[18] However, the massive expansion of these organizations and their legal entrenchment in the German welfare system only took place after World War II and the end of the Nazi regime.

Post-war Germany saw a steep resurgence of religiosity after the moral havoc of Nazi dictatorship and the Holocaust.[19] An allied survey from March 1946 indicates that 65 percent of all Catholics attended church regularly.[20] Many Germans thought that the "third Reich originated in the increasing alienation from God."[21] The Christian Democratic Party picked up on this. Their founding manifesto states that "[f]rom the chaos of guilt and disgrace, in which the deification of a criminal adventure has thrown us, an order in freedom can only evolve, if we remember the cultural, ethical and moral force of Christianity."[22]

In line with the resurgence of religiosity, the churches were to play a major role in the new post-World War II democratic system. German basic law, adopted in 1949, reflects a "positive neutrality"[23] that grants privileges to the churches recognizing their positive role in public life.[24] Article 140 incorporates a number of articles form the Weimar constitution (Art. 136, 137, 138, 139, 141) from 1919, including the provision that there is no state church; that Sundays and religious holidays are protected; that church organizations have autonomy and public legal status; and that the state collects a church tax on behalf of the churches from its members. These prerogatives are important for a number of exemptions that faith-based welfare providers have, as they are part of the two churches. However, for the entrenchment of faith-based welfare provision in the German welfare system, a series of reforms from the 1950s were even more important.

The 1950s and 1960s saw the introduction of the subsidiarity principle into the German welfare state. Catholic family doctrine and the experiences of Nazi totalitarianism had assured that the patriarchic social entity of the family was made largely impermeable for state or societal control. This impermeability was reinsured through the subsidiarity principle. *Quadragesimo Anno* states that:

> [t]he supreme authority of the State ought, therefore, to let subordinate groups handle matters and concerns of lesser importance, as occasion requires and necessity demands. Therefore, those in power should be sure that the better a graduated order is kept among the various associations, in observance of the principle of "subsidiary function."[25]

In other words, the lowest entity in society should always have the responsibility. Only if the lowest entity fails does the next higher entity step in and help out. This is how Diakonie and Caritas became firmly entrenched in the German welfare system.[26] Not that the state should step in if the family fails to provide care tasks, as in Sweden, other Nordic countries, or in France; rather, intermediary institutions like Caritas and Diakonie should do so.[27] In general, through their social doctrines, the two churches provided much of the ideational blueprint for the reestablishment of the German welfare state after World War II.[28]

The onset of German partition reinforced the independent status of the two charitable organizations from state oversight. The consensus in West Germany was that the churches in East Germany had to be shielded from influence from the communist state.[29] The Adenauer government granted Diakonie and Caritas an exemption from federal labor law codification. In 1952, Adenauer exempted them from parts of federal labor law.[30] This releases Caritas and Diakonie from having to comply with collective wage bargaining and allows them to negotiate wages in the so-called third way, in commissions (*Arbeitsrechtlichen Kommissionen*) where employer and employees sit together and decide consensually. This, so the churches argue, makes strikes and unions superfluous and therefore illegal with Caritas and Diakonie.[31] Moreover, the two churches and their welfare organizations enjoy exemptions from discrimination and equal treatment clauses and the labor representation law.[32] Hence, these exemptions allow Caritas and Diakonie to dismiss employees who do not live their life in accordance with the Christian worldview of their employer.

The welfare law of 1961 (*Bundessozialhilfegestz*) cemented the subsidiarity principle. It gave Caritas and Diakonie (and the other semi-public welfare organizations like Arbeiterwohlfahrt, Paritätischer Wohlfahrtsverband, Rotes Kreuz, and Zentralwohlfahrtsstelle der Juden) a privileged position in public welfare, establishing the reimbursement principle (*Kostendeckungsprinzip*) and thereby opening a path-dependent growth phase for these organizations along with the expansion of the German welfare state.[33] Among these six privileged associations of the German free welfare, or "freie Wohlfahrtspfelge," Caritas and Diakonie enjoyed an even more privileged position. Being part of the two churches gave them the exemptions listed above, and they profited from being politically extremely well connected.[34]

The familial- and subsidiarity-oriented welfare system was very much in line with the values of West German society in the 1950s and 1960s. Caritas and Diakonie enjoyed high acceptance and esteem. The connection to the Christian Democratic Party was especially strong. During the 1940s, 71 percent of all regular church-going Catholics and 40 percent of regular church-going Protestants displayed an affinity to the Christian Democratic Party.[35] Things started to change from the 1960s onward. The share of women in Germany that wanted to be "housewives" had diminished between 1961 and 1973 from 57 to 29 percent.[36] Between 1970 and 2013, female labor market participation increased from 46.5 to 72.4 percent. The male breadwinner model started to erode on the "behavioral level"[37] and with it the "private patriarchy"[38] of German society.

The process of societal liberalization of family values went hand-in-hand with a decrease in church attendance: In 1950, 50.4 percent of all Catholics attended Sunday Mass on a regular basis. In 1973, the figures had dropped to 35 percent. Of Protestants, only 7 percent in West Germany attended Mass on a regular basis[39] (see Fig. 9.3).

Whereas the churches were hemorrhaging members and church attendance dropped, ever more people started to work for and receive care from Caritas or Diakonie. In the 1970s and 1980s, faith-based welfare providers saw their largest expansion. Caritas and Diakonie almost doubled their employees from 245,967 to 451,717. The subsidiarity principle institutionalized in the German welfare state allocated care tasks to the six large charitable providers with special status when the family could not provide care anymore. Since Caritas and Diakonie were the largest, and

a. Protestant Church

b. Catholic Church

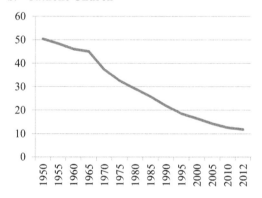

Fig. 9.3 Frequent church attendance, Protestant Church and Catholic Church. (a) Protestant Church. (b) Catholic Church. Sources: Sekretariat der Deutschen Bischofskonferenz 2013. *Katholische Kirche in Deutschland: Katholiken, Gottesdienstteilnehmer 1950–2013*, 2013, http://www.dbk.de/fileadmin/redaktion/Zahlen%20und%20Fakten/Kirchliche%20Statistik/Katholiken%20und%20 Gottesdienstteilnehmer/2013-Tabelle-Katholiken-Gottesdienstteilneh mer_1950-2013.pdf; Detlaf Pollack and Gert Pickel, "De-institutionalization of religion and religious individualization in eastern and western Germany," *KZfSS Kölner Zeitschrift für Soziologie und Sozialpsychologie* 55, no. 3 (Fall 2003): 447–74; 458

best connected politically, they got most of the care contracts. Their child care, elderly care, and disabled care sectors expanded and, along with technical progress, so did the medical sector.

What Do Religious Actors Intend to Achieve in Their Public Agency?

The German churches see their major welfare organizations as essential instruments for evangelization. The preamble of the Caritas states that "essential for its actions is the ambition of the Gospel and the belief of the church" and that Caritas "forms its action in accordance with Christian social ethics and the social teachings of the church."[40] The code of practice of the Diakonie states that its work is "a living expression of the Protestant Church."[41]

This also implies that if you want to work for Caritas or Diakonie, you must act and live in accordance with their worldview. That means that homosexuals, divorcés, or employees who exit the church can be instantly fired (the Protestant Diakonie relaxed this in the 1990s). The modernization of values in German society, which also impacted the workforce of Caritas and Diakonie, has led to a series of conflicts between Caritas, Diakonie, and their employees.[42] Public criticism targets the legitimacy of the faith-based provider's claim that their personnel must live and act in accordance with their worldview. As indicated in the introduction, over two-thirds of the operation of Caritas and Diakonie are funded by the federal government.

This is a new development. In the 1950s, employees of Caritas and Diakonie did not mind the worldview requirements of their employers, simply because most of their employees were religious personnel. In 1950, 60,447 friars and nuns worked for Caritas, while 45,611 of the employees were professional lay care providers.[43] In 1960, Diakonie employed 47,918 professional care workers backed up by 25,011 deacons and nuns.[44] In 1970, the religious personnel had decreased to 15.7 percent. At Caritas, the professionals increased from 137,938 in 1970 to 251,010 in 1980, while religious personnel decreased to 13 percent.[45] In 1990, only 6.5 percent of all employees of Caritas were religious personnel and at the Diakonie only 2.3 percent. A survey of 2600 employees of Caritas and Diakonie between 2006 and 2007 shows that only 11.2 percent chose their employer based on their own religiosity, and only 20.1 percent said that they had consciously considered the religiosity of their employer when choosing to work for the faith-based organization.[46]

This has led since the 1980s to a series of conflicts between the largely professionalized staff (in the 2000s, Caritas stopped collecting statistics on its religious personnel, as the numbers became negligible) with largely secularized ideas about marriage, divorce, religion, patriarchy, and homosexuality and the conservative ideas of the faith-based employers. In the 2010s, this created a strong public blowback with a series of negative articles in federal press.

In 2012, a lesbian educator was dismissed during her parental leave.[47] In the same year, Bernadette Knecht, a female child care facility manager in the city of Königswinter, was dismissed after she had divorced and moved in with her new partner.[48] In 2014, a Muslim nurse wearing a headscarf was dismissed by the Diakonie. In 2015, a lesbian manager of a Catholic youth club had to go because she had married her girlfriend.[49] In 2015, an educator of a Protestant disability care facility who acted in amateur porn movies during her spare time got dismissed by the Diakonie.[50] In 2010, a social worker of the Catholic Kolpingwerk lost his job because he had a profile on a homosexual dating site.[51]

These are just the cases that made it into the federal press. Between 2000 and 2015, 39 cases of conflicts between employees of Caritas and Diakonie were discussed in German courts.[52] In almost all cases, the highest courts defended Caritas's and Diakonie's prerogatives on the basis that they were members of the church and therefore enjoyed an especially constitutionally protected status.

Most of the discrimination cases never make it to court because employees know that their cases do not stand a chance.[53] Employees who divorce and remarry, or marry their homosexual partner, often preemptively terminate their contracts, as in the case of a child care facility manager in Holzkirchen,[54] or do not get the job in the first place, as in the case of Tanja Jungerer in Ulm.[55] *Der Spiegel* also reported on a hospital bought by the Protestant Diakonie whose employees, in fear of losing their jobs, started a mass-baptism.[56]

So, how do religious actors operate in the German public square? We have seen above that since the 1950s Diakonie and Caritas have become essential part of the welfare state and have expanded along the lines of German social security expansion. They are the executing agents independent of but acting on behalf of the state, shouldering a significant part of the care the German welfare state provides. No precise figures exist on the total volume of faith-based care in Germany in contrast to the amount of total care, but one can approximate it with the figures from the federal statistical agency on the total number of care workers in Germany. This leaves the impression that around one-fifth of the care is delivered by faith-based providers in Germany.

WHAT ARE THE CONSEQUENCES OF RELIGIOUS ACTORS' POLITICAL/PUBLIC INVOLVEMENT IN GERMANY?

German reunification led to a boost in faith-based welfare provision in the early 1990s. West German faith-based organizations were able to expand their services to the East and take over most of the formerly state-run care facilities. German reunification was not only an opportunity to expand the care services further, but also a challenge. East Germany was both more Protestant and more secular than the West. The denominational balance shifted from half Protestant and half Catholic in post-war West Germany to one-third Catholic, one-third Protestant, and one-third not belonging to any of the two churches in post-reunification Germany. The communist East German state had a gender policy that officially contrasted with the West German male breadwinner model. Women's share of employment had been much higher than in the West, and the attitudes toward working mothers were much more favorable than in the West.[57] The sudden care crisis in the East triggered by the collapse of the East German state fueled an expansion of faith-based providers. However, East German secularism also undermined their legitimacy. In addition, the 1990s saw recalibration and retrenchment of the service sector of the German welfare state. The automatic cost reimbursement principle for the six large publicly acknowledged charitable institutions that provide welfare service on behalf of the state (*Kostendeckungsprinzip*) was abolished, a marketization of the care sector started, and European integration opened the German care market to non-German competitors. After a short spike due to reunification, the 1990s therefore saw a leveling out of faith-based welfare expansion. With reference to the loss of many institutional and legal vantage points, many commentators saw this as the end of faith-based welfare growth.[58] However, this trend was reversed through a federal child care and elder care reform that expanded services and offered Caritas and Diakonie the opportunity to grow in these sectors. As shown above, this expansion has sparked a series of conflicts regarding the two employers' worldview loyalty principle that twice reached the highest German court, the Bundesverfassungsgericht.[59] Moreover, the strong expansion of the two major faith-based providers made them vulnerable to criticism from private competitors and unions of having abused their exclusive status as members of the two churches in wage bargaining and the disciplining of staff. Caritas and Diakonie both set wages independently from federal collective bargaining processes in special bipartite commissions. While this so-called third way often used to work in favor of the employees, since the liberalization of the care market, it has been increasingly accused of leading to wage dumping.[60]

Moreover, since 80 percent of faith-based employees are women,[61] they are negatively impacted not only because of the conservative church doctrine but also because care is a field characterized by precarious working conditions. Feminist welfare analysts have long argued that care jobs are "worse paid, all else equal, then other types of work," with "continental Europe report[ing] the highest gaps" in wages between men and women.[62] Since the 1980s, part-time work in faith-based organizations has increased dramatically. While in 1980 only 20 percent of the employees had part-time contracts, the numbers grew to 45 percent in 2004. In 2008 72 percent of Diakonie staff had a part-time contract, which shrank to 60.1 percent in 2012. The expansion of faith-based welfare contributes more strongly to negative implications of "gendered occupational regimes"[63] than does the employment in other care providers. Moreover, in contrast to the female-dominated workforce, men make up 80 percent of the wage-setting commissions. In the words of Herman Lührs, "540 men decide the working conditions of one million women."[64] A recent report on the wage-bargaining system of Protestant faith-based welfare providers predicts a further "worsening of the negotiated wages of women" due to the increasing economic rationalization of faith-based welfare organizations triggered by declining church tax revenues due to decreasing church membership.[65]

Negative press, recruitment problems, pressure from the unions, and a court sentence from the Bundesarbeitsgericht led to reform of church labor law in 2013 in both churches. Unions are no longer forbidden to enter Caritas facilities, and according to the churches, 10–15 percent of the members of the *Arbeitsrechtliche Komissionen* should be union members in the future. The value commitment was eased but only with regards to married homosexual couples and people who have been remarried. Moreover, value commitments are still in place for professionals involved in evangelization (*verkündungsnahe Berufe*), an expansive term involving child care workers as well as head physicians. For all other groups of employees, neither homosexuality nor remarriage any longer automatically leads to suspension or demission, but they are instead subject to rigorous case-by-case analysis.

The reception of the reform was mixed. Alois Glück, the head of the Catholic lay organizations, said it was a paradigm shift. Three bishops initially refused to implement the reforms in their constituency but eventually relented.[66] Catholic youth organizations criticized the reforms for being too timid. The piecemeal concessions confirm that the Catholic Church and Caritas try to have it both ways: they expand their care empire because it secures political and social influence, and at the same time, they cling to traditional values when using their care providers for evangelization efforts. Caritas and Diakonie have not made a transition toward a fully market-based enterprise as many of their critics argue, but the value requirements are becoming increasingly costly in terms of public approval and increasing legal conflicts with their largely secularized employees.

But is there an alternative to faith-based welfare providers in Germany? What would happen if Caritas and Diakonie suddenly stopped their services due to negative public, political, or legal backlash? The figures presented throughout this chapter show that one-fifth of all care work in Germany would no longer be carried out. Since two-thirds of funding for Caritas and Diakonie come from the state, it is likely that the state could find other providers to do the job, as it did when the East German care service provision broke down during reunification in the early 1990s. Given the development of the German welfare state since the late nineteenth century, this would be a paradigmatic rupture. Since new providers that step in would most likely be profit-oriented, this paradigmatic shift would have consequences for the quality of the services offered. Market-based providers would likely operate with fewer personnel and more remotely from people in need. In general, trust in Caritas and Diakonie to provide high-quality services is still high. The question is why the two do not make more out of social capital as "other" care providers compared to market- or municipality-based services in order to expand further but instead rely on a somewhat outdated disciplining strategy enabled through their special status as parts of the two great churches.

How Are State-Sponsored Health and Welfare Services Viewed in Germany?

Has the "positive neutrality" enshrined in German basic law that sets the relationship between state and churches and their faith-based welfare organizations morphed into a conflictual partnership (*Konfliktpartnerschaft*) given the increased number of labor law disputes before court or negative press, as some commentators have called it?[67] As documented above, conflict exists, but the conflict largely plays out between the churches and the public. Courts that regulate this conflict as arbitrators on behalf of the state are overwhelmingly on the side of the churches when it comes to the interpretation of labor law disputes between employees and employers.

There is an exemption worth mentioning: refugee and asylum politics that result from the influx of approximately one million refugees between 2015 and 2016 during the so-called German refugee crisis. When after September 4, 2015, a greater number of refugees were allowed to travel from Hungary to Germany, the Catholic cardinal Reihard Marx and Heinrich Bedford-Strohm, the head of the German Protestant church, personally welcomed the arriving refugees in Munich, calling it an "ecumenical welcome culture."[68]

Subsequently, a fight over church asylum erupted in which the federal Minister of Interior De Maziere compared church asylum to Sharia. With the German established parties coming under ever more pressure from the newly formed and quickly rising right-wing party Alternative für Deutschland, which entered parliament in 2017 with a 12.6 percent vote share, other parties try to respond with a harsher stance on immigration, including open criticism of the churches' welcoming gestures toward asylum seekers and their work with refugees.

To sum up, the strong position of the two great faith-based welfare providers within the German welfare system will continue. Plummeting church membership and service attendance did not show any impact on these organizations' steep growth throughout the second half of the twentieth century. The strong changes in values that gripped German society from the 1970s onward and its effect on female labor market participation did however leave an impact. With it came a time-lagged expansion of care services of the German welfare state, especially in the fields of elder, child, and disability care services. As a consequence, faith-based welfare providers managed well to profit from the expansion and remodeling of the

German welfare state, but they will also suffer once this welfare state and its ample care provision becomes retrenched in the future. Moreover, their positive stance on refugees and asylum seekers makes them ever more often the target of populist political critique. In general, it is not clear how the dominance of traditional Protestant and Catholic faith-based organizations will evolve in a rapidly pluralizing religious environment. Open questions remain as to whether they will lose their outstanding legal prerogatives and their pampered political treatment or if also other faith-based organizations—orthodox Christian, Free Church Evangelical, or Muslim—will be granted the same special rights to deliver their care services. So far, no discussion of the issue has taken place in scholarly circles or in the wider public sphere, but it seems that it is time to start one.

Notes

1. Caritas, "Geschäftsbericht 2016," https://www.caritas.de/diecaritas/deutschercaritasverband/verbandszentrale/geschaeftsbericht/2016/geschaeftsbericht-des-deutschen-caritasverbandes-2016.
2. Caritas, *Die katholischen Sozialen Einrichtung und Dienste der Caritas Erhebung 31.12.2014 Einrichtungsstatistik Gesamtübersicht*, 2015, http://www2.caritas-statistik.de/; Diakonie, *Einrichtungsstatistik zum 1. Januar 2016. Statistische Informationen 04.2017*, 2017, https://www.diakonie.de/fileadmin/user_upload/Diakonie/PDFs/Statistiken_PDF/Einrichtungsstatistik_2016_Web.pdf.
3. Josef Hien, "Competing Ideas: The Religious Foundations of the German And Italian Welfare States" (PhD diss., European University Institute, 2012); Helmut W. Smith, *German Nationalism and Religious Conflict* (Princeton, NJ: Princeton University Press, 1995).
4. Hans-Ulrich Wehler, *Deutsche Gesellschaftsgeschichte. Bd. 4: Vom Beginn des Ersten Weltkrieges bis zur Gründung der beiden deutschen Staaten 1914–1949* (Munich: C.H. Beck, 2008).
5. Detlef Pollack and Gert Pickel, "De-institutionalization of Religion and Religious Individualization in Eastern and Western Germany," *KZfSS Kölner Zeitschrift für Soziologie und Sozialpsychologie* 55, no. 3 (Fall 2003): 447–74.
6. FOWID, "Religionszugehörigkeit Bevölkerung 1970–2011," https://fowid.de/meldung/entwicklung-religionszugehoerigkeiten-nach-bundeslaendern-1950-2011.
7. BAMF, "Wie viele Muslime leben in Deutschland? Eine Hochrechnung über die Anzahl der Muslime in Deutschland zum Stand 31. Dezember 2015," 2016, https://www.bamf.de/SharedDocs/Anlagen/DE/Publikationen/WorkingPapers/wp71-zahl-muslime-deutschland.pdf?__blob=publicationFile.

8. Wolfgang Schroeder and Kiepe Lukas, "Konfliktpartnerschaft zwischen konfessionellen Wohlfahrtsverbänden und Staat in der Krise des Migrationsstaates 2015/2016," *Politische Vierteljahresschrift*, forthcoming.
9. Wolfgang Schroeder, *Konfessionelle Wohlfahrtsverbände im Umbruch: Fortführung des deutschen Sonderwegs durch vorsorgende Sozialpolitik?* (Wiesbaden, Germany: Springer, 2017); Karl Gabriel, "Von der Caritas zum sozial-caritativen Handeln der Kirche. Transformation im Selbstverständnis der Caritas in den 60er Jahren," in *Caritas und Diakonie im "goldenen Zeitalter" des bundesdeutschen Sozialstaats. Transformationen der konfessionellen Wohlfahrtsverbände in den 1960er Jahren*, ed. Traugott Jähnichen, 56–73 (Stuttgart: Kohlhammer, 2010).
10. Florian Tennstedt, "Peitsche und Zuckerbrot oder ein Reich mit Zuckerbrot?: der Deutsche Weg zum Wohlfahrtsstaat 1871–1881," *Zeitschrift für Sozialreform* 43, no. 2 (Summer 1997): 88–101.
11. DESTATIS, "Die Generation 65+ in Deutschland," https://www.destatis.de/DE/PresseService/Presse/Pressekonferenzen/2015/generation65/Pressebroschuere_generation65.pdf?__blob=publicationFile.
12. DESTATIS, "Die Generation 65+ in Deutschland."
13. Josef Hien, "Unsecular Politics in a Secular Environment: The Case of Germany's Christian Democratic Family Policy," *German Politics* 22, no. 4 (Winter 2013): 441–60.
14. Josef Hien, "From Private to Religious Patriarchy: Gendered Consequences of Faith-Based Welfare Provision in Germany," *Politics and Religion* 10, no. 3 (Fall 2017): 515–42.
15. Michael Minkenberg, "The Policy Impact of Church—State Relations: Family Policy and Abortion in Britain, France, and Germany," *West European Politics* 26, no. 1 (Spring 2003): 195–217; Josef Schmid, "Verbändewohlfahrt im Modernen Wohlfahrtsstaat: Strukturbildende Effekte des Staat-Kirche-Konflikts," *Historische Sozialforschung* 20, no. 2 (Summer 1995): 88–118; Ipek Göcmen, "The Politics of Religiously Motivated Welfare Provision" (PhD diss., Universität zu Köln, 2011); Birgit Fix and Elisabeth Fix, *Kirche Und Wohlfahrtsstaat: Soziale Arbeit Kirchlicher Wohlfahrtsorganisationen Im Westeuropäischen Vergleich* (Freiburg, Germany: Lambertus-Verlag, 2005).
16. Karl Gabriel, "Religiöser Pluralismus in Deutschland als Herausforderung für Wohlfahrtsverbände—ein Problemaufriss, in *Religiöse Pluralisierung: Herausforderung für konfessionelle Wohlfahrtsverbände*, ed. Traugott Jähnichen, Alexander-Kenneth Nagel, and Katrin Schneiders, 19–29 (Stuttgart: Kohlhammer, 2016); Christoph Sachße and Florian Tennstedt, *Geschichte der Armenfürsorge in Deutschland, Band 4: Fürsorge und Wohlfahrtspflege in der Nachkriegszeit* (Stuttgart: Kohlhammer, 2012);

Christoph Sachße and Florian Tennstedt, *Geschichte der Armenfürsorge in Deutschland. Band 2: Fürsorge und Wohlfahrtspflege 1871 bis 1929* (Stuttgart: Kohlhammer, 1988); Ipek Göcmen, "The Politics of Religiously Motivated Welfare Provision" (PhD diss., Universität zu Köln, 2011).
17. Paul Misner, "The Predecessors of 'Rerum Novarum' within Catholicism," *Review of Social Economy* 45, no. 4 (Winter 1991): 444–64.
18. Catherine Maurer, *Der Caritasverband zwischen Kaiserreich und Weimarer Republik Zur Sozial- und Mentalitätsgeschichte des caritativen Katholizismus in Deutschland* (Freiburg: Lambertus, 2008); Gabriel, "Religiöser Pluralismus," 26.
19. Anna J. Meritt and Richard L. Meritt, *Public Opinion in Occupied Germany, The OMGUS Surveys* (Urbana: University of Illinois Press, 1970); Detlef Pollack, "Einleitung," in *Religion und Lebensführung im Umbruch der langen 1960er Jahre*, ed. Claudia Lepp, Harry Oelke, and Detlef Pollack, 9–28 (Göttingen, Germany: Vandenhoeck & Ruprecht, 2016).
20. Florian Tennstedt and Günther Schulz, *Geschichte Der Sozialpolitik in Deutschland Seit 1945, Band 3: Bundesrepublik Deutschland 1949–1957. Bewältigung Der Kriegsfolgen, Rückkehr Zur Sozialpolitischen Normalität* (Baden-Baden, Germany: Nomos, 2007), 78.
21. Frank Bösch, *Die Adenauer-CDU: Gründung, Aufstieg Und Krise Einer Erfolgspartei. 1945–1969* (Stuttgart and München: Deutsche Verlags-Anstalt, 2001), 30.
22. CDU, "Gründungsaufruf Der CDU Berlin 26. Juni 1945," http://www.kas.de/upload/ACDP/CDU/Programme_Beschluesse/1945_Gruendungsaufruf-Berlin.pdf, 1945.
23. Stephen Monsma and J. Christopher Soper, *The Challenge of Pluralism. Church and State in Five Democracies* (Lanham, MD: Rowman & Littlefied, 2013).
24. Michael Minkenberg, "The Policy Impact of Church—State Relations: Family Policy and Abortion in Britain, France, and Germany," *West European Politics* 26, no. 1 (Spring 2003): 195–217, 202.
25. Pius XI, "Quadragesimo Anno," par. 80, http://w2.vatican.va/content/pius-xi/en/encyclicals/documents/hf_p-xi_enc_19310515_quadragesimo-anno.html.
26. Sachße and Tennstedt, *Geschichte der Armenfürsorge in Deutschland. Band 2*; Sachße and Tennstedt, *Geschichte der Armenfürsorge in Deutschland. Band 4*.
27. Hans Günter Hockerts, "Sozialpolitische Reformbestrebungen in der frühen Bundesrepublik. Zur Sozialreformdiskussion und Rentengesetzgebung 1953–1957," *Vierteljahrshefte für Zeitgeschichte* 25, no. 3 (Fall 1977): 341–72; Werner Abelshauser, "Erhard oder Bismarck? Die Richtungsentscheidung der deutschen Sozialpolitik am Beispiel der

Reform der Sozialversicherung in den fünfziger Jahren," *Geschichte und Gesellschaft* 22, no. 3 (Fall 1996): 376–92; Kees Van Kersbergen, *Social Capitalism. A Study of Christian Democracy and the Welfare State* (London and New York: Routledge, 1995); Hien, "Competing Ideas."

28. According to Kuller, the Protestant Church up until the 1970s was of the opinion that the state should largely not interfere actively in the welfare sector. Christiane Kuller, "Der Protestantismus und die Debatten um den deutschen Sozialstaat" in *Teilnehmende Zeitgenossenschaft*, ed. Christian Albrecht and Reiner Anselm, 53–64 (Tübingen, Germany: Mohr Siebeck, 2015).
29. Hartmut Kreß, *Der Sonderstellung der Kirchen im Arbeitsrecht—sozialethisch vertretbar? Ein deutscher Sonderweg im Konflikt mit Grundrechten* (Baden-Baden, Germany: Nomos, 2014).
30. Betriebsverfassungs- und Personalvertretungsrecht §118 Abs. 2 BtrVG, §112 BpersVG; see also Kreß, *Der Sonderstellung der Kirchen im Arbeitsrecht* and "Das Arbeitsrecht der Kirchen im Meinungsstreit. Neuralgische Punkte auf evangelischer und katholischer Seite," *Materialdienst des Konfessionskundlichen* 3 (2012), 53–56.
31. BVerfGE 70, 138; BVerfGE 46, 73 and 53, 366. See also Hermann Lührs, *Die Zukunft der Arbeitsrechtlichen Kommissionen: Arbeitsbeziehungen in den Kirchen und Ihren Wohlfahrtsverbänden Diakonie und Caritas Zwischen Kontinuität, Wandel und Umbruch* (Baden-Baden, Germany: Nomos, 2010).
32. Betriebsverfassungsgesetz and Personalvertretungsrecht §118 Abs. 2 BtrVG §112 BPersVG.
33. Rolf Heinze and Katrin Schneiders, "Vom Wohlfahrtskorporatismus zur Sozial-wirtschaft? Zur aktuellen Situation der freien Wohlfahrtspflege in Deutschland," *Archiv für Wissenschaft und Praxis der sozialen Arbeit* 2 (2013): 4–17.
34. Karl Gabriel and Hans-Richard Reuter, "Religion und Wohlfahrtsstaatlichkeit in Deutschland. Korporatistischer Sozialversicherungsstaat mit konfessioneller Prägung," in *Religion und Wohlfahrtsstaatlichkeit in Europa*, ed. Karl Gabriel, Hans-Richard Reuter, Andreas Kurschat, and Stefan Leibold, 93–140 (Tübingen, Germany: Mohr Siebeck, 2013), 97.
35. Meritt and Meritt, *Public Opinion in Occupied Germany, The OMGUS Surveys*, 81–3.
36. Frank Rusciano, "Rethinking the Gender Gap: The Case of West German Elections, 1949–1987," *Comparative Politics* 24, no. 3 (Fall 1992): 335–57, 351.
37. Jane Lewis, "Gender and Welfare Regimes: Further Thoughts," *Social Politics: International Studies in Gender, State & Society* 4, no. 2 (Summer 2017): 160–77.

38. Hien, "From Private to Religious Patriarchy."
39. Pollack and Pickel, "De-institutionalization of Religion and Religious Individualization," 458.
40. Caritas Deutschland, "Leitbild Des Deutschen Caritasverbandes," http://www.caritas.de/glossare/leitbild-des-deutschen-caritasverbandes, 5, 15.
41. Diakonie Deutschland, "Satzung Des Evangelischen Werkes Für Diakonie Und Entwicklung," http://www.diakonie.de/satzung-9285.html.
42. Sascha Kneip and Josef Hien, "The times, are they a-changin'? Die besondere Stellung konfessioneller Wohlfahrtsverbände in Zeiten gesellschaftlicher Pluralisierung," *Leviathan* 45, no. 1 (Spring 2017): 81–110.
43. Hermann Lührs, "Kirchliche Arbeitsbeziehungen: Die Entwicklung der Beschäftigungsverhältnisse in den Beiden Gro\s Sen Kirchen und Ihren Wohlfahrtsverbänden," *WiP Working Papers* 33 (2006): 37–8.
44. Lührs, "Kirchliche Arbeitsbeziehungen," 37–8.
45. Lührs, "Kirchliche Arbeitsbeziehungen," 37–8.
46. Hermann Lührs, "Arbeit in der Kirche. Analyse Einer Bundesweiten Befragung von Beschäftigten in den Beiden Grossen Kirchen und Ihren Wohlfahrtsverbänden Diakonie Und Caritas," *WiP Wirtschaft un Politik Workingpaper* 41 (2008): 52.
47. Stefan Mayr, "Bistum Augsburg: Lesbische Erzieherin Siegt Gegen Kirche," *Sueddeutsche Zeitung*, June 20, 2012, http://www.sueddeutsche.de/bayern/lesbische-erzieherin-siegt-vor-gericht-wer-fuer-die-kirche-arbeitet-ist-selber-schuld-1.1387341.
48. Matthias Kamann, "Warum die Kirche Lesbische Erzieherin Entlassen Darf," *Welt Online*, August 11, 2012, http://www.welt.de/politik/deutschland/article108575212/Warum-die-Kirche-lesbische-Erzieherin-entlassen-darf.html.
49. *Die Welt*, "Erzieherinnen Wegen Ihres Privatlebens Gekündigt," *Welt Online*, April 21, 2015a sec. Regional, http://www.welt.de/regionales/bayern/article139876549/Erzieherinnen-wegen-ihres-Privatlebens-gekuendigt.html.
50. Dario Nassal, "Julia Pink spricht über ihren Jobverlust als Erzieherin." *Süddeutsche Zeitung*, 28 (October 2014), http://www.sueddeutsche.de/bayern/jobverlust-wegen-pornodrehs-das-ist-doch-laecherlich-1.2193358.
51. Karin Schädler, "Diskriminierung in Katholischen Einrichtungen: Tendenz Schwulen- Und Lesbenfeindlich," *Die Tageszeitung*, May 12, 2010, http://www.taz.de/!5142797/.
52. This reveals a search in the juris database, a database sponsored by the German government that contains the majority of court cases from 1990 to the present. https://www.juris.de/jportal/index.jsp. For full analysis, see Kneip and Hien, "The times, are they a-changin'?"

53. Corinna Gekeler, *Loyal Dienen: Diskriminierendes Arbeitsrecht bei Caritas, Diakonie und Co.* (Aschaffenburg, Germany: Alibri Bücher, 2013).
54. *Die Welt*, "Erzieherinnen Wegen Ihres Privatlebens Gekündigt."
55. Kamann, "Warum die Kirche Lesbische Erzieherin Entlassen Darf."
56. Eva Müller, "Arbeitgeber Kirche: Getauft Für Den Job," *Der Spiegel*, January 14, 2013, http://www.spiegel.de/karriere/berufsleben/kirche-als-arbeitgeber-angestellte-lassen-sich-fuer-den-job-taufen-a-876868.html.
57. Michael Braun, Jacqueline Scott, and Duane F. Alwin, "Economic Necessity or Self-Actualization? Attitudes toward Women's Labour-Force Participation in East and West Germany," *European Sociological Review* 10, no. 1 (Spring 1994): 29–47.
58. Lührs, "Kirchliche Arbeitsbeziehungen," 37–8; Amos Zehavi, "Religious Supply, Welfare State Restructuring and Faith-Based Social Activities," *Political Studies* 16 (2013): 516–79.
59. For full analysis, see Kneip and Hien, "The times, are they a-changin'?"; for an insightful analysis from the 1950s to the 1980s, see Joseph Listl, "Die Arbeitsverhältnisse der Kirchlichen Dienstnehmer in der Rechtsprechung der Gerichte der Bundesrepublik Deutschland," *Jahrbuch Für Christliche Sozialwissenschaften* 27 (1986): 131–58.
60. Kreß, *Der Sonderstellung der Kirchen im Arbeitsrecht*; Lührs, *Die Zukunft der Arbeitsrechtlichen Kommissionen*.
61. Lührs, "Kirchliche Arbeitsbeziehungen," 27.
62. Ann Shola Orloff, "Gendering the Comparative Analysis of Welfare States: An Unfinished Agenda," *Sociological Theory* 27, no. 3 (Fall 2009): 317–43, 326; Daniela Kroos and Karin Gottschall, "Dualization and Gender in Social Services," in *The Age of Dualization: The Changing Face of Inequality in Deindustrializing Societies*, ed. Patrick Emmenegger, Silija Häusermann, Bruno Palier, and Martin Seeleib-Kaiser, 100–24 (Oxford: Oxford University Press, 2012); Kendra Briken, Karin Gottschall, Sylvia Hils, and Bernhard Kittel, "Wandel von Beschäftigung und Arbeitsbeziehungen im Öffentlichen Dienst in Deutschland—zur Erosion Einer Sozialstaatlichen Vorbildrolle," *Zeitschrift Für Sozialreform* 60, no. 2 (Summer 2014): 123–48.
63. Orloff, "Gendering the Comparative Analysis of Welfare States," 327; Margarita Estevez-Abe, "Gender, Inequality, and Capitalism: The 'varieties of Capitalism' and Women," *Social Politics: International Studies in Gender, State & Society* 16, no. 2 (Summer 2009): 182–91, 186.
64. Lührs, "Kirchliche Arbeitsbeziehungen," 2; Lührs, *Die Zukunft der Arbeitsrechtlichen Kommissionen*.
65. Heinz-Jürgen Dahme, Gertrud Kühnlein, Anna Stefaniak, and Norbert Wohlfahrt, "Leiharbeit und Ausgliederung in Diakonischen

Sozialunternehmen: Der 'Dritte Weg' Zwischen Normativem Anspruch und Sozialwirtschaftlicher Realität. Hans-Böckler-Stiftung," Abschlussbericht Eines Forschungsprojektes im Auftrag der Hans-Böckler-Stiftung, Bochum, Dortmund, Magdeburg, 2012, 89.

66. *Die Welt*, "Drei Bayerische Diözesen Lenken Ein," *Welt Online*, October 13, 2015b sec. Regional, http://www.welt.de/regionales/bayern/article147554159/Drei-bayerische-Dioezesen-lenken-ein.html.
67. Kiepe and Schroeder, "Konfliktpartnerschaft zwischen konfessionellen Wohlfahrtsverbänden."
68. DBK, "Kardinal Marx und Landesbischof Bedford-Strohm begrüßen Flüchtlinge am Bahnhof," http://www.dbk.de/presse/details/?presseid=2884&cHash=0e4030ad358c762e549c00ce37497b11.

Index[1]

A
Abortion, 2, 3, 36, 39, 40, 82, 83, 96, 103, 126, 148, 150, 151, 188, 196
Acli (the Christian Associations of Italian Workers), 64
Adenauer, Konrad, 212
Alleanza contro la povertà (Alliance against poverty), 64, 65
Arikan, Gizem, 4
Austerity, 12, 13, 24, 31, 32, 54, 55, 63, 64, 68, 84, 89, 95, 96, 106, 115, 117, 121, 125, 126, 131n40, 169, 177, 186, 190, 197

B
Bedford-Strohm, Heinrich, 220
Blair, Tony, 185, 189, 200n29
Bloom, Pazit Ben-Nun, 4, 17n13
Blunkett, David, 190
Bourdieu, Pierre, 32, 43n33, 186

C
Caritas, 64, 66, 84–90, 93, 95, 101n63, 101n69, 205–207
Casse Mutue, 54
Catholic, 6, 14, 22, 23, 26–30, 33–36, 38–41, 48, 50, 52, 56, 59–63, 65, 75–79, 81–84, 87–90, 92, 93, 95, 101n68, 101n72, 104–115, 120, 126, 127, 137, 140, 142, 207, 208, 211–213, 216, 217, 219–221
Celtic Tiger (approx. 1995–2005), 23, 24
Centesimus Annus (hundredth year), 62
Charity, 6, 41, 53, 56–60, 62, 75, 119, 137, 144, 151, 188, 191, 192, 195
Child, 22–25, 27–29, 34, 113, 115, 116, 120, 138, 142, 145, 171, 172, 176, 177, 206, 210, 220
Christian Democratic Party, 127n4, 211, 213
Church affiliation, 208, 209, 218, 220

[1] Note: Page numbers followed by 'n' refer to notes.

Church of Sweden, 162–168, 172–177, 180n7
Church tax, xii, 13, 25, 26, 31, 69n17, 80, 81, 115, 118, 139, 148, 151n2, 166, 206, 211, 218
Civil society, xii, 4, 8, 11, 14, 15, 62, 81, 82, 92, 103, 111, 117, 120, 131n40, 147, 165, 169–171, 189, 190
Coleman, James, 186
Conservative-Liberal Democrat, 189, 190
Corporal acts of mercy, 110, 112, 114, 124, 126, 128n9

D
Deepening democracy, 1, 4, 103, 117, 126
de Valera, Eamon, 26, 29
Diakonie, 205–207
Disabled, 57, 58, 151, 206, 210, 215
Divorce, 2, 3, 14, 26, 30, 39, 40, 49, 82, 83, 103, 216

E
East German, 212, 217, 219
Elder, 23, 49, 50, 53, 66, 138, 144, 146, 151, 172, 173, 209, 210, 220
Englund, Steven, 2, 16n2, 17n5
Etatisme, 5
Evangelical, 142, 209, 221
Evangelization, 215, 219

F
Fahey, Tony, 27, 42n4, 43n18, 43n20
Family, 22, 24–29, 40, 47, 49, 50, 55, 58, 60–62, 83, 85, 88, 115, 116, 141, 150, 176, 177, 187, 188, 190, 206, 210, 212, 213
Financial crisis, 24, 115, 144–147, 151

Fishman, Robert, 4
Fomento de Estudios Sociales y de Sociología Aplicada Foundation (FOESSA), 84–86
Foundation Compromiso y Transparencia (Commitment and Transparency), 96
Fung, Archon, 4, 17n11

G
Glorious Thirty, 53, 55, 59
Great Recession (2007–2008), 24
Greek Orthodox Church, 12, 13, 135

H
Hervieu-Léger, Danielle, 77, 97n4, 97n12
Hirst, Paul, 4, 17n12, 119, 131n41
Hollenbach, David, 33, 43n36
Homeless, 6, 24–25, 27, 33, 66, 84, 174, 175, 177
Homosexual, 2, 3, 14, 39, 40, 62, 83, 96, 103, 126, 143, 148, 196, 215, 216, 219

I
Instituições Particulares de Solidariedade Social (IPPS, Private Institutions of Social Solidarity), 111, 118
Italian Bishop, 64

J
Jewish, 22, 140, 142, 165, 173, 207
John Paul II, Pope, 62, 72n59, 82

K
Kennedy, Stan (Sister), 27

L
Laïcité, 5
Law of separation (1905), 5
Lutheran, 2, 161, 162, 168

M
Marx, Reihard, 220
McQuaid, John Charles (Archbishop), 26, 28, 29
McVerry, Peter, 27
Medical, 3, 13, 29, 30, 32, 35–37, 50, 55–57, 85, 87, 89, 94, 96, 115, 117, 120, 146, 171, 187, 190, 206, 215, 220
Member, 30, 57, 61, 71n47, 85, 94, 103, 104, 112, 114, 117, 119, 126, 127n4, 139, 141–143, 145, 150, 162, 163, 165, 166, 170, 172, 179, 186–189, 192–196, 198, 206, 208, 209, 211, 213, 216, 218, 220
Misericórdia, 110–112, 114, 115, 119–121
Mitterrand, Francois (President), 5
Moore, Louella, 6, 18n16, 18n17
Muslim, xi, 8, 14, 23, 79, 140–142, 171–173, 176, 178, 188, 190, 209, 210, 216, 221
Muted vibrancy, 1–3, 6, 75–79, 103, 104, 126

N
Nazi, 138, 208, 211, 212
New Labour, 185, 189
Nordic, 161–171, 177, 212

O
Observatorio de la realidad social (Observatory of Social Reality), 84
Opere Pie, 53, 54, 56

Orthodox Christianity, 136, 188
Ottoman, 137

P
Pérez-Agote, Alfonso, 77, 97n2, 97n3, 97n5, 100n56, 132n48
Poor, 1, 3, 4, 6, 12–14, 24–25, 27, 31–33, 50, 53, 56–59, 63–68, 69n13, 84–86, 88, 90, 113, 116, 124–126, 138, 145, 147, 151, 154n39, 206
Popular Party, 82, 95
Protestant, 13, 14, 22, 28, 34, 79, 81, 142, 173, 205, 207–209, 211, 213–218, 220, 221, 224n28
Public funding, 81, 87, 119, 168, 177
Putnam, Robert, 3, 17n7, 186, 199n6

R
Recalibration, 50, 55, 217
Reddito di inclusione sociale (REIS, income for social inclusion), 65
Refugee (asylum/immigrant), xi, 3, 6, 23, 25, 33, 66, 79, 86, 94, 110, 113, 138, 141, 146, 151, 162, 167, 171, 173, 175, 179, 209, 220, 221
Religious variables, 1
Retrenchment, 15, 48, 54, 55, 86, 93, 198, 217, 221
Revolution of 1789, 5
Rodríguez, José Luis, 83

S
Scandinavian pattern, 53
Schmitter, Philippe, 4, 17n8
Schools, 27, 28, 34–40, 52, 54, 59, 93, 118, 131n40, 139, 143, 148, 152n5, 154n39, 156n59, 172, 174, 175

Secours Catholique, 6
Secours Populaire and Restaux du Coeur, 6
Secular, xi, xii, 4–6, 8, 10, 12, 14, 15, 22, 28, 34, 35, 38, 40, 41, 53, 56, 60, 82, 83, 87, 89, 93, 95, 101n62, 104, 105, 110–112, 127, 129n16, 143, 161–180, 188, 191, 192, 206, 217
Separation (of church and state), 5, 79–81, 148, 150, 151, 165
Social capital, 1, 3, 15, 76, 86, 178, 185–198, 219
Social-democratic, 11, 53, 161, 168
Social Emergency Program, 116
Spanish Basque Country, 76, 77, 89, 93, 94
Stepan, Albert, 4, 17n9, 127n4
"Strategic actor" model, 3
Strategic silence, 1–15, 83, 95–96
Swedish Agency for Support to Faith Communities (SST), 162, 163, 166, 167, 172

T
Trocaire, 33

U
Unemployment, 13, 24, 47, 53, 85, 116, 145, 146

V
Valadier, Paul, 2, 16n2, 16n3
Villagrán, Gonzalo, 2, 16n4, 102n73
Volunteer, 6, 13, 15, 50, 62, 85, 119, 144, 188, 195, 197

W
Warner, Carolyn, 3, 17n6, 95, 102n74
Weimar, 207, 211
Women, 3, 21, 25, 29, 36, 49, 55, 195, 210, 213, 216, 218, 220
Workers' Mutual Aid Societies, 53, 71n47

CPSIA information can be obtained
at www.ICGtesting.com
Printed in the USA
LVHW07*1847170618
581000LV00009B/517/P